The Exceptional Manager

The Exceptional Manager

Making the Difference

Rick Delbridge, Lynda Gratton, and Gerry Johnson

OXFORD
UNIVERSITY PRESS

Great Clarendon Street, Oxford OX2 6DP

Oxford University Press is a department of the University of Oxford.
It furthers the University's objective of excellence in research, scholarship,
and education by publishing worldwide in

Oxford New York

Auckland Cape Town Dar es Salaam Hong Kong Karachi
Kuala Lumpur Madrid Melbourne Mexico City Nairobi
New Delhi Shanghai Taipei Toronto

With offices in

Argentina Austria Brazil Chile Czech Republic France Greece
Guatemala Hungary Italy Japan Poland Portugal Singapore
South Korea Switzerland Thailand Turkey Ukraine Vietnam

Oxford is a registered trade mark of Oxford University Press
in the UK and in certain other countries

Published in the United States
by Oxford University Press Inc., New York

© Oxford University Press 2006

The moral rights of the authors have been asserted
Database right Oxford University Press (maker)

First published 2006

British Library Cataloguing in Publication Data
Delbridge, Rick.
The exceptional manager / Rick Delbridge, Lynda Gratton, and Gerry Johnson.
p. cm.
Includes bibliographical references and index.
ISBN-13: 978-0-19-929222-6 (alk. paper)
ISBN-10: 0-19-929222-1 (alk. paper)
1. Management by exception. 2. Strategic planning. 3. Executive ability 4.
Industrial management. I. Gratton, Lynda. II. Johnson, Gerry. III. Title.
HD30.6.D45 2005
658.4–dc22
2005027339

Typeset by SPI Publisher Services, Pondicherry, India
Printed in Great Britain
on acid-free paper by
Biddles Ltd., King's Lynn, Norfolk

ISBN 0-19-929222-1   978-0-19-929222-6

This book is dedicated to the memory of our friend and colleague Sumantra Ghoshal who brought wisdom, insight, and inspiration to the AIM Fellowship.

Contents

List of Figures   viii
List of Tables   ix
Abbreviations   x
Acknowledgements   xi
Notes on the Authors   xii
Introducing the AIM Initiative   xvi

Part I. Setting the Scene   1

   1. Making a Difference   3

   2. Building on the National Context   18

Part II. The Building Blocks   41

   3. Transforming Strategy   43

   4. Managing Employment Relations   62

   5. Innovating Beyond the Steady State   87

   6. Measuring Performance in Innovative Firms   107

Part III. The Reflective Practitioner   135

   7. Adopting Promising Practices   137

   8. Learning in Organizations   156

   9. Making Intelligent Decisions   178

   10. Cooperating across Boundaries   199

   11. Overcoming Busyness   223

   12. Taking the First Steps   243

Index   251

List of Figures

1.1. Strategic drift   9

2.1. Product and labour market regulation, 1998   26

2.2. Regulation over time, by country   27

2.3. Output per worker and per hour worked   30

2.4. Comparison of output per worker and employment rate   31

2.5. US productivity advantage over the UK   32

2.6. Value added per worker, UK manufacturing plants   34

2.7. Business operations in relation to government, other
     businesses, and institutions   35

7.1. The service–profit chain   146

8.1. Four phases of the learning models adopted at
     Chaparral Steel   161

8.2. Knowledge-management strategies and context   167

9.1. Example of a frame-analysis worksheet   186

9.2. A causal cognitive map from framing experiments   188

10.1. The journey of corporate renewal   202

10.2. A typology of conversations   212

10.3. The self-fulfilling prophecy   216

List of Tables

2.1. UK net public investment as % of GDP   25

2.2. Bibliometric analysis of share in the the science base   25

2.3. The productivity spread   32

9.1. How selected heuristics and biases affect strategic
     decision-making   181

9.2. Illustration of the framing bias   185

11.1. Overcoming the traps of non-action   224

Abbreviations

AIM	Advanced Institute of Management
BPR	business process re-engineering
CBI	Confederation of British Industry
DTI	Department of Trade and Industry
ERM	exchange rate mechanism
FDI	foreign direct investment
GDP	gross domestic product
HMT	HM Treasury
IKMN	International Knowledge Management Network
JIT	just-in-time
MNE	multinational enterprise
MSC	Manpower Services Commission
NGO	Non-Governmental Organization
NHS	National Health Service
OECD	Organization for Economic Cooperation and Development
OFR	operating and finance review
PBIT	profit before interest and taxation
SNA	UN System of National Accounts
TEC	Training and Enterprise Council
TFP	total factor productivity
TPM	total productive maintenance
TPS	Toyota Production System
TQM	total quality management
TUC	Trades Union Congress
WERS	Workplace Employment Relations Survey
WIP	work-in-progress

Acknowledgements

As lead authors on this collaborative project we owe debts to a number of people. First, we thank our AIM colleagues for their tremendous work, both as authors of chapters and in the conceptual development of this book. AIM is an innovative and ambitious project bringing together scholars from different disciplines within management research. Its success lies in the spirit of collaboration and the willingness to go that bit further, think more widely, that has characterized the Fellows. First among equals in this endeavour was our dear friend and colleague Sumantra Ghoshal. He inspired us and continues to do so. We dedicate this book to his memory.

Second, we thank those who have taken the lead roles in directing AIM—Anne Sigismund Huff and Robin Wensley—for their work in establishing and guiding the overall AIM project. Third, we thank David Musson and his excellent staff at Oxford University Press for their enthusiasm, support, and professionalism.

Finally we would like to extend our deep gratitude to Simon Caulkin who has worked closely with us in preparing this book. His skill as a writer, insightful comments, and camaraderie have played a major role in bringing this book to publication, and in keeping us sane.

RD, LG, and GJ

Notes on the Authors

Elena Antonacopoulou is a Professor of Organizational Behaviour at the University of Liverpool Management School. She is currently joint Editor-in-chief of the international journal *Management Learning* and serves on the editorial board of the *Academy of Management Learning and Education Journal*. She is an active member of the Academy of Management in the USA and has served as member of the Board of Governors (2000–3), Chair of the Academy's Ethics Committee (2001–3), and held several Executive positions in the Management Education and Development (MED) Division leading to her role as Division Chair in 2002–3.

John Bessant is Professor of Innovation and Technology Management at Imperial College, London where he is responsible for a major EPSRC 'Grand Challenge' Programme on 'Innovation and Productivity' involving a consortium including Imperial, Cambridge, Cranfield, Liverpool, and Loughborough Universities and AIM. His most recent books include *High Involvement Innovation* and *Managing Innovation* (3rd edition), both published by John Wiley and Sons.

Julian Birkinshaw is Professor and Chairman of Strategic and International Management at the London Business School. His recent books include *Transnational Management* (2003), *Inventuring* (2003), *Entrepreneurship in the Global Firm* (2002), and *Leadership the Sven Goran Eriksson Way* (2002).

Ian Clarke is Professor of Marketing at Lancaster University Management School. He has worked as an internal consultant to Tesco PLC and since returning to academe his work has focused on organizational decision-making and sense-making processes. He has been Principal Investigator for two EPSRC-and ESRC-funded projects. He is a Council member of the British Academy of Management. He is also an editorial board member for the Routledge journal *International Review of Retail, Distribution and Consumer Research*.

Rick Delbridge is Professor of Organizational Analysis at Cardiff Business School. He is the author of *Life on the Line in Contemporary Manufacturing* (OUP) and Associate Editor of *Organization*. His co-authored paper 'Systems of exchange' was adjudged the Academy of Management Review Best Paper in 2005.

Mark Easterby-Smith is Professor of Management Learning at Lancaster University Management School and President of the British Academy of Management. He has published widely on organizational learning, and is co-editor of the *Blackwell Handbook of Organizational Learning and Knowledge Management*.

Paul Edwards is Professor of Industrial Relations at Warwick Business School, University of Warwick. He is a Fellow of the British Academy. Research interests include employment relations in small firms and the personnel policies of multinational companies. His books include *Managers in the Making* (with John Storey and Keith Sisson, 1997) and *The Politics of Working Life* (with Judy Wajcman, 2005).

Lynda Gratton is Professor of Management Practice at London Business School where she directs the school's executive programme, 'Human Resource Strategy in Transforming Organisations'. She is author of a number of books including *Living Strategy: Putting People at the Heart of Corporate Purpose* and *The Democratic Enterprise*. Her co-authored article 'Integrating the Enterprise' won the Sloan Management Review best article of the year award, and her case of BP, the ECCH award for the best case of 2005.

Rachel Griffith is Deputy Director of the Institute for Fiscal Studies (IFS) and Reader in the Economics Department, University College London. She is on the editorial board for the *Review of Economic Studies*, on the Council of the European Economic Association, a fellow of the Centre of Economic Policy Research, and an academic consultant to HM Treasury and the Competition Commission.

Jonathan Haskel is a Professor of Economics at the Department of Economics, Queen Mary, University of London. Jonathan is a fellow of the Centre of Economic Policy Research, and a research associate of the Institute of Fiscal Studies. He is on the editorial panel of *Economica* and *Economic Policy*. He is currently an academic consultant to HM Treasury and a member of the UK Competition Commission.

Gerard Hodgkinson is Professor of Organisational Behaviour and Strategic Management at Leeds University Business School. Gerard is the

Editor-in-Chief of *the British Journal of Management,* a Consulting Editor of the *Journal of Occupational & Organizational Psychology,* and an Editorial Board Member of the *Academy of Management Review.* He is also a member of the Research Grants Board of the ESRC.

Chris Huxham is Professor of Management at the University of Strathclyde Graduate School of Business. She was a member of the Scottish Executive Task Force on Community Planning, and is a Council member of the British Academy of Management (BAM) with responsibility for research policy. She is convenor of the BAM Directors of Research Network and was the initiating convenor of the BAM Special Interest Group on Inter-organizational Relations. Chris is on the Advisory board for *Public Management Review* and the Editorial Board of *Organization Studies.*

Gerry Johnson is Professor of Strategic Management at the University of Strathclyde Graduate School of Business in Glasgow. He has published a number of books and written numerous papers in the field of strategic management. *Exploring Corporate Strategy,* of which he is co-author, is the best-selling text on strategy in Europe and regularly appears in the Top 10 Business Books in the UK. He is a member of the editorial board of the *Strategic Management Journal* and the *Journal of Management Studies* and a council member of the Society for the Advancement of Management Studies.

Andy Neely is Deputy Director of AIM, the Advanced Institute for Management Research, Chairman of the Centre for Business Performance at Cranfield School of Management, and a Visiting Professor at London Business School. He chairs the Performance Measurement Association, an international network for those interested in performance measurement and management, and has authored over 100 books and articles, including *Measuring Business Performance,* published by the *Economist,* and *The Performance Prism,* published by the *Financial Times.* He sits on the Treasury's Performance Information Panel and the Accounting Standards Board Advisory Committee for the Operating Financial Review.

Mari Sako is Peninsular and Orient Steam Navigation Company Professor of Management Studies at Said Business School, University of Oxford. Mari's books include *Prices, Quality and Trust* (1992), *Japanese Labour and Management in Transition* (1997), and *Shifting Boundaries of the Firm* (forthcoming from Oxford University Press). She serves on the editorial boards of several leading journals, including *Industry and Innovation* and the *Political Quarterly.*

Chris Voss is Professor of Operations and Technology Management at London Business School, and Director of the Centre for Operations and Technology Management. Chris also leads the 'International Service Study', and is the founder and former Chairman of the European Operations Management Association and consultant to a wide range of companies.

George Yip is Professor of Strategic & International Management at London Business School. He has also taught at Harvard, Stanford, Cambridge, and Oxford. His book, *Total Global Strategy,* has been published in ten languages. Hs articles have appeared in the *California Management Review, Columbia Journal of World Business, Harvard Business Review, Sloan Management Review, and Strategic Management Journal.* He worked for ten years in business in the United States and Britain, for multinational companies such as Unilever and Price Waterhouse.

Introducing the AIM Initiative

'The extraordinary complexity of management:
Getting the right people in place
Creating structures and lines of reporting
Correcting and adapting when things go wrong
Applying common sense.'
Hamish McRae, *Independent*, 6 July 2005

The central dilemma in researching management is the extent to which the core elements of effective management are relatively easy to describe in words, yet 'extraordinarily complex' when it comes to putting them into practice.

This book—the first synthesis of our joint work on the issue of management and UK competitiveness within the AIM research initiative—is (we believe) a ground-breaking attempt to address this central dilemma of relating research to a practical, in this case national, management agenda.

Jointly funded by Economic and Social Research Council (ESRC) and the Engineering and Physical Sciences Research Council (EPSRC), the Advanced Institute of Management research initiative was established in November 2002 as a novel and ambitious initiative designed to address academic concerns within the framework of real economic needs. On the academic front, it had the parallel aims of boosting the UK's output of international-quality social science research in management and strengthening the capacity of the higher-education sector to sustain that quality and quantity in the future. These academic objectives were set in the context of a concern about the international competitiveness of UK industry and the role of management within it: how far was the latter a determining factor and to what extent could it benefit from evidence-led improvement?

One of the key developments within the overall initiative was the appointment of sixteen competitiveness fellows, each of whom made a three-year commitment to a role combining individual research with collective effort. These leading academics and researchers have together crafted, written, and produced the book that you have in your hands.

A critical part was a sustained and challenging attempt to develop an overall perspective that was both multidisciplinary and closely engaged with management practice.

This book, centred on the concept of 'the exceptional manager', represents the start of this journey. It would be wrong (as well as diminishing of the effort and ambition involved) to imply that even at this stage the journey has not been challenging and sometimes controversial. It has had its saddening aspects, too, most obviously the early loss of Sumantra Ghoshal. As those who knew him would have expected, Sumantra had already proved to be one of the most stimulating and forceful participants in the venture; he was also one of the most committed to its ambitious aims. We should also note the debt we owe to the groundwork carried out by AIM's founding director, Professor Anne Huff, in appointing and knitting together the fellows as a functioning and effective team.

Our Basic Schematic Model

The task for the fellows was how in research and theory terms we should link the general issue of management, that is, broadly speaking what goes on inside the 'black box' of the organization itself, to productivity and the overall competitiveness of the UK economy. Why do UK firms appear to perform poorly in terms of productivity, and in what ways can and does this influence the international competitiveness of the UK economy as a whole?

We developed an initial schema within which we could articulate our differing perspectives on and understandings of these issues. It is important to make explicit here the implications of this schema for our subsequent work—in particular, as illustrated in the latter parts of the book, the way in which it enables us to focus more clearly on our central question but also inevitably marginalizes certain other broader issues.

Initially, we decided to build the work on three pillars or themes, rather than just the single strand of productivity. Bearing in mind the essential process of innovation and imitation in the competitive evolution of firms, we introduced the twin notions of innovation itself and then the transfer of best practice between organizations. The basic model is circular. Innovation that delivers improved performance and productivity at the firm or sub-firm level is taken up as a promising practice and imitated by other parts of the firm and by competitors. The cycle continues with further innovation. This is much like the process of choice described by Jim March as 'exploitation' versus 'exploration'.[1] What remains unclear is how far we can expect a single organization to engage in both aspects simultaneously, or see this as a balance which is achieved over time by a system of firms in both competition and collaboration.[2]

In linking these three themes to the competitiveness of the national economy, we need to find a way of relating what goes on within a firm with what happens between firms. Again, we adopt a somewhat simplistic three-way distinction between workers, managers, and firms. We might suggest that worker performance is a function of skills and work organization, manager performance is a function of both the older (strategy, structure, and systems) and the newer (people, purpose, and process) capabilities,[3] and firm performance links to the economy through market growth, regulation, and mergers and acquisitions, as well as the overall market-based processes of innovation, imitation, and, of course, selection.[4]

We also recognize that management itself, as an activity or set of activities, can be seen from very different perspectives. We are interested in how these relate to each other and the extent to which competence in any or all of them is reflected in managerial performance as a whole. The three aspects that we focus on are:

- decision-making and the forms of analysis and the nature of the processes that managers undertake before and after the decisions themselves;
- action-taking and the ways in which managers use sequences of actions to resolve uncertainties and ensure direction and intent;
- sense-making and learning and the role of stories and narrative in providing not only a useful synopsis of the past but guidance in terms of change and the future.

Although these can be regarded, as above, as a linear sequence from decision to action to learning, we believe it is more appropriate to picture them in a relationship where each can be mapped independently from the chronological perspective.[5] We should add that many actions in the corporate and competitive market domain must be seen as incorporating substantial elements of both intention in terms of desired future states and anticipation in terms of the future actions of others.[6]

Finally, we see two underlying foundation concepts: one related to individual initiative, the other to collective action. We associate the former with entrepreneurship (although we recognize that in practice much so-called entrepreneurial action is at least as much if not more collective than individual), and the latter with cooperative behaviour. Of course, the balance between these two motivations is a subject of wide debate and discussion. We only enter into this from a rather limited perspective, in the context and nature of the managerial activities that we are studying.

Our focus on the role of management in understanding the nature and detail of UK competitiveness inevitably means that this book leaves out a number of broader questions which can and should be addressed by social-science research.

First and most obvious, we have not addressed the wider question of other explanations for the UK's competitive shortcomings. We have therefore not added significantly to the wide body of previous work which has adduced causes as varied as the long-term impact of the British class system to the the lack of specific skills in the UK workforce. While we believe there is a strong prior case that management comprises a significant component in the explanation,[7] we would in no way wish to claim that it is the sole and exclusive factor.

Second, our central bias towards management clearly influences the perspective we take on a range of specific phenomena. For instance, our general method of aggregating from work organization to managerial direction to firm performance means that questions of both the distribution of economic rewards and the broader sociological nature of management and managers as a potential privileged class are not subjected to critical scrutiny. Further, questions of the institutional relationship between business schools, consultancies, and industry itself are generally absent from the specific analyses and therefore again we do not directly address some of the critical commentaries in this area.[8] We unashamedly focus on management, and even more so managers, as the locus of our interest; the book stands as a summary of our collective understanding, at this stage of our research, of the ways in which the active manager can make a difference to the performance of the firm.

As we noted above, AIM was set up with a clear objective to focus multidisciplinary management research on a critical and long-established policy question. As a representation of our work, therefore, this book reflects a rather unusual collective endeavour. While the lead authors had the job of pulling together the contributions, the book as a whole represents the collective effort of all the competitiveness fellows. All contributed in terms of both individual research expertise and many discussions about other related work in small groups and the whole fellowship.

We trust you, our readers, will find the subsequent chapters interesting, challenging, and well informed. Ever more we hope this book can play a small part in the route to overall improvement in the UK economy, the benefits of which would be very real.

Robin Wensley,
Director of the AIM Initiative.

Notes

1. March, J. 1996. 'Exploration and Exploitation in Organizational Learning'. In M. Cohen and L. Sproull (eds.), *Organization Science*: 101–123. Thousand Oaks, CA: Sage Publications.

2. Of course, as in many things relating to managerial practice, the mainstream tendency is to espouse the view that the individual firm can indeed 'have its cake and eat it' by being successful at both imitation and innovation, but often at the cost of managing a serious paradox (see Smith and Tushman, 'Managing Paradoxically: A Senior Team Model for Simultaneously Exploring and Exploiting', AOM Conference, New Orleans, August 2004).

3. See the three key articles by Chris Bartlett and Sumantra Ghoshal: 'Changing the Role of Top Management: Beyond Strategy to Purpose', *Harvard Business Review*, Nov/Dec 1994, Vol. 72, Issue 6, pp. 79–88 ; 'Changing the Role of Top Management: Beyond Structure to Processes', *Harvard Business Review*, Jan/Feb. 1995, Vol. 73, Issue 1, pp. 86–96; 'Changing the Role of Top Management: Beyond Systems to People', *Harvard Business Review*, May/Jun 1995, Vol. 73, Issue 3, p. 132–42.

4. This reflects what could be termed a strong Schumpeterian perspective as to be found for instance, in, Stanley Metcalfe, *Evolutionary Economics and Creative Destruction*, (Routledge: London, 1998).

5. Indeed in terms of much management research which involves active engagement with practice, and can be seen broadly as action research, notions of timing and causality arise in the very questions about the nature of the reliability of our research itself (Kirk, J. and Miller, M.L. (1986) *Reliability and Validity in Qualitative Research* (Qualitative Research Methods Series, Vol. 1) Beverly Hills) Sage.

6. For a more detailed review see Wensley, R, 'Strategy as Intention and Anticipation', in Wilson, D and Cummings, S. (eds.) *Images of Strategy*, Oxford, Blackwell: 2003.

7. See, for instance, N. Bloom, S. Dorgan, J. Dowdy, J. Van Reenen, and T. Rippin, *Management Practices Across Firms and Nations*, Centre for Economic Performance, LSE, June 2005.

8. See, for instance, Henry Mintzberg, *Managers not MBAs*, London: FT/Prentice Hall, 2004.

PART I

Setting the Scene

Making a Difference

IN the 1970s, the UK was known as the 'sick man of Europe'. It had an ailing economy, a troubled workforce, and, it was generally accepted, below-average managerial capability. During the next decade, it went through something of an economic and business revolution. Many people applaud this time; others abhor it. Yet few would argue that it did not make a difference. It affected the structure of the country's economic and financial institutions, the nature of society, the role managers play within it, and their relationship with organized labour. By the year 2000 the UK was hailed as one of the more successful economies in Europe, if not in the world. Yet there remained major challenges for the managers of the new millennium. This book is about those challenges and what managers might do to address them.

Like many of the world's mature economies, the UK faces a strategic problem. The shedding of the post-war malaise was partly the result of some major structural and institutional changes, but another important element was the emphasis placed on greater efficiency, the reduction of costs in often sloppily managed businesses, and the construction of an economic infrastructure that, at least on the face of it, should provide the basis of a successful economy. We develop this theme in more detail in Chapter 2.

However, in time the focus on greater efficiency and lower cost set up a new challenge of its own. It is impossible to build a successful economy for the future on the basis of competing on cost alone. For the UK to be successful, the economy needs to be based on international competitiveness built on added value, achieved through innovatory products and services. The reason is straightforward. Mature economies such as the UK have a fixed cost base—wages, taxes, the cost of materials and utilities, and so on—which is much higher that that of competitors located in, for example, eastern Europe, the Indian subcontinent, and the Far East. While UK firms may be more efficient, any productivity advantages that they enjoy are liable to be short-lived. They are unlikely to prove significant enough to allow them to remain competitive on price alone in the longer term.

The problems posed for the UK are twofold. Indigenous firms find it increasingly difficult to survive against international competition; and the UK itself is becoming a less attractive site for foreign direct investment (FDI) in operations founded on low cost. Take the example of FDI in manufacturing. During the 1980s, the Conservative government prioritized the attraction of FDI over support for UK firms, and major investments, particularly from Japan, were heralded with great fanfare as the source of economic regeneration in areas such as the north-east of England and south Wales, where traditional domestic industry was in decline. Such investment was welcome and provided much-needed employment for a period, but its roots were shallow and could not sustain long-term economic regeneration. Over the last few years, Japanese consumer-electronics firms have shifted production to eastern Europe as the region has become a viable location from which to supply the western European market. Global car assemblers such as Nissan and Toyota are outstanding examples of manufacturing efficiency and make major contributions to the economy; but increasingly they are seeking cost reductions and sourcing components and systems (generally at least 70 per cent of the total value of the vehicle) from outside the UK.

This shift confronts the UK with the challenge of fundamental strategic change. An economy that has earned its success through becoming more efficient needs to metamorphose into one that retains the efficiency but does much more besides: an economy which develops greater capabilities for adding value and creating and developing innovation. These are not new challenges; the state of, and prospects for, the UK economy have been the focus for numerous studies, not least by economists who make similar points. Our focus, however, is particular and novel: the role of management in the raising of UK competitiveness. Here studies are much less exact. They suggest that managers should surely make a difference, but are less than precise about how. The issues raised by this book are all linked to this question. Just what are the challenges that managers face both in their own roles and in contributing to the wider economic wealth of the UK? Where is the evidence as to how they might do this, both strategically and in terms of their managerial roles? And what does this mean in terms of their behaviour as managers? The argument we develop is that, indeed, managers do matter and can make a difference—but that the ways in which they do so are not always straightforward or self-evident.

The New Managerialism

At the dawn of the new millennium, management seemed to have become *the* career aspiration of the UK working population. By 2004 it had become the single most popular course for undergraduate students, and the four MBA courses on offer in the early 1970s had grown to more than seventy. The role of the 'manager' and the significance of management had both grown enormously in the contemporary economies of mature nations. Official figures for the UK showed that in late 2003 18 per cent of all men and 10 per cent of all women were managers, senior officials, professionals, or associated professional or technical staff.[1]

In terms of aspirations, this was perhaps understandable. Apart from the undoubted high earning potential of top managers, managerial success surely meant making a real difference to something. Judging by the popular business press, the success—or failure—of firms is down to corporate heroes like Steve Jobs, Jack Welch, or Richard Branson. They are not just the subject of press attention; they write books themselves or have books written about them and about how their experiences can help other managers. They have become both business gurus and social icons. According to a 1996 survey, 95 per cent of UK consumers were able to name Richard Branson as the founder of Virgin, and in the 1997 'Think Different' advertisements for Apple computers, Branson was featured together with Einstein and Gandhi as a 'shaper of the 20th century'. A survey of students in 2000 found that Branson was their number-one role model. We appear to be in an age of aspirational managerialism.

The implication is that managers matter; that they make a real difference to the fortunes of organizations. We begin this book by asking how and to what extent this is so. At first sight that seems an odd question. Of course, getting things done, managing efficiency, ensuring continuity, and the like 'matter' in the sense that organizations cannot do without them. But this kind of routine management is not enough to give a business competitive advantage. In chapters that follow, we consider this challenge in relation to management practice in general. In this chapter, however, we begin with an acid test: whether managers matter and make a difference *strategically*. In this context we are certainly concerned with top management, but also with any manager who has an influence on the strategy of his or her organization; who heads a division, runs a major project, or heads a team that has an impact on company performance. As we shall see, we are also concerned with people in organizations—managers or not—who can hinder strategic development. The conclusion we come to is that managers can indeed make a difference—but those who do so strategically are the exception rather than the rule.

We believe that, if the challenges outlined above are to be met, we need more managers who can make a strategic impact. In this chapter we seek to pin down the challenge more specifically by explaining why it is so difficult to make a difference, why 'difference-makers' are the exception, and behind that what being 'exceptional' actually entails. We also offer views on what managers need to focus on to make a strategic difference and invite readers to consider how the lessons drawn in the chapters that follow might also help develop 'exceptional' managers.

Of Course Management Matters

The starting point is that businesses can and do make impressive improvements in strategic and financial performance. In 1992 BP, at that time the UK's largest industrial enterprise, was in trouble. A combination of rising debts and unit costs, falling oil prices, and bitter internal strife was reflected in seriously deteriorating results. In response, the board slashed the dividend and sacked the then CEO Bob Horton. Fast-forward ten years and the situation could hardly have been more different. Consistently among Europe's most admired companies, over the intervening decade BP had successfully acquired and integrated its rivals Amoco, Arco, and Castrol. It had jumped from second-tier to 'super-major' status in the oil industry, boasting the lowest unit costs and the highest return on capital employed among comparable firms. It was delivering after-tax profits at the rate of $1 billion a month.

As BP was confronting meltdown in London, a small Scottish bank in Edinburgh was wrestling with big problems of bad debt and poor profitability. Costs amounted to 63 per cent of income. By 2002 the same bank had become the fifth largest in the world by market capitalization, ahead of such familiar names as Merrill Lynch, Goldman Sachs, and UBS. As with BP, a proportion of the Royal Bank of Scotland's remarkable growth derived from acquisitions, including NatWest in the UK and Citizens Financial Group in the US. But during the same period, when RBS's growth was the best of all significant banks in Europe, its cost–income ratio, down from 63 per cent to 45 per cent, was one of the lowest among comparable companies. This performance was crucial to all its stakeholders. Over the five-year period from 1997 to 2002, RBS was the world's best-performing bank in terms of total shareholder return.

Much of the popular management literature concentrates on 'explaining' corporate success stories like these. In most books on top management, leadership, or strategy, success is ascribed to either careful or insightful strategic planning, or gifted or charismatic leaders, or a peculiarly dynamic top team. Less often, but perhaps as important, it may be recognized that it is not only top management that makes a difference. After the delayering of the 1980s, middle managers can be seen to play a vital role, too,[2] a role that goes beyond the implementation and control of strategies set at the top. Middle managers also act as a crucial bridge between senior management and people at lower levels in the organization, reinterpreting and adjusting strategic responses as events unfold on the ground in terms of relationships with customers, suppliers, the workforce, and the community. And they make a difference through the advice they feed upwards, for example on likely organizational blockages and requirements for change.

So of course managers make a difference, and therefore matter a great deal.

Well, Really?

For every success story like BP or RBS, there are at least as many examples of failure. For decades Marks & Spencer was one of the best-performing companies in the UK. Long considered the benchmark for retailers, it was as much admired as BP later became. It was therefore with real shock that M&S's management and industry observers watched its plummeting fortunes in the 1990s. Yet, with hindsight, was it so surprising? This was the retailer that until the early 1990s had no changing rooms for clothes buyers, accepted no credit cards other than its own, and was regularly caught out of stock of its main selling lines. This was the management that failed to recognize that competitors were not only catching up with its product offering, but were undermining its strategic advantage by creating new ways to compete. With hindsight, it seems remarkable that such highly regarded management failed to see what was coming. Even when it did in the late 1990s, there was no rapid resolution, but rather a protracted bout of infighting among the board.

Or take the decline of Marconi, of which one journalist observed: '[Its] transition from UK corporate colossus to overindebted pigmy must count as one of the swiftest-ever exercises in value destruction. It is also one of the great corporate governance fiascos of all time.'[3] This is the story of a once-great company that in pursuit of a strategic decision to become one of the world's leading telecommunications businesses—arguably a defensible aspiration in itself—sold off what by that definition were peripheral businesses to invest as fast as possible in a string of acquisitions in areas that the management did not fully understand. To compound the errors, managers failed to anticipate the impending bursting of the telecom bubble. Indeed, the view of the then finance director, later to become deputy chief executive, was that Marconi's real mistake was in failing to sell the business at the height of the telecom boom. In short, reputable managers of a long-established and previously successful UK company took a wildly over-optimistic view of the market and the industry, failed to understand the basis of long-term value creation for shareholders, moved into businesses they did not understand, and excused themselves for it afterwards. The picture overall, then, is that managers may indeed make a difference—but for ill just as much as for good. Indeed, looking at the broader picture, the evidence is that the success of most businesses is short-lived. Consider, for example, the fate of the UK's largest businesses since the 1980s. Of the 100 companies comprising the FTSE 100 in 1984, twenty years later, just twenty-three remained. Some had gone out of business. Others had been acquired. There is little to suggest that a history of success is a guarantee of future success. Indeed, as we shall see, it could be that a record of success is inherently part of the problem.

How do we account for this bigger picture?

Patterns of Strategy Development and the Propensity for Strategic Drift

Historical studies reveal a pattern in the life and death of businesses in which long periods of relative strategic continuity characterized by little or incremental change alternate with periods of flux where strategies change but in no clear direction. These are punctuated by infrequent bouts of transformational change, in which strategic direction is fundamentally modified.[4] This pattern has become known as 'punctuated equilibrium',[5] and is illustrated in Fig. 1.1.[6]

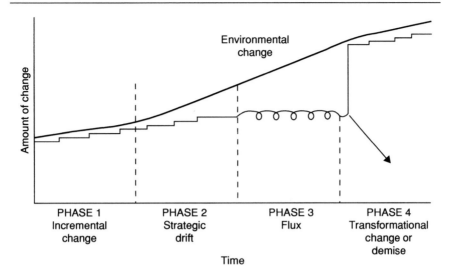

Figure 1.1.   Strategic drift

Source: Adapted from exhibit 1.4 in Gerry Johnson, Kevan Scholes, and Richard Whittington, *Exploring Corporate Strategy* (London: FT/Prentice Hall, 2005), 27.

There are a number of important points to be made about this pattern. Most often companies do not die because of dramatic changes in their environment. Instead, they succumb to a gradual 'strategic drift' from the realities of the business environment.[7] With hindsight, retail observers could see signs of drift in the M&S of the late 1980s—the arrogance of assuming that consumers would adapt to M&S assumptions about shopping behaviour rather than vice versa, for example. The problem is that the drift may be imperceptible at the time, not only to managers but to other stakeholders too, not least because there is a lagged effect on performance: M&S may have begun to drift in the 1980s, but the consequences for performance became evident only a decade later.

Even the most successful companies may be subject to strategic drift. Indeed, Danny Miller formulated what he calls the 'Icarus paradox' to suggest the tendency of businesses to become victims of their own past success.[8] Entrapped by the formula that has delivered good results in the past, they are unable to look beyond it in the present.

Transformational change tends to occur when performance has fallen off significantly, that is, at times of crisis. This is an important point, because it is transformational change that is often the source of the most trumpeted management success stories: transformation is where managers most visibly make a difference. Yet ironically, from the point of view of market position, shareholder wealth, and jobs, this is too late. The time to 'make a difference'—when management really matters most—is in phase 2 in Fig. 1.1, the moment when the organization begins its drift, before performance suffers—and, very likely, before most people inside and outside the organization have spotted that there is a problem at all. In this perspective, the exceptional manager might be defined as the one who can see what others cannot and can persuade them to do something about it.

Why Managers Might Not Make a Difference[9]

There are long-standing explanations of how this propensity for incremental change and strategic drift occurs.

Strategy Development

Consider how organizational strategies come about. You might think that strategy involves major decisions about the future taken at an identifiable point in time at the top of the organization resulting in significant one-off changes to direction or structure. Think again. Research suggests that more typically strategies develop in an adaptive fashion, changing gradually as they build on the existing strategic direction. An apparently coherent strategy may in fact develop stepwise from a series of strategic moves, each of which makes sense in terms of previous steps. A product launch or significant investment decision establishes a de facto strategic direction, which itself guides decisions on the next strategic move—an acquisition or further product line extension, say. This in turn helps to consolidate the strategic direction, and so on. Over time, this can lead to quite significant strategic shifts, but incrementally. In many respects, gradual change makes sense. No organization can function effectively if it is constantly chopping and changing strategy; and while change occurs in the environment, this too is likely to be gradual. In a positive sense, therefore, incremental change looks like sensible adaptation to the opportunities arising from a continually changing environment.

The problem, however, is that all too easily 'good decisions' as seen by managers become those that are consistent with past decisions and current strategy rather than those most appropriate for the current and future situation of the organization.

The Nature of Managerial Decisions

Incrementalism also results from the very challenge of decision-making in complex and unpredictable circumstances. A prescriptive rational decision-making model might suggest that managers clarify objectives, make an exhaustive search for alternatives, carry out a full evaluation of the various options, and then select the optimal course against desired outcomes. In practice, this is often unrealistic. Organizational objectives are themselves often the subject of political disagreement and compromise. Moreover, the 'problem' is frequently defined in terms of past actions and current strategy rather than a wider assessment of the organization's position. A further limiting factor is that identifying and evaluating all the alternatives may require more than the available time and resources. This is why organizational theorists talk of 'bounded rationality',[10] or of 'trial-and-error' decision-making models when trying to capture what actually happens in organizations. Bounded rationality recognizes that in the face of resource constraints search processes are necessarily less than exhaustive. Managers search until they find a satisfactory solution to a particular problem. So the outcome of decision-making processes in complex situations is generally 'satisficing' rather than optimizing; finding a decision that is 'good enough'—and this is likely to be good enough in terms of what is practical or expected in relation to what has worked in the past. The result, again, is incremental change on the basis of what has gone before.

Experience and Bias

When taking decisions, managers are expected to bring their experience to bear. Human beings are able to function effectively because they have the cognitive capability to make sense of the problems or issues that confront them. They recognize and articulate these on the basis of past experience and what they come to believe to be true about the world. More formally, individual experience can be explained in terms of the mental (or cognitive) models people build over time to help make sense of their situation.[11]

Managers are no exception. When they face a problem, they make sense of it in terms of the mental models that are the basis of their experience. This has major advantages: it means they are able to relate such problems to prior events and therefore have comparisons to draw on; it means they can interpret one issue in the light of another, giving them bases for making decisions founded on experience. If they did not have such mental models, they could not function effectively; they would meet each situation as if they were experiencing it for the first time.

There are, however, downsides, too. The same mental models, the same experience, can lead to bias. People make sense of new issues in the context of past issues; they are likely to address a problem in much the same way as they dealt with a previous similar one. Moreover, they are likely to search for evidence that supports those inclinations. So some data will be seen as more important than other data, and some may not be taken on board at all. The important points are:

- The interpretation of events and issues in terms of prior experience is inevitable. The idea that managers approach strategic problems and issues entirely dispassionately and objectively is unrealistic.
- Such interpretation and bias arise from experience of the past, not least with regard to what is seen to have worked or given rise to problems. So the future is likely to be made sense of in terms of the past.

Collective Experience and Organizational Culture

As with individuals, so also with groups. Managers do not operate purely as individuals; they work and interact with others, and at the collective level, too, there are reasons to expect experience to count. This is reflected in the taken-for-granted assumptions and ingrained organizational routines that are collectively referred to as 'organizational culture'. Such taken-for-granted assumptions and routines can be especially important as an influence on the development of organizational strategy.[12] For a group or organization to operate effectively, there has to be such a generally accepted set of assumptions; in effect, it represents the collective experience without which people would have to 'reinvent their world' for different circumstances. As with individual experience, this shared understanding allows the collective experience gathered over years to be brought to bear to make sense of a given situation, to inform a likely course of action, and to gauge the likelihood of the latter's success.

Obvious as this may seem, it has significant implications. The important point is precisely that the underlying assumptions are taken for granted; they are unlikely to be considered as problematic. But suppose the organization needs or expects to undergo significant change. Core assumptions and routines are difficult to change just because they *are* taken for granted; and managers may therefore find themselves unable to adjust to such pressures.

Suppose newspapers find their revenue coming mainly from advertising rather than newsstand sales. Suppose the government expects the police to concentrate more on preventing crime than on 'catching criminals'. In terms of what is taken for granted, newspapers are about news and the police are about catching criminals. Even if editors and police chiefs accept intellectually the need for their assumptions to change, they do not readily do so. The notion that reasoned argument necessarily changes deeply embedded assumptions rooted in collective experience is not borne out by events in the real world. Readers need only think of the difficulty of persuading others to rethink political, religious, or even sporting allegiances to realize how far from reality it is.

Institutional Norms and Resource Dependence

Such collective thinking typically stretches even beyond the organization. Managers may assume that they can manage the environment, but the evidence is that the environment largely determines managerial action. Institutional theorists point to the striking similarities in assumptions and practices, including strategy, among organizations in the same industry.[13] Accountancy firms resemble each other, likewise firms in engineering or firms in publishing. It is often not difference but similarity of strategies that defines competitors. Accountancy firms offer similar services and seek to enhance those services and build relationships with clients in similar ways. Long-haul airlines or car manufacturers tend to follow similar strategies and imitate each other's innovations. Successful strategies tend to be copied, especially where organizations face uncertainty and ambiguity. Why? There are several reasons.

First, where one organization has achieved success, others obviously hope to do the same. Secondly, over time people in competing companies begin to think alike in terms of organization and the environment they operate in, including the nature of customers, suppliers, and competitors. Hence the phenomenon of 'organizational fields'[14]—networks of related organizations in which common assumptions, values, and ways of doing things become so institutionalized that it is hard for people to question or change them. Thirdly, organizational fields often develop norms and practices that confer 'legitimacy' and to which powerful stakeholders such as government, professional bodies, and customers expect organizations to conform.

There is, moreover, evidence that such conformity and mimicry may make sense in performance terms.[15] In the long term, organizations conforming to the strategic norms of the organizational field tend to stand more chance of survival than those that choose to differentiate themselves. A few differentiators may outperform rivals, but for others being different will be their undoing. So imitation and conformity may be a safe bet. In turn, suppliers, financiers, and potential employees may privilege the safe bets, giving them further benefits. Arguably, this is a lesson learned by the banks, for example. There may be some winners from doing things very differently, but on the whole there is more similarity than difference in their strategies.

As well as being subject to institutional pressures to conform, organizations are dependent on the source of the resources they need to operate—raw materials, components, expertise, technology, and finance, for example. This 'resource dependence' creates further constraints on managerial action,[16] particularly where resources are important and scarce. So the broad picture that emerges is one of managers captured by their own experience and constrained by reliance on others. The assumptions and routines of their organizational culture, in turn embedded within a wider institutional framework, tend to encourage conformity. There are also forces for conformity in the activities that managers prioritize.

Management Control

Managers are charged with ensuring efficiency, meeting objectives and deadlines, reporting honestly and transparently to shareholders, and setting out procedures to ensure that others do the same. In other words, they perceive the need to exert control. Unfortunately, high degrees of control and the associated hierarchical structures are more likely to foster conformity than the variety that gives rise to new ideas. So innovation is less likely the more extensive and elaborate the control.[17] Indeed, some complexity theorists argue that innovation and creativity emerge at 'the edge of chaos',[18] where there is just enough order to make things happen but not so much that it stifles the errors and experiments that generate fresh thinking. This 'edge of chaos' is an uncomfortable space to inhabit; it cannot be readily controlled—at least in conventional terms—from the top. So the natural tendency is tighter rather than looser control, the consequent loss of innovation, and bias to conformity.

The Exception Rather than the Rule

Perhaps surprisingly, therefore, far from being a matter of 'of course they do', making a difference is a major challenge for managers. Unless they are exceptional, or in exceptional circumstances such as a crisis, the norm is that they do not make a great deal of difference. Of course, managing efficiently and delivering good customer service are important—but managing continuity is not the same as making a difference. And it is change, not continuity, that is needed. The point of departure for this book is that for the UK economy to compete successfully over the long term, firms will need to add more value and operate at the higher end of markets. The UK is home to a number of companies that appear on the world stage—BP, RBS, Cadbury Schweppes, GlaxoSmithKline, Smith & Nephew, Tesco, Vodafone—but they are exceptions. Our argument is that the currently 'exceptional' levels of innovativeness and value added achieved by these firms need to become the norm, and that the role of management in making it happen is absolutely crucial, at all levels of the organization. Many UK firms seem content to aim for survival, operating in the most cost-sensitive sectors of the market, without sufficient commitment or aspiration to innovation and improvement in business performance. The fear is that the majority of these firms are doomed to fail. To avoid that fate, UK managers must take up the challenge of making the exceptional commonplace.

What does it take to be exceptional? There are unlikely to be ready, off-the-shelf answers, and indeed managers should be sceptical of any that are offered. While first articulating the challenge, this book is also an attempt to provide some insights into how managers might respond to it, drawing on different fields of research in business and management and considering what lessons can be learned from them.

The book consists of three parts. The first part sets the scene. Chapter 1 puts forward the need for the exceptional manager, while Chapter 2 develops the theme for the need for the UK economy to migrate to higher-added-value activities. The evidence on competitiveness in productivity and innovation is that many UK firms are not only a long way from achieving this qualitative shift; they may not even be aware of the necessity. The chapter argues that after two decades of market-orientated policy and institutional reform, policies now need to be revised to build economic and political institutions that encourage businesses to innovate their way upmarket. It also discusses the importance of management in making the shift happen.

The second part of the book provides same building blocks by unpacking what managing for high value added entails. It examines the challenges within organizations and draws out the implications for key areas of management: the management of organizational strategy, the management of employee relations, the management of innovation, and the measurement of performance. All these are areas of management where inappropriate or ineffective practice can undercut legitimate ambitions to shift the firm's trajectory to a higher level of performance.

The third part of the book considers in more detail the notion of the 'reflective practitioner'. How can managers make the best of the 'promising practices' that become available to them while avoiding the traps of faddism? How should they think about their role in creating organizations capable of learning and reflection, and the implications of learning both for organizational systems and for human behaviour? In turn, we consider the insights from cognitive science that might inform management decision-making. Then we look at the need to manage across conventional boundaries and develop the skills of reflective conversation. And finally, we consider how managers might achieve the space and time to do these things in the context of their everyday behaviour.

Notes

1. Labour Market Trends, February 2004.
2. S. Floyd and W. Wooldridge, *The Strategic Middle Manager: How to Create and Sustain Competitive Advantage* (San Francisco: Jossey-Bass, 1996); and S. W. Floyd and B. Wooldridge, 'Middle Management's Strategic Influence and Organizational Performance', *Journal of Management Studies*, 34/3 (1997), 465–85.
3. J. Plender, *Financial Times*, 19 January 2002, 13.
4. This is based on the explanation of emergent strategy by H. Mintzberg and J. A. Waters, 'Of Strategies Deliberate and Emergent', *Strategic Management Journal*, 6/3 (1985), 257–72.
5. The concept of punctuated equilibrium is explained in E. Romanelli and M. L. Tushman, 'Organisational Transformation as Punctuated Equilibrium: An Empirical Test', *Academy of Management Journal*, 37/5 (1994), 1141–61.
6. This figure is from G. Johnson, K. Scholes, and R. Whittington, *Exploring Corporate Strategy*, 7th edn. (London: FT/Prentice Hall, 2005), but was originally developed by G. Johnson, 'Rethinking Incrementalism', *Strategic Management Journal*, 9/1 (1988), 75–91.
7. Strategic drift was the term coined by G. Johnson in the paper 'Rethinking Incrementalism' (see above).
8. D. Miller, *The Icarus Paradox* (New York: Harper Business, 1990).
9. This section of the chapter is based on arguments made in Johnson, Scholes, and Whittington, *Exploring Corporate Strategy*, 45–8, 567–8.
10. H. A. Simon, *The New Science of Management Decision* (London: Prentice Hall, 1960).

11. For a more thorough explanation of the role of cognitive processes in strategy, see G. P. Hodgkinson and P. R. Sparrow, *The Competent Organization* (London: Open University Press, 2002).

12. For a discussion of the links between organizational culture and the development of strategy, see Johnson, 'Rethinking Incrementalism'; and G. Johnson, 'Managing Strategic Change—Strategy, Culture and Action', *Long Range Planning*, 25/1 (1992), 28–36.

13. See e.g. R. Greenwood and C. R. Hinings, 'Understanding Strategic Change: The Contribution of Archetypes', *Academy of Management Journal*, 36/5 (1993), 1052–81; and J. Porac, H. Thomas, and C. Baden-Fuller, 'Competitive Groups as Cognitive Communities: The Case of Scottish Knitwear Manufacturers', *Journal of Management Studies*, 26 (1989), 397–416.

14. See P. DiMaggio and W. Powell, 'The Iron Cage Revisited: Institutional Isomorphism and Collective Rationality in Organizational Fields', *American Sociological Review*, 48 (1983), 147–60.

15. See D. Deephouse, 'To be Different or to be the Same? It's a Question (and Theory) of Strategic Balance', *Strategic Management Journal*, 20 (1999), 147–66.

16. See J. Pfeffer and G. R. Salancik, *The External Control of Organizations: A Resource Dependence Perspective* (New York: Harper and Row, 1978).

17. This is discussed, for example, by K. M. Eisenhardt and D. N. Sull, 'Strategy as Simple Rules', *Harvard Business Review*, 79/1 (2001), 107–16.

18. S. L. Brown and K. M. Eisenhardt, *Competing on the Edge* (Boston: Harvard Business School Press, 1998).

2

Building on the National Context

I⟨T⟩ could be argued that UK management has never had it so good. Over the last twenty years the economic landscape of the UK has been transformed beyond recognition. Huge swathes of industry have been stripped out of the public sector and privatized. Trade union power and membership have significantly diminished, particularly in the private sector. Trade and regulatory protection of preferred industries and firms is a thing of the past. Politicians like to boast that Britain has turned itself into one of the most market-orientated and business-friendly economies in the world, in comparison with more stolid, slower-growing countries such as France and Germany.

But despite the political drum-beating, the changes leave something of a puzzle. Business-friendly and market-orientated the environment may be, but judged overall the economic results are less impressive than might have been expected. With some exceptions, companies do not seem to have made up competitive ground on their foreign counterparts. National productivity and prosperity have improved absolutely, but still obstinately lag those of direct rivals. The feeling persists that the UK is a weaker performer than it should be relative to less market-orientated economies. Why is this the case? Is it management's fault? And where do we go from here?

This chapter argues that the widespread market reforms have succeeded in creating a powerful institutional framework that encourages managers and workers to operate efficiently and effectively. But that we now face new challenges, to build new institutions that help focus attention on developing skills and promoting innovation.

The world has moved on since the reforms of the 1980s, and so has the management agenda. As Michael Porter reported to the Secretary of State for Trade and Industry in 2003:

There is a growing need for the UK to move to a new competitiveness agenda. This should be seen as a necessary transition to the next stage of economic development, not a failure of past strategy. The role of management, prominent in recent discussions of competitiveness, cannot be separated from the overall competitiveness issues facing the country.[1]

What exactly is new in this competitiveness agenda? In our view, it is the greater role cast for management in evolving UK competitiveness. This is not just management in its familiar role of improving corporate performance—although even that is less straightforward than often supposed, as the previous chapter has argued. Equally critical in today's conditions, however, is managers' ability to influence events on a less obvious dimension: creating the institutions for cooperation and coordination with policy-makers that will serve as guide-rails as they climb the value added ladder—responding more quickly to market opportunities, becoming more innovative, and creating higher-value-added products and services.

Although this particular management perspective is informed by the contemporary context, a brief account of the UK's legacy of economic underachievement is enough to show that today's competitive concerns include similarities with, as well as differences from, the past. High on the agenda for reform of the Thatcher era were macro economic instability as a cause of inflation and unemployment, and the notion that powerful trade unions were holding back productivity through restrictive practices and industrial disputes. These are no longer major preoccupations. At the same time, the shortfall of well-educated managers in business (as opposed to finance) and the lack of workers with intermediate skills are continuing worries, despite policy reforms. These two-speed outcomes are clear evidence that performance results—'competitiveness'—are more than a matter of pulling a single lever. Rather, they emerge from the interplay of a number of factors: government policy, management action, and underlying socio-economic changes in labour markets and technology. Although this book is largely about management for managers, a theme of this chapter is the importance of understanding the wider context and how these elements interact.

To set the scene, we begin by tracking the key policy interventions that have transformed the market-orientation and business-friendliness of the UK's institutional framework. In the second section, we show that, despite the reforms, the UK overall economic performance has been unimpressive compared with that of other advanced countries, although the average hides a wide range of performance within sectors and regions. Given this chequered experience, what are the challenges now facing managers and policy-makers? In subsequent chapters, we look more closely at the demands the new agenda makes of traditional performance factors that are directly under managers' own control—the challenges of creating a sustainable, high-value-adding enterprise, and the qualities that that requires of managers themselves. First, however, we open up the less familiar challenges involved in moving UK business as a whole to a different performance level: the need to craft instruments of cooperation with policy-makers that will help arrest and reverse the vicious circles in low skills, underinvestment in infrastructure, and lagging innovation that currently discourage companies from moving upmarket.

The Institutional Framework

Government policies have a major impact on the way national institutions function through legislation and by altering the economic incentives that managers, workers, and consumers respond to. Whitehall and Brussels have subjected British and European institutional structures to major overhauls over the past two decades. As a result, the UK, along with the US and New Zealand, is now conventionally speaking one of the most market-orientated and business-friendly economies in the world.

Coordinated versus Market Economies

Ideas about the optimal institutional framework for promoting national competitiveness have varied substantially over time and from place to place. In the early part of the twentieth century many countries, including the UK, nationalized large chunks of industry in the belief that central planning and government ownership could produce fuller employment and greater economies of scale than the unregulated private sector. In France, 1960s indicative planning spawned 'national champions' as a half-way house between centralized public ownership and decentralized market control (an idea that has recently made something of a comeback in French, and German thinking). Oil-shock-induced stagflation in the 1970s, and the UK's later entry into the ERM, the precursor of the euro, prompted some policy-makers to propose a variation on Scandinavian-style corporatism—a tripartite forum of employers, trade unions, and government—as a remedy for the UK's continuing competitiveness issues. With the rise of

Germany and Japan as competitive powerhouses in the 1980s, economic and business-school theorists, including Michael Porter, bemoaned Anglo-Saxon short-termism as manifested in the City of London and on Wall Street and talked up the virtues of Japanese and German institutional arrangements. More recently, people have been casting envious glances at the entrepreneurial dynamism and quick-fire innovation which have flourished in the institutional framework of the US, which seems to many a perfect fit with the opportunities thrown up by the rapid technological advances of the new economy.

We can contrast the 'ideals' of a coordinated economy with a deregulated market economy. The idea is not so much that one set of institutions is bad and the others good; rather that there is more than one engine of growth, and that different settings require different institutions.[2] In less advanced economies growth relies heavily on 'factor accumulation'—investments in physical capital, labour, and human capital or education—and on imitating and adapting technologies from more advanced countries. Both factor accumulation and imitation can flourish in economies when competition is limited and the birth rate of new firms low—that is, under regulated regimes.[3] However, in advanced knowledge-based economies, where the growth potential of factor accumulation and imitation has been exhausted, innovation at the technological frontier becomes the main source of growth. To the extent that leading-edge innovation is spurred by vigorous competition among many firms in a free market, as suggested by the US model, countries should move from a less competitive to a more competitive regime to sustain high growth rates as they evolve. But competition is not the only feature of the economic environment that affects how companies perform. Workers need the right skills, and firms must be able to access the ideas emanating from the science base.

In a liberal market economy the key economic role of the government is to ensure that markets function efficiently, while in a coordinated market model the government's task is promoting and safeguarding institutions of coordination and long-term relationships—professional and industry bodies, public–private collaborations, industry–education links, and so on. Trade theory of comparative advantage tells us that a nation specializes in goods that use the nation's relatively abundant resource. By analogy, it is easy to see that a nation can exploit 'comparative institutional advantage' by specializing in industries that make best use of the existing institutions.[4] So a liberal market economy such as the US specializes in high-technology sectors that compete on radical innovation and/or low cost—a specialization made possible by flexible financial and labour markets (plentiful venture capital and active stock markets, a mobile and entrepreneurial workforce) that enable managers to acquire and dispose of resources with low switching costs. By contrast, a coordinated market economy like Germany specializes in sectors such as precision engineering that compete on incremental innovation, requiring more cumulative adaptation and learning. However, institutions can change, and a key objective of UK and EU reform has been to move away from the old institutions favouring imitation, towards those favouring innovation—in other words, towards a more market-based economy.[5] What have the big institutional changes been?

Privatization

Since the 1980s, successive UK governments have consistently pursued policies designed to push UK institutions towards the liberal market end of the spectrum. One of the most enduring legacies of the 1980s was the programme of privatizations set in train by the Thatcher government. Privatization took various forms. Some state-owned enterprises such as Unipart, the component division of BL, were bought by their employees; others, such as British Telecom, were sold to the public at large in an attempt to turn Britain into a 'share-owning democracy'. Some public services were contracted out to the private sector, while others were hived off as independent agencies. As a result of these programmes the share of the public sector in GDP fell from around 12 per cent in 1979 to 2 per cent in 1997. Even the Post Office, spared privatization by Mrs Thatcher because the Queen's head appears on postage stamps, is being opened up to competition, bringing to an end 300 years of monopoly. More recently, the government has introduced commercial incentives into the public sector through the Private Finance Initiative (PFI) and the creation of NHS trusts. Private firms have also gained a foothold in schools and prison management.[6]

Labour Markets

Governments have worked to loosen up the functioning of labour markets. Interventions have included curbing trade union power, abolishing minimum wages (and reintroducing them at comparatively low levels), and dismantling tripartite arrangements for skills training. Perhaps the most obvious headline change was in relations with the trade unions. One of the Thatcher government's first actions on taking office was to end direct consultation with the trade unions—so-called 'beer and sandwiches at Number 10'. This abruptly curtailed relationship was reflected more subtly in the abolition of the tripartite Manpower Services Commission (MSC) and the creation of an employer-led network of Training and Enterprise Councils (TECs) in its stead. Starting with the 1980 Employment Act, Parliament passed a series of measures drastically reducing trade union power vis-à-vis both the general public and their own members, restricting picketing, tightening the use of pre-strike ballots, making trade unions susceptible to legal action, and empowering employers to resist industrial action. Wage Councils that set sector-specific minimum wages were abolished in 1993.[7]

The results of these legal and institutional changes were dramatic. The proportion of employees belonging to a trade union fell from a peak of around 56 per cent in 1979 to 29 per cent in 2003. Union membership is now a mainly public-sector phenomenon, with membership in the private sector estimated at 18 per cent compared to the public sector's 59 per cent. Meanwhile, the proportion of employees whose pay was set through collective bargaining fell from 75 per cent in 1980 to 40 per cent in 1998. Levels of strike activity fell even more sharply; the number of strikes in the period 1997–2002 was about one-tenth that of 1975–9, while numbers of days lost were a mere one-twentieth. Strikes in the private sector are now extremely rare.[8]

More recently, the Labour government has launched a large number of welfare-to-work schemes designed to get low-income individuals into work and introduced a national minimum wage. There have also been a number of efforts to reform education and training via a national curriculum and greatly increased spending on schools. However, while the proportion of school-leavers going on to higher education has risen sharply from 19 per cent in 1990/1 to 35 per cent in 2001/2, basic skills levels remain low.[9] In a comprehensive international literacy audit measuring adult proficiency in handling prose, documents, and numbers, the UK ranked respectively 13, 16, and 17 out of 22 developed economies.[10]

In parallel with these reforms, the nature of the labour market has changed substantially. In 1980 8 per cent of UK employees were self-employed. By 2001 this had increased to 11 per cent, while 24 per cent worked part-time (four-fifths of them women). Moreover, around 3 million people were working mainly at or from home. Only 35 per cent of employees now work 'standard' nine-to-five, Monday-to-Friday hours.[11] At the same time, income inequality rose considerably over the 1980s and 1990s, generating significant levels of poverty.[12] Further discussion of these developments and their implications for the management of employees are the subject of Chapter 4.

Competition Policy and Macro-stabilization

European competition policy has historically been weak, with decisions by competition authorities subject to ministerial approval, and many sectors, in particular professional services, exempt from competition law. More recently policy in the UK and EU has been tightened up. The EU's Single Market Programme has dramatically lowered barriers to the movement of goods and services and labour and financial capital.[13] In the UK the Enterprise Act 2000 gave full review powers to the Competition Commission, taking politicians out of the regulatory process, and stronger, independent regulators were recruited to oversee regulated industries.[14]

When Labour came to power in 1997, one of its first acts was to set the Bank of England a 2.5 per cent inflation target and make it independent, thus freeing economic policy-making from the influence of the political cycle. Self-imposed fiscal rules—the 'golden rule', which means borrowing only to invest over the cycle, and the sustainable investment rule, requiring net debt to be kept below 40 per cent of GDP—further emphasized stability, largely successfully: since 1997 there has been a period of uninterrupted, low-inflation growth.

The Conservatives had already deregulated the financial services industry, allowing commercial banks to compete in the market for housing loans in the retail sector, and abolishing capital controls. In the securities market, the 'Big Bang' did away with previous restrictions on firms acting as both brokers and jobbers. The process of financial liberalization was speeded up by increased demand for home loans as council houses were sold off and by mass-privatizations of many publicly owned companies.

Infrastructure

Lastly, as the Table 2.1 shows, public investment was low for the last quarter of the twentieth century, falling sharply from the mid-1970s and only recently staging a partial recovery. One response to this has been to involve the private sector in public investment projects via the PFI. So far the PFI has funded £15 billion of investment in roads, prisons, hospitals, schools, and railways—about 20 per cent of the government's capital spending over the period—the results of which are judged to be mixed.[15]

The science base is an important part of any innovation infrastructure. The UK looks rather poor on many measures of innovation, both companies and government, for example, being unenthusiastic spenders

Table 2.1. *UK net public investment as % of GDP*

Apr.–Mar. financial years	% GDP
1963–76	5.9
1976–80	3.2
1980–5	1.7
1985–90	0.9
1990–7	1.3
1997–2001	0.6
2001–7	1.6 (planned)

Note: After 1985 numbers fall in part due to movement of utilities out of the public sector into the private sector.

Source: HM Treasury, quoted in, Nickells. 'The Assessment: The Economic Record of the Labour Government since 1997', *Oxford Review of Economic Policy*, 18/2 (2002), 1–107.

on R&D compared with other G5 countries.[16] On other measures, the UK performs better, for instance scoring quite well in its share of cited papers and world papers (although the figures may be skewed by the fact that English is the international scientific language). Nonetheless, inability to convert the science base into national wealth is an enduring problem.

The Overall Picture

These reforms have undoubtedly been substantial, but what do they add up to and how do they compare with other advanced economies?

Table 2.2. *Bibliometric analysis of share in the science base*

Country	% world papers	% world citations
United States	34.2	47.9
United Kingdom	8.2	9.2
Japan	7.8	5.8
Germany	7.4	6.2
France	5.5	4.7
Canada	4.5	4.6
Italy	3.0	2.3

Source: Office of Science and Technology, *Investing in Innovation: A Strategy for Science, Engineering and Technology*, www.hm-treasury.gov.uk/spending_review/spend_sro1 spend_sro2_science.cfm.

The OECD has recently attempted to measure product- and labour-market regulation across countries, and the results are shown in Figure 2.1. It demonstrates that the UK has the least regulated product markets and one of the most liberalized labour markets in the developed world.

The picture was very different two decades ago. Figure 2.2, produced by the Fraser Institute and the World Economic Forum and based on a number of indicators (regulatory burden, product and labour market flexibility) for France, Germany, the UK, and the US, shows that by 2000 UK institutions were among the most market orientated in the world.[17] Evident too is the faster pace of institutional change in the UK than in other major economies.

These macro economic institutional reforms are important because they set the system conditions within which firms and managers can operate—but they are not in themselves enough to ensure economic growth. The behaviour of managers and workers in innovating and adopting new

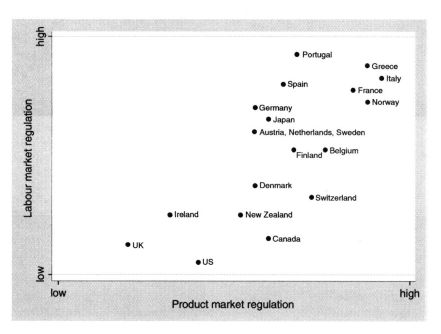

Figure 2.1. Product and labour market regulation, 1998. These measures are a composite of a large number of indicators

Source: G. Nicoletti, S. Scarpetta, and O. Boylaud, *Summary Indicators of Product Market Regulation with an Extension to Employment Protection Legislation*, OECD Economic Working Paper 226 (2000) Paris: OECI.

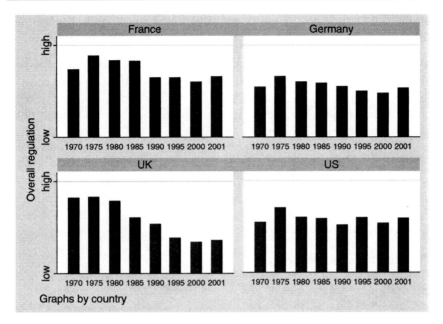

Figure 2.2.   Regulation over time, by country

Source: Fraser Institute, *Economic Freedom of the World: 2002 Annual Report* (Vancower, 2002).

technologies is also a key ingredient. National institutions matter to managers to the extent that they affect the cost and benefit of pursuing certain strategies. Some of the reforms have opened up new business opportunities. For example, lower barriers to entry have been seized on by new European 'no-frills' airlines such as Ryanair and easyJet—which have also benefited from a flexible, non-unionized workforce whose pay is set in deregulated labour markets.[18]

Overall, it can be argued that the reforms have left the UK with both strengths and weaknesses. On the credit side, firms benefit from markets that are open to international trade and investment, an unregulated economy, and sophisticated equity markets. On the other hand, they are held back by a fragile and deteriorating physical infrastructure, a shortfall in skills and education, limited access to debt finance, and low levels of R&D and innovation, in particular feeble commercial exploitation of the strong science base. In short, where the UK framework falls down is in institutions for collaboration—for example, effective industry associations or research consortia—and in encouraging management to adopt new and promising practices. The challenge of new practice adoption is further considered in Chapter 7. As Porter observes:

> The government effort to create a network of industry forums is believed to have had some success in the automotive cluster, but little impact on other clusters. There are large numbers of organizations concerned with improving general management quality, but their impact in terms of the uptake of modern management techniques appears to be low.[19]

So how are these strengths and weaknesses reflected in measures of UK national competitiveness and productivity?

How Competitive is the UK?

What is National Competitiveness?

National competitiveness is about the effective functioning of the economic system and its ability to generate wealth. A key aspect of competitiveness is productivity—the value of goods and services produced per unit of human and capital inputs. Productivity embraces firm performance but is broader than that; other contributors, for example, are the degree to which workers are matched to the most appropriate jobs and have the skills to perform them, levels of investment in physical and human capital, and innovation.

The key is not so much *which* goods and services we produce, but how *well* we produce them. The idea of comparative advantage is that, in a world where nations trade in goods and services, we are all better off if economies specialize in activities that they are good at. Comparative advantage can be driven by differences in the relative abundance of factors of production—labour, capital, raw materials, and so on. However, it is not only the cost of the inputs but also their quality that matters. Cheap labour is no advantage if the labour force is unproductive—firms just have to hire more workers to get the same job done. Put the other way round, despite much higher wage levels, a UK firm can still compete with an Indian or Chinese firm so long as its productivity is correspondingly higher. In other words, it is unit labour costs rather than wage levels as such that are important. Of course, countries cannot do much directly about the size of the workforce or their endowment of raw materials—but they can choose to invest in workers' skills through education and training, and they can choose to adopt institutions that favour investment or entrepreneurship.

The key insight of comparative advantage is that while no country can be the best at everything, there are still gains from specializing and trading. What matters is that a country is good at some things. It is the argument of this chapter that UK managers have become used to specializing in, and competing on the basis of, low-cost labour and other inputs. As we have suggested in Chapter 1, whether or not that was sensible at the time, it is no longer a viable specialization for an advanced economy. The factor advantages of India, China, and some parts of eastern Europe, for example, are so great that competing with them for low-cost, price-sensitive commodity product markets is likely to be a losing game. For the UK to compete head-to-head in these markets, as the productivity of firms in less advanced countries improves, so UK wage levels would have to fall. This is not a winning strategy. Where the UK can compete with China and India is in higher-added-value, knowledge-intensive products where smarter manufacturing and greater management know-how can compensate for the raw factor disadvantages. This is where the institutional framework comes in. Moving up the value-added ladder depends not only on the ambition and 'animal spirits' of individual entrepreneurs and firms, important though those are, but also on, for example, available skills, access to good ideas (R&D, university departments, the science base), alert and demanding customers, and sophisticated long-term investors—in other words, flexible and responsive institutions.

It is time to see how the present institutional framework stacks up in terms of UK competitiveness over a longer period.

The Competitiveness of the UK as a Whole

The wealth of an economy is usually measured by the value of goods and services it produces (GDP). To compare this across countries, we need to look at GDP per citizen. GDP per worker, or per hour worked, is a measure of labour productivity. Figure 2.3 shows GDP per hour worked and per worker in France, Germany, the UK, and the US, with the UK indexed to 100. From it we can see that, with the exception of German output per worker, on both measures the UK substantially lags its rivals.

Why should British workers produce 20–40 per cent less than those in the three other countries? There are three possible factors. One is differences in investment in, and use of, capital machinery, or capital intensity. A second could be differences in the skills of the labour force. Third—which is where management comes in—is Total Factor Productivity (TFP),

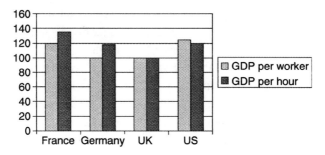

Figure 2.3. Output per worker and per hour worked in 2002

Source: ONS, http://www.statistics.gov.uk/articles/nojournal/Feb_ICP.pdf.

which comprises the rest of the variation in output levels that is not accounted for by the first two.[20] The two most important components of TFP are generally thought to be innovation and differences in technology, and the organizational efforts and skills of managers.[21]

Research by Mahoney and de Boer shows that the productivity differences between the UK and Germany are due in roughly equal measure to each of these three factors, with Germany using more capital, having higher-skilled workers, and employing more advanced technology. In France, capital intensity is more important. Comparison with the US suggests that US employees are backed by more capital, but the big difference is that they have access to substantially better technology and/or are better organized and managed. In addition, UK workers on average have lower education and skill levels than workers in France, Germany, and the US.[22]

As a matter of arithmetic, GDP per person changes along with GDP per person working and the participation rate—the proportion of people in work. Over the long term, changes in GDP per person are the most important. Is there a trade-off between the two—so that countries with higher participation rates tend to have lower productivity, perhaps because they employ a larger proportion of less productive workers? Leaving aside the US for a moment, Figure 2.4 suggests that in some circumstances this may be the case: the corollary being that if a trade-off exists, countries should be able to choose what balance between participation and productivity to strike. There is a notable exception, however. The US has managed to combine high productivity with high participation, which means that the rule is not necessarily hard and fast.[23]

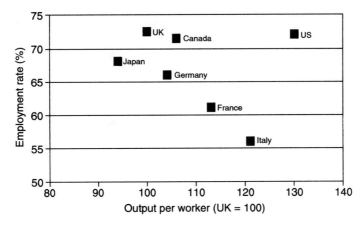

Figure 2.4. Comparison of output per worker and employment rate in 2002

Source: HMT, http://www.hm-treasury.gov.uk/media/B3A/4C/pbro3chap3_197.pdf.

The Competitiveness of Sectors within the UK

The picture above gave an impression of the whole economy, but there is great diversity between industries (and between firms within industries). Some industries in the UK are world leaders, while others lag well behind. And while on average business in the US is more productive than in the UK, the top UK firms are up there with the best in the world.

Figure 2.5 shows value added per worker in the US relative to the UK. As is clearly visible, the UK is less productive than the US in every sector except mining and quarrying, and electricity, gas, and water. The size of the productivity gap varies considerably across sectors. The gap is largest in machinery and equipment, where the US is more than twice as productive. Next largest are the gaps in hotels and restaurants, and financial intermediation.

The Competitiveness of UK plc

The data above show that on average the UK is lagging. But when we look across establishments operating within the geographic boundaries of the UK, the essential fact about productivity that emerges is its huge variation.

Table 2.3 shows differences in plant-level productivity (measured as value added per worker) for all UK manufacturing plants. It is a remarkable picture. Stripping out possibly misleading extremes and comparing the productivity of the plant at the 90th and 10th percentiles of the ranking

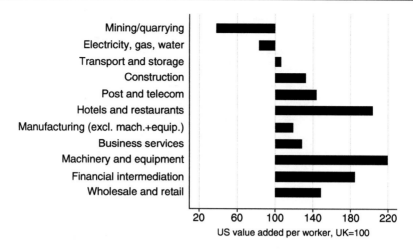

Figure 2.5. US productivity advantage over the UK in 2000

Source: R. Griffith, R. Harrison, J. Hastel, and M. Safo, 'The UK Productivity Gap and the Importance of the Service sector', AIM Briefing Note, London, 2003, www.aimresearch.org/publication/rabrief.pdf./

(i.e. the plant producing more per worker than 90 per cent of the others and the plant producing more than only the worst 10 per cent), the first row of the table indicates that in 1980 of 13,024 manufacturing plants the plant at the 90th percentile was four times as productive as that at the 10th percentile. The second row shows that by 2000 the number of plants had fallen by one-third and the value of output per head had quadrupled—but the difference between the 10th and 90th percentile was still the same. So overall the differentials had not narrowed.

These data are for all manufacturing plants, covering an enormous range of industries which have very different intrinsic productivity levels.

Table 2.3. *The productivity spread*

	Number	Mean plan productivity[a]	90/10 ratio[b]
Plants in 1980	13,024	8.6	4.0
Plants in 2000	8,119	32.3	4.2
Plants in 2000, vehicles	336	31.5	3.4
TFP	20	4.2	1.5

[a] Measured as value added per worker.
[b] Ratio of 90th percentile to 10th percentile.

Source: Calculations from the ARD dataset.

Row 3 recalculates the differentials for a single industry, vehicles (comprising motor vehicles, trailers, and semi-trailers). There are 336 plants in this industry, and, as the table shows, they display similar average productivity to the picture overall. However, despite narrowing the range of plants included,there are still enormous differentials with the top (90th percentile) plant still producing over three times as much as the bottom (10th percentile) plant.

Now let us look at inputs, concentrating just on data from the twenty plants making vehicle bodies. Row 4 of the table shows the differential in terms of TFP (output per unit of capital and labour), which is 1.5 for the vehicle body plants that we have data for. This is clearly less than the productivity difference, which is partly due to differences in capital. But row 4 still demonstrates a very important fact. Walk round these plants in the same region, in the same industry, and allow for different capital: you will still find that the top plants are 50 per cent more productive than the bottom ones.[24]

There is one other comparison to make. Consider foreign-owned manufacturing firms operating in the UK with the same infrastructure, the same pool of workers, and the same regulations as domestic companies. Operating in the same environment, foreign-owned plants do better, with US firms particularly productive. However, care is needed with these comparisons. Foreign firms are, by definition, multinational enterprises (MNEs), while only a small subset of domestic plants are owned by MNEs. Thus the comparison of foreign firms with *all* UK firms is not a like-with-like comparison. It would be more informative to compare foreign MNEs with UK MNEs, not with all UK firms. This produces a very different picture, as set out in Figure 2.6.

Two points stand out. First, UK MNEs are much better performers than UK domestics on both productivity measures. Secondly, when one compares UK MNEs with other MNEs, the UK disadvantage does not look quite so great. What are the causes for these productivity differentials? They are complex and vary according to the industries and types of firms involved. Ongoing research is looking at a number of explanations but, as we have indicated above, poor infrastructure, a lack of appropriate basic skills, limited levels of investment in R&D, and a failure to commercialize basic science are all likely to play a part.[25] But, in combination, what the figures presented here also affirm is that the organizational efforts and skills of management play a significant role in the UK's performance deficit.

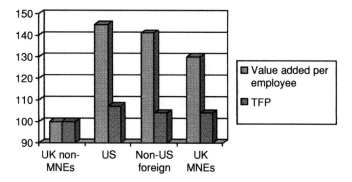

Figure 2.6. Value added per worker, UK manufacturing plants, 2000

Source: C. Criscuolo and R. Martin, *US Productivity Leadership: Evidence from Britain*, CeRiBa working paper (2004), www.ceriba.org.uk.

The Challenge

Successful implementation of market-based reforms through privatization, deregulation, and competition policy has shifted the UK economy out of its pre-1980 trajectory of economic stagnation on to a new track. Compared to many European economies, the UK is now a notably market-orientated and 'business-friendly' location, as demonstrated by both measures of the national institutional framework and macroeconomic indicators showing the gains from the changes in terms of growth, low inflation, and relatively full employment.

But, as we have seen, 'business-friendliness' is not everything—otherwise UK productivity would by now have overtaken that of apparently less friendly locations such as France and Germany. The difficulty is that competitiveness is a moving target. The terrain on which businesses operate is constantly shifting. UK companies now have to compete with rivals from low-cost nations such as China, India, central and eastern Europe, and other emerging economies which enjoy substantial factor advantages. In the face of this competition, the gains from the past two decades of UK reform—reform that created market institutions best suited to the exploitation of low costs as a source of competitive advantage—are running out. Technology and adaptability (with a strong management component) are becoming increasingly important.[26] To stay competitive, the UK needs a new approach that reflects today's imperatives: to move upmarket, to create higher-value products and services, to be more innovative, to come up with unique strategies and ways of competing.[27]

These changes provide challenges to both policy-makers and managers. The competitiveness agenda facing UK leaders in business and government is couched in terms of developing new institutions that reflect the interrelated nature of the two and can keep pace with the changing economic environment. This requires a fundamental shift in management attitudes, in particular managers' views on how their business operations relate to the government, other businesses, and institutions such as universities. Figure 2.7 is an aid to thinking about these issues.

The focus of this book is on the role of managers. We can draw two broad conclusions from the review presented in this chapter. The first is that adjusting corporate strategy to existing institutions is necessary but not sufficient for firms to remain competitive. Recall that the Porter report identified three key UK management weaknesses:

- investment: failure to invest enough in capital assets and innovation;

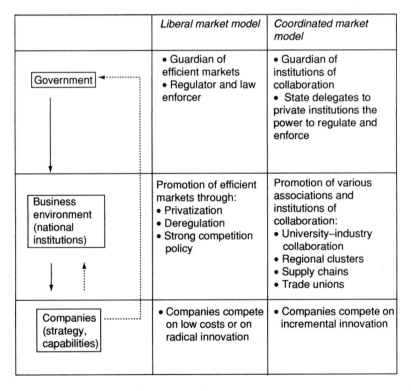

Figure 2.7. Business operations in relation to government, other businesses, and institutions

- strategic positioning: choosing to compete with products that rely on low input cost rather than high value or innovation;
- management: reluctance compared with rivals to adopt modern management techniques.

In the context of the deregulated markets created by UK policy reforms, these characteristics are unsurprising. Policies to cut down red tape and lower labour and other costs of doing business encouraged companies to centre their competitive position on low input costs; reluctance to invest in R&D and new management techniques can be explained in the same way. The two downward arrows connecting the three boxes in Figure 2.7 describes this mindset, in which managers see the government setting policies that create an institutional framework that in turn is taken as given: 'this is the environment in which we have to do business'. Implicit in this mindset is that managers can do little to create new institutions for innovation and higher added value; it is for the government to take the initiative and for managers to respond. The response may well include voting with their feet—locating out of the UK where the institutions are more favourable. Outsourcing to India is a good example of companies continuing to play the low-cost input card.

The second conclusion is that policies and management practices are complementary, so getting out of a competitiveness problem requires proactive working to create new policies and practices together. Despite—or perhaps because of—the government's policy record on market liberalization, the World Economic Forum's Global Competitiveness Report (2003) also points to UK weaknesses in relatively low levels of public investment in infrastructure, public R&D, and education. These features of public policy are related to and complement national management characteristics. For instance, corporate emphasis on low input cost creates less demand for well-educated and highly skilled workers, while the limited supply from the education system makes it harder to alter the strategy. Similarly, low levels of public-sector R&D are reflected in weak R&D spending and a low innovation count in the private sector.

How do we get out of this vicious circle—a self-reinforcing spiral linking public policy and corporate strategy? The government may attempt to create financial and other incentives to increase the supply of highly educated workers. But what of the role that might be played by managers seeking to make a difference? A shift in corporate strategy to one that puts more reliance on skills will in itself create effective demand for workers who possess them. In addition, managers can create or support educational initiatives to improve the quality of both managers and workers, or strengthen company links to universities through collaborative R&D. Managers can transform relations with competitors, customers, and suppliers, through the creation of new industry clusters and associations. In other words, UK management has a constructive and proactive role to play in altering the character of the national institutions to reflect the need for innovation and risk-taking. Figure 2.7's two upward arrows, connecting companies to institutions and the government, illustrate this mindset.

In the past two decades, UK companies have done quite well to adjust to the business environment they have found themselves in—an environment created by a government which has seen its role above all as promoting efficient markets, dismantling institutional obstructions to their working, and strengthening its position as regulator and enforcer of strict competition policy. Now, however, the challenge lies in making the leap to the next stage, by enhancing investment in technology and skills, and making companies more competitive through innovation and high-value-added operations. How, and whether, this goal is achieved depends in part on the ability of the UK government to evolve from being a guardian of efficient markets to a promoter of institutions of collaboration working in partnership with companies. In transition, managers can either wait and see (or lobby for) what the government might do; or they can proactively work to transform their business environment by creating new institutions, for instance collaborative linkages in research, training, certification, and marketing. As discussed in Chapter 1, for managers to make a real difference even within companies is more of a challenge than often assumed. The implication of this chapter is that working to improve external conditions and incentives such that the UK institutional context fits with the goals of higher-value-added businesses may turn out to be as critical to evolving competitiveness as the more familiar managerial role of performance improvement.

Notes

1. Michael E. Porter and Christian H. M. Ketels, *UK Competitiveness: Moving to the Next Stage*, DTI Economics Paper 3 (2003).
2. For recent academic work on this see EU Sapir Report, 'An agenda for a growing Europe: Making the EU economic system deliver', report of an independent

high-level study group (2003), http://europa.eu.int/comm/lisbon_strategy/pdf/sapir_report_en.pdf.

3. This relates to the well-known infant-industry argument; see e.g. P. Krugman and M. Obstfeld, *International Economics, Theory and Policy* (Reading, MA Addison Wesley, 2003).

4. P. Hall and D. Soskice (eds.), *Varieties of Capitalism: The Institutional Foundations of Comparative Advantage* (Oxford: Oxford University Press, 2001).

5. EU Lisbon agreement documents and Sapir Report, *An Agenda for a Trawing Europe* (Oxford: Oxford University Press, 2004).

6. There is a substantial literature on privatization and performance. Most agree that productivity is boosted by market liberalization and by pre-privatization restructuring; see e.g. W. L. Megginson and J. M. Netter, 'From the State to the Market: A Survey of Empirical Studies on Privatization', *Journal of Economic Literature*, 39 (2001), 321–89. For data across countries; and the UK, R. Green and J. Haskel, 'Seeking a Premier Economy: The Role of Privatization', in R. Blundell, D. Card, and R. Freeman (eds.), *Seeking a Premier Economy* (Chicago: University of Chicago Press for NBER, 2004.

7. Low Pay Commission, First Report, appendix 5, http://www.dti.gov.uk/er/low-pay/.

8. See P. Blyton and P. Turnbull, *The Dynamics of Employee Relations* (Basingstoke: Palgrave, 2004).

9. See C. Crouch, D. Finegold, and M. Sako, *Are Skills the Answer?* (Oxford: Oxford University Press, 2000).

10. Quoted in 'Full And Fulfilling Employment: Creating the Labour Market of the Future', DTI report, http://www.dti.gov.uk/er/emar/fullemp.pdf.

11. Labour Force Survey, reported in http://www.dti.gov.uk/er/emar/fullemp.pdf.

12. The Gini coefficient, a measure of inequality, rose from around 0.25 in 1979 to 0.38 in the late 1990s (T. Clark et al., 'Taxes and Transfers 1997–2001', *Oxford Review of Economic Policy*, 18/2 (2003), figure 7).

13. The Single Market Programme consisted of around 300 measures in six main areas of action, namely (1) unified markets in goods and services, (2) unified factor market, (3) promotion of competition, (4) monetary integration, (5) social protection, and (6) united response to external challenges.

14. For a discussion of the literature on the impact of competition on managerial incentives, innovation, and performance, see P. Aghion and R. Griffith, *Competition and Innovation* (Cambridge, MA: MIT Press, 2005).

15. See P. Grout, 'The Economics of the Private Finance Initiative', *Oxford Review of Economic Policy*, 13/4 (1997), 53–66; M. Pollitt, 'The Declining Role of the State in Infrastructure Investments in the UK', in M. Tsuji, S. V. Berg, and M. G. Pollitt (eds.), *Private Initiatives in Infrastructure: Priorities, Incentives and Performance* (Tokyo: Institute of Developing Economies, Japan External Trade Organization, 2000).

16. For recent evidence see R. Griffith and R. Harrison, 'Understanding the UK's Poor Technological Performance', IFS Briefing Note 37 (2003). The UK's R&D performance over the period 1981–2000 was poor relative to the USA and other

G5 countries. Over the 1980s, reductions in government-funded R&D account for three-quarters of the UK's poor R&D performance relative to the USA. Roughly two-thirds of these reductions are associated with cuts in defence spending. Weak growth in R&D funded and conducted by business accounts for only one-sixth of the UK's poor performance relative to the USA over the 1980s, but accounts for all of the UK's poor performance over the 1990s. The UK's poor business R&D performance relative to the USA was due to weak within-sector growth in R&D rather than a shift in output towards low-R&D sectors. The relative decline in within-sector R&D intensity was particularly extreme during the mid-1990s. The UK's within-sector decline in R&D intensity relative to the USA was in both the manufacturing and the non-manufacturing sectors. During the mid-1990s, it was largely concentrated in the manufacturing sector. However, towards the end of the 1990s, the USA experienced a large increase in non-manufacturing R&D intensity that was not seen in any of the other G5 countries. The relative decline in R&D intensity within the UK manufacturing sector was concentrated in a few industries, particularly those related to machinery, equipment, and transportation. In contrast, pharmaceuticals were responsible for a large positive contribution to growth in R&D intensity compared with the USA.

17. Other indicators reveal a similar picture, e.g. the data cited in the Sapir Report, *An Agenda for a Growing Europe: The Sapir Report* (Oxford: Oxford University Press, 2004).

18. There is a union recognition agreement for only the pilots union (BALPA) at easyJet since 2001.

19. Porter and Ketels, *UK Competitiveness.*

20. Blundell, Card, and Freeman explore this question in depth: David E. Card and Richard B. Freeman, 'What Have Two Decades of British Economic Reform Delivered?', in R. Blundell, D. Card, and R. Freeman (eds.), *Seeking a Premier Economy: The Economic Effects of British Economic Reforms, 1980–2000* (Chicago: University of Chicago Press for NBER, 2004).

21. We focus on private-sector productivity here. Although the public sector is a significant part of the UK economy—government output accounts for 20 per cent of GDP—measuring productivity is difficult. The United Nations System of National Accounts (SNA), to which the UK subscribes, suggests that government output should be measured in terms of the outputs produced (for example, the number of healthcare treatments) rather than the inputs consumed (the number of doctors). Changes in its quality should be reflected in the output measure. The Atkinson Review is currently looking at this issue.

22. Porter and Ketels, *UK Competitiveness.*

23. There is a difficult measurement problem here: if one is measuring output per person without adjusting for the skills of those persons, then it is likely to fall as the less skilled enter work. But it might be argued that it would be more appropriate to measure output per person controlling for skills.

24. See J. Haskel and R. Martin, 'The UK Manufacturing Productivity Spread', Centre for Research into Business Activity Paper, 2002, available at http://www.ceriba.org.uk.which maps the productivity progress of all plants between 1980 and 1990. This shows that 31.5% of employment in plants that were in the top quintile of productivity in 1980 were still in the top quintile a decade later; that 12.9% of plants in the top quintile in 1980 were in the second quintile in 1990. Only 4.6% of plants descended into the third quintile. That 49.8% of plants from the top quintile in fact exited. That the fraction of plants in the bottom quintile in 1980 making it to the top quintile in 1990 was very small, 0.4%. That 21.5% of plants in the bottom quintile in 1980 were still there in 1990. Of plants in the bottom quintile in 1980, 70.8% exited by 1990. The fraction of plants in the top quintile in 1990 who entered at some point over the decade was 58.7%. Interestingly, the fractions are rather evenly spread with plants that enter spread over the productivity distribution.

25. There is large literature looking at differences in performance between multinationals and domestic firms. See R. Martin and C. Criscuolo (http://www.ceriba.org.uk/) and R. Griffith and H. Simpson, 'Characteristics of Foreign-Owned Firms on UK Manufacturing Productivity', in R. Blundell, D. Card, and R. Freeman (eds.), *Seeking a Premier Economy* (Chicago: University of Chicago Press for NBER, 2004).

26. The Sapir Report.

27. Professor Michael Porter of Harvard Business School, quoted in 'Why Costing on Past Gains will Leave us Washed up', *Financial Times*, 23 January 2003.

PART II

The Building Blocks

3

Transforming Strategy

How did British Airways go from 'Bloody Awful' in the 1970s, to 'Bloody Awesome' and 'the world's favourite airline' in the 1980s, then back into the doldrums by the turn of the millennium? Why is Marks & Spencer, historically one of Britain's most successful and admired companies, now regularly held up as a model of corporate failure? How has easyJet been so successful in the late 1990s and early 2000s? The answer lies in the management of corporate and business strategy.

In the first two chapters, we looked at the need for UK companies to move up the value chain and, within that context, at the challenge for managers in 'making a difference' strategically. Now it is time to give closer consideration to strategy itself. What is strategy? There is surprisingly little agreement.[1] An underlying theme, however, is that strategy is the means for achieving sustainable competitive advantage resulting in superior returns to shareholders (and the achievement of other stakeholder objectives). In this chapter we review some classic strategy approaches and conclude that almost all of them suffer from being overly static. Static strategies are better viewed as 'business models'. We argue that, if managing strategy is really about the long-term creation of value, then fundamental to strategic management is the need to change business models. Sustaining higher added value than competitors, almost by definition, means changing strategies over time. UK firms face many sources of market and other changes that require corresponding strategy changes: accelerating globalization, increasing European integration, further deregulation of protected sectors, abrupt technological change such as the Internet and other information technologies, and the continuing influx of foreign firms, many with highly effective management methods and talent.

This chapter argues, then, that if businesses are to be successful in the long term, it is the management of strategic transformation that is the prime challenge. Strategies have to be dynamic, not static. Simple rules of thumb, such as 'stick to the knitting', can lead to a dead end—particularly at a moment when managers are seeking to develop higher-order sources of advantage rather than low input costs. Finland's Nokia did not become internationally successful as a producer of rubber boots (its original business), but as the world's leading producer of mobile telephones. Furthermore, the reflective manager needs to beware of simplistic strategy formulas and rules. Successful new strategies and business models require creative insights to break away from conventional approaches.

Put Strategy before Financial Performance

Many companies make financial performance, especially enhancement of shareholder value, their primary focus. This may be correct—but only so long as companies do not neglect the strategies that actually drive superior financial performance. Getting the strategy right is the first requirement. Financial performance will follow—as such, it is an essential measure of just how good the strategy is. To paraphrase former US President Bill Clinton's election guide in 1992, 'It's the strategy, stupid'. A simple way to think about the link from strategy to financial performance is that a successful strategy allows a firm to do at least three things:

- extract financial returns from its activities that are greater than its cost of capital—otherwise shareholders and other investors will withdraw their funds;
- achieve financial returns that are greater than those of its competitors—otherwise competitors will be able to reinvest more, thereby tilting the balance of competitive advantage in their direction;
- achieve superior financial returns that are sustainable in the long run—financial markets price a firm's shares on the basis of expected long-term returns, even if individual owners hold shares for relatively short periods.

How then does a firm achieve the nirvana of a successful strategy?

The Classic Answers to Strategic Success

Forty years of research by management academics and consultants have generated many ideas about what constitutes strategic success. These prescriptions can be grouped under the following headings:

- deploy strategic planning;
- choose an 'attractive' industry or the right 'position' or 'strategic group' in an industry;
- employ generic strategies (such as differentiation or low cost) or a focused strategy;
- think of strategy as resources and competencies;
- outsmart the competition by making fast strategy changes;
- diversify.

What do we know about how these ideas about strategy relate to performance?

Make Use of Strategic Planning

One school of thought has stressed the *process* of developing strategy rather than the strategies themselves. In particular, strategic planning and its predecessor, long-range planning, held sway from the 1960s through the 1980s, until increased turbulence in markets and other aspects of the environment made formal planning less popular. There is increasing evidence that where formal planning systems exist, they are more about the coordination and control of strategies that have developed in other ways.[2] Indeed, when executives describe what they mean by 'strategic planning' nowadays, they often talk about 'away days', strategy workshops, 'think tanks', and the like, rather than formal planning processes. Also, it has been almost impossible to demonstrate that companies that do plan strategically achieve any better results than those that do not—which is perhaps not surprising, given that such studies do not take account of the content of the strategies themselves.[3] Moreover, it was often the already well-managed and superior performing companies that made the most use of formal strategic planning.

Our view is that companies do need some way to deal with the complexity of strategy-making. But how they do this—more or less formally—depends on the nature of the business, the context it operates in, and the expertise and nature of managers.[4] To sum up: all companies need some form of strategic planning, but it is reflective and questioning strategic thinking that underpins the management of strategy.

Choose an Attractive Industry

Industries differ in the level of company performance they permit over time. Research suggests that this 'industry effect' arises from industry conditions, especially the level of competition.[5] Take US airlines, for example. The industry allowed most of its participants to enjoy superior performance for three decades from the late 1940s until the late 1970s. Then came deregulation in 1978, which allowed an influx of new entrants, in turn provoking a profitability collapse for many carriers. A similar pattern is emerging in Europe.

However, it turns out that within nearly every industry some firms do much better (or worse) than the average. Even in a 'bad' industry it is still possible to be a winner. In airlines a few discounters, such as Ireland's Ryanair, easyJet in the UK, and Southwest Airlines in the US, all perform very well indeed. Conversely, a company can also be a loser in a 'good' industry. SSL International, formed from the 1999 merger of Seton Scholl Healthcare and London International, formerly London Rubber Group, is one of the UK's major healthcare companies. Because of its haphazard corporate-level strategy, SSL has greatly underperformed relative to its industry—between the merger date and mid-2004 its share price halved—and it has done even worse compared to the healthcare-sector index. This poor performance is particularly surprising given the company's participation in highly attractive segments of the healthcare market, including footcare, surgical products, and condoms, where Durex is the world's market leader.

Much recent academic research now questions the contribution to firm performance of industry effects as opposed to company or business-unit effects (which in theory are under management's control).[6] The reality seems to be that the average company shares the fate of its industry, but companies at the extreme can under- or overperform.[7]

Conceptually, a neater prescription seems to be to position a company within the 'right' strategic group within an industry. For example, no-frills airlines constitute a strategic group within the airline industry, and their performance is currently far better than that of their full-fare, full-service competitors. So the key may be to get into the attractive part of an industry, with a business model that works for that segment or strategic group. In many ways, the strategic group argument is a sub-case of the industry argument, both of them being about selecting the right arena for competition. But the evidence for the effect of strategic group membership on performance is even thinner than that for industry membership.[8]

So while it certainly helps to be in a good industry and the right strategic group, managers still need to work at developing advantages relative to competitors.

Use Generic Strategies

For a while, it was popular to think that there were a few simple 'generic' strategies that would result in superior performance. One combination was the 'low-cost', 'differentiation', or 'focus' set of options, and avoiding being 'stuck in the middle'.[9] But there has been a great deal of confusion over just what these generic strategies mean.

- Low cost is not a basis for competitive advantage if everyone is striving for it. Indeed, the idea of 'low cost' as a strategy is dangerous, precisely because firms fail to see that low cost is usually a threshold requirement in an industry. As we saw in Chapter 2, this is particularly relevant to the UK. Everyone is searching for low cost—it is a necessary requirement to be an effective player in the game. It is not, however, a basis for competitive advantage. It would only be an advantage if it were *lowest* cost, such that competitors knew they could not compete effectively against it; and that is extremely hard to achieve without extraordinary scale or market-share advantages or unique factor–cost benefits—for example, access to some uniquely beneficial resource.
- Low price is often confused with low cost. A business following a low-price strategy is often referred to as following a 'low-cost' strategy. But clearly cost and price are not the same. And businesses following a low-price strategy need to learn the lesson described above: success is likely to depend on lowest, not low, cost.
- Until recently, the notion of differentiation was not even conceptually clarified. It was translated as 'being different', which in itself is of no benefit. It is only of benefit if the difference is both valuable to buyers and capable of being sustained against competitors. For instance, in the 1990s Sainsbury's promoted itself as being 'different', using its old slogan, 'good food costs less at Sainsbury's'. It argued that price competition was unnecessary, since customers would pay for superior quality. By the 1990s, however, 'good food' had become a basic customer expectation. Incapable of providing buyers with a difference

that was valuable in terms of either quality or price, and confronted with the emergence of higher-performing competitors such as Tesco, Sainsbury's supermarket business model found itself facing serious questions by the end of the 1990s.

Not surprisingly, research which has sought to make a link between ill-defined generic strategies and performance has been doomed for these and other reasons.[10] In any case, it is not *differences* but *similarity* of strategies which tends to describes competitors.[11]

In Chapter 1 we noted that accountants, long-haul airlines, and car manufacturers tend to resemble each other strategically and imitate each other's innovations. Indeed, the whole idea of strategic groups builds on the idea of strategic similarity among directly competing firms. We also saw that successful strategies are often copied, as less successful rivals climb on a better bandwagon and industry norms and practices assert themselves.[12] There is a logic to this: reproducing successful industry strategy may not only be a 'safer bet' than differentiation in itself, it may also be perceived as such, gaining the mainstream a privileged position with suppliers, investors, and potential employees, for example.

Some commentators have argued that a 'strategic balance' between differentiation and similarity may be a sensible approach; and there is some evidence that balance does result in higher levels of return than more extreme differentiation or imitation.[13] Some of the most successful UK companies seem to pursue a strategic balance. BA usually outperforms full-service rivals Lufthansa and Air France through a strategy of being first with a continuing stream of minor points of difference, such as beds in business class or dinner in the business-class lounge before a flight.

So there may be good reasons for following the industry conventional wisdom unless a company can find a superior and defensible strategy. The fact that mainstream UK banks share very similar business models did not prevent most of them from posting record profits in 2004. The danger is that, in time, an existing industry player, or more likely a new one, decides to defy industry norms and practices and thereby changes the rules of the game. (We describe the case of the no-frills carriers in the airline industry later in the chapter.) So even though adopting standard industry practice may be sensible in the short term, it is unlikely to provide for long-term success. Deciding when to change and how to do it becomes the challenge.

Focus on a generic strategy can thus work for a time, but it may cause managers to become strategically blinkered as industry conditions change.

Strategy as Resources and Competencies

A dominant influence on the strategy debate is the idea that it should be based on a thorough understanding of the organization's resources and competencies—its strategic capabilities. In the 'resource-based view' of strategy,[14] businesses gain competitive advantage by developing products or services, or selecting markets, that allow them to capitalize on the things they are good at, especially where these qualities are difficult to imitate and can therefore be expected to last. At the most obvious level, resources might be the technology of BAE Systems, the branch network of HSBC, or Unilever's brands. Competencies might be Ryanair's operational capabilities or Tesco's logistics systems. This approach, however, is not as straightforward as it might appear.

One problem is that it is circular. Saying that an organization is successful because it has capabilities that are superior to those of another is unenlightening and close to tautology.[15] Moreover, how can a firm know in advance which resources and competencies are required for success? Even if it does know—from observing competitors, say—it might find them difficult if not impossible to imitate.[16]

The difficulty is that competencies responsible for the strategic success of the organization are likely to reside not so much in physical assets as in a myriad of routine behaviours and activities that have built up over time. The chances of being able to imitate the entire business system of a rival are slim indeed.[17] Indeed, advantage may dwell in competencies embedded in organizational systems of which managers are not even fully aware. This raises the uncomfortable question of just how readily managers of firms can deliberately engineer such embedded competencies. As two academics have put it with some understatement: 'It is likely to be quite difficult for practitioners to effectively manipulate that which is inherently unknowable.'[18]

Further, strategies based on embedded competencies may outlive their usefulness, ending up damaging performance rather than supporting it. As we noted in Chapter 1, past success is no guarantee for the future: core competencies can easily become core rigidities.[19] With hindsight, it is possible to see that the demise of many organizations was rooted in their very success.[20]

We can conclude, therefore, that resources and competencies can be significant bases of competitive advantages—but only so long as they do not become core rigidities and lead to strategic inertia.

Outsmart your Competitors or Make Fast Strategy Changes

An emerging school of thought is less concerned with long-term sustainable bases of strategy and competitive advantage, focusing instead on 'hyper-competition' or 'hyper-competitive strategy'.[21] Here the argument is that the search for lasting competitive advantage is vain, because competitors can more rapidly imitate or circumvent strategies than ever before. In other words, advantage lies in agility or speed of thought. The most obvious example is high-tech businesses where innovations have shorter and shorter shelf-lives. But even in relatively steady-state industries, such as accounting, advantages tend to be short-lived and easily replicated. In such circumstances, how should strategists behave?

Richard D'Aveni argues that, having created a basis of competitive advantage, managers must change it again before it is imitated: 'eat your own lunch before someone else eats it for you'. But here again, the assumption is that change occurs within the existing business model. Nike launches a successful new trainer, but before competitors can imitate it, it brings out another model. Arguably, the orientation is again the short term. In our terms, unless hyper-competitive strategies build on lasting competencies of innovation and creativity that can serve as the bases of building and rebuilding competitive advantage over time, this is tactics, not strategy.[22] There is little evidence to suggest that firms are able to achieve sustained higher performance in this way over time.

Making fast competitive changes may help. But competitive advantage built this way requires rare strategic capabilities of speed, creativity, and innovation, which are in short supply in the UK. It will also be difficult to sustain. More fundamental strategic changes may sometimes still be needed.

Diversify

The strategies we have discussed so far all concern a single business or business model. In fact many, perhaps most, businesses seek to extend or stretch their business model, believing that they can thereby build on their existing competencies. They launch new products, seek new markets, or acquire new businesses in the belief that those moves will fit with their current business model; that they are somehow 'related'. Studies of diversification have focused a good deal on the extent to which 'related' or 'unrelated' diversification makes more or less sense.[23] The main lesson from these studies: while moderate levels of diversification appear to have positive results, stretching the business too far into a multitude of related business activities does not work. One dilemma is that companies do not recognize the 'diversification too far' until it is done. The UK brewing companies of the 1980s argued themselves from brewing and pubs, through hotels, into holiday camps and eventually gambling—all in the name of relatedness. And Saatchi & Saatchi, having become the world's largest advertising agency, overstretched itself with a foray into management consulting and a failed lunge at banking. By contrast, WPP, set up by Saatchi's previous finance director, Martin Sorrell, has prospered with a much more focused series of diversifications into related marketing services.

A second problem, however, is the difficulty of being clear about just what 'moderate' levels of diversification, 'related', or 'focused' diversification mean in practice. Related to what? Focused on what? Here research is rather less helpful. We can, however, generalize to the extent that problems arise when the conglomeration of businesses becomes too complex to manage. Putting it another way, competencies can be stretched only so far. Trying to build businesses that are unrelated suffers from similar problems. Having diversified 'far enough', the organization is faced with the need to manage the business model it has evolved or developed to that point.

In summary, the right kind of diversification strategy can work well. The trick is to avoid overdiversifying.

The Need for Dynamic Strategies

The previous section suggests that managing strategy is a constant balancing and rebalancing act, complicated by the need for managers to make long-term commitments while walking the tightrope of competition. Successful strategic formulas in the form of business models are constantly challenged by changes in the environment: customers, competitors, markets, technology, and the economy in general. It is tempting to believe that success is about exploiting the current business model—and so it is to a point. The dilemma is deciding when to change. Poker is a good analogy. A poker hand is good or bad only relative to what other players hold. A flush beats a straight but loses to a full house. Marks & Spencer had a winning hand until speciality retailers came along. Like rash poker players, many companies attempt near-impossible strategies: the odds against 'drawing to an inside straight' are 10 to 1. The decision 'when to hold and when to fold' also applies in business.

The biggest criticism of the classic strategies is that most of them are static, while sustaining competitive advantage requires a dynamic approach. One way to reconcile this contradiction is to think of the distinction between routine and transformational approaches to managing strategy. Pursuing competitive advantage by exploiting the existing business model is a routine approach. Changing the business model to achieve long-term value creation and survival—the challenge now facing many UK companies—is transformational. Based in the UK's very open economy, British firms face stiff challenges from foreign competitors. At one extreme is the low-cost threat from countries such as China and India, at the other, competition from US companies enjoying the scale advantages of a much bigger domestic economy. Competition is also intensifying from European companies that are modernizing themselves under the spur of EU integration. Even in sectors where foreign competition is limited, such as retail, UK firms are up against many strategic challenges—witness the tribulations of Marks & Spencer and Sainsbury's. Systematic, professional, and aggressive management has become the norm for UK industry leaders. Laggards must improve or die.

Business Model versus Strategy

We noted that although strategy is one of the most important fields of business enquiry, there has been little agreement on what it really is.[24] By introducing the term 'business model', the Internet boom may have inadvertently helped to clear up the confusion. In essence, we can say that companies use *transformational* strategies to change their business models and *routine* strategies to change their market positions. Companies employ routine strategies, such as a marketing strategy to increase market share, all the time. But they have recourse to transformational strategies only rarely—usually when changes in the environment make their current business model untenable. Few firms voluntarily choose to embrace a new business model.

The root cause and rarity of transformational strategies explain their low rate of success. First, replacing a business model is a giant step that is inherently risky. Secondly, most companies and executives have little experience of devising and implementing transformational strategies. After all, many business models work successfully for decades. For example, IBM's mainframe computer business model functioned effectively from the mid-1960s to the PC revolution of the mid-1980s. Marks & Spencer's business model was finely honed from its early development at the end of the nineteenth century through decades of success until the late 1990s.

In a few rare cases, companies seek to change their business model from a position of strength (although typically facing incipient environmental challenges and threats). Portfolio management is one way of doing this. In the late 1980s Whitbread was a successful UK brewing company with developing interests in restaurants and hotels. By 2004 it was no longer a brewing business at all. It did not even own any pubs, having moved decisively into leisure with the purchase of health clubs, coffee shops, and hotels.

Change may also come through diversification. Up to the mid-1980s, Smith & Nephew was an inconspicuous UK supplier of unrelated, low-margin medical products. Over the next two decades, the company trans-formed itself into the leading provider of high-margin technological prod-ucts in the US 'wound management' market.

Companies can sometimes achieve a switch of business model organic-ally, as shown by Tesco's successful move away from its original 'pile it high and sell it cheap' formula of the 1970s. By centralizing its distribution system and through a transformational strategy based on low-cost probes in technological, service, and foreign market areas, Tesco has built a reputation as a highly innovative company with a focused international strategy.

Finally, a company can craft a mix of approaches to achieve the same end: through a combination of organic development, experimental acqui-sitions, and joint ventures; for example, the Royal Bank of Scotland has transformed itself in less than two decades from a provincial niche player—a holding company for two regional banks—into a diversified global financial services provider.

It must be emphasized, however, that the ability to change business models is the exception rather than the rule. All transformational strat-egies are inherently risky, since they involve moving from equilibrium, through disequilibrium, to another position of balance.

Strategy always involves managing change to some degree, whether to a market, a business's position in a market, or a business model. In the case of routine or incremental strategies, nearly every business seeks to improve its position incrementally. A company usually wants to improve its market share, cost and quality position, and profitability, and commonly all of them, generally by means of routine strategies that do not change the underlying business model. For example, by boosting advertising, intro-ducing new products, enhancing customer satisfaction, and the like, a company might hope to increase its market share by 10 or 15 per cent. More lofty ambitions—doubling or tripling market share—on the other hand may require a fundamental change in the business model, such as targeting entirely new customer groups by changing the nature of the value proposition, altering the scope of the business significantly, and so on.

To change the business model, a radical strategy is needed. A business model can be broadly defined as comprising the following elements:

- value proposition;
- nature of inputs;
- how to transform inputs (including technology);
- nature of outputs;
- vertical scope;
- horizontal scope;
- geographic scope;
- nature of customers;
- how to organize.[25]

Moreover, there is evidence that the most successful forms of what we call radical strategy involve multiple rather than singular changes to elements of the business model.[26] As we have noted, it is no easy matter to change a business model—which explains why it is often new entrants to industries rather than incumbents that innovate in this way. The airline industry, where easyJet and Ryanair have done what the traditional carriers could not—or would not—do, is a good example. Indeed, even when the latter have tried to imitate the low-cost model, they have failed.

EasyGroup's Business Model

EasyJet is the UK's Internet-based version of Southwest Airlines in the US. Founded in 1995 by a young Greek-Cypriot entrepreneur, Stelios Haji-Ioannou, the firm grew very rapidly. Initial success in airlines has allowed the parent company, easyGroup, to expand geographically and horizontally all over Europe and in the US, into car rental (easyCar) and Internet cafés (easyInternet). EasyJet's 2000 initial public offering in London was ten times oversubscribed. Its business model abandoned virtually all the elements of the traditional airline model. It has these key features:

- A clear value proposition. The 'easy' concept brings cheap and efficient services to the mass market.

- Very simple inputs. Like Southwest Airlines, easyJet operates only one type of aircraft, the Boeing 737, while the easyCar fleet has just two or three car models.
- A common, pervasive technology, the Internet. Most customers book online. The easyGroup companies pursue constant and common goals of cutting unnecessary costs, bolting on the efficiencies of new technologies, maintaining very high customer satisfaction, and creating strong brand awareness.
- Simple outputs. All easyGroup companies offer no-frills, stripped-down service.
- Horizontal scope based on commonalities in low-cost, efficient service to mass-market customers, where Internet technology and the 'easy' brand provide more relatedness than the actual services themselves: easyGroup diversified in 2002 into financial services with easyMoney, undercutting margins on credit card and unsecured loans.
- A geographical scope that increases in opportunistic fashion: wherever established players with overpriced operations dominate markets, easyGroup sees a niche. Originally established in London, easyInternet cafés now operate throughout Europe and in the US.
- A common type of customer. Most easyGroup customers are young, urban, and hip (or think of themselves that way), with more time than money.
- Focused and lean organization under the charismatic, hands-on leadership of Stelios Haji-Ioannou, a tireless marketer of the company's brands. The company achieves the winning combination of low costs with high quality by putting people at the top. With a low-cost model, there is very little left except people. The company has developed a learning and culture-building process that emphasizes learning, innovation, and speaking up.

The easyGroup story illustrates the truth that most companies do not have strategies other than routine ones. Rather, they hit on or deliberately develop a successful business model that they try to maintain for as long as possible, as the full-service carriers in the airline industry did.

However, it should be noted that easyGroup's expansion from airlines into car rental, Internet cafés, and financial services represents incremental rather than radical change to its own core business model, different as that is. Interestingly, easyGroup's first possible stumble, easyCinema, launched in 2003, departs from its core business model. By contrast with the self-sufficiency of its other businesses, easyCinema depends on cooperation from film distributors. Distribution companies are mostly owned by film producers, who balk at undercutting the high prices on which their own business model depends.

Successful as it has been overall, there remain some unanswered question marks over easyGroup's business model. First, can it survive head-to-head competition with rivals following the same formula? Initially easyJet found pickings easy against the fatter business model of the full-fare airlines. As for other discounters, easyJet hoped that its low prices would deter competition, and until 2004 that was the case. By 2004, however, easyJet was coming up against other low-cost competitors and traditional carriers which were beginning to imitate its methods. As the discount sector becomes more crowded with direct competitors, does easyJet have a business model that will allow it to survive and prosper? The second question is whether easyGroup's one business model is transferable to other markets. Not all the group's businesses have been equally successful. Will it, too, face the challenge of strategic transformation?

Conclusion: The Challenge of Strategic Transformation

If the real business of managing strategy is to achieve long-term success and create long-term value, managers cannot assume that their business model will endure indefinitely. In the end, either the model will run out of steam, or extending it will become too complex, or intensifying competition will mean that it can only provide the basis for tactical variants and temporary advantage. The challenge for strategists, therefore, is transformational: changing business models rather than strategy in the traditional sense; deciding when to do it, how to do it, and what ways business models may change.[27]

Researchers studying the subject have begun to recognize the new configuration. A growing number of explanations of strategy development assume the redundancy of business models—or more precisely they accept that business models have finite life, and that managing strategy means simultaneously managing continuity of the existing business model and looking for a new one. So, for example, 'real options',[28] or the idea of low-cost strategic probes,[29] suggest ways in which organizations can search for quite different approaches or business models, while still maintaining the current one. RBS attributes much of its success to its experience of strategic probes. Its alliance with Spain's Bank of Santander, for example, allowed it to learn about European banking and European scope with little initial commitment or capital outlay. What caused it to act was not so much a grand vision of the bank as it is now, as an awareness that it needed to be fundamentally different from what it was then. The alliance set in train options that had the potential to galvanize or facilitate fundamental change.

This chapter has advanced a critical view of what we know about strategy and performance. It argues that managers should recognize the limits of the strategic recipes commonly advocated, to the extent that:

- they tend to be about managing existing business models rather than about changing them;
- their relationship to organizational performance is equivocal at best and rather limited;
- case studies tend to be short- or medium-term in scope—there are few that have looked at organizational performance linked to strategy over the long term.

Strategic transformation provides a different and promising perspective through which to view a firm's viability and value-adding capacity over time.[30] In the perspective of strategic transformation, managers operate a business model within a strategic position. These positions are inherited from previous managers. This means that managers have two jobs. One is to operate the current system as efficiently and profitably as possible. They may well see this as not rocking the boat. The second job, however, is to adopt a new business model when needed—as we noted in Chapter 1, *before* the company drifts into decline. As we have seen, such considerations are especially relevant for UK companies, whose traditional modes of competing are coming under ever greater pressure from a variety of different business models. The real UK strategic challenge is therefore not singular but double: to develop the ability to manage both routine and transformational strategic change. This is indeed a challenge for the exceptional manager.

Notes

1. A classic definition is 'corporate strategy is the pattern of major objectives, purposes, or goals and essential policies and plans for achieving those goals, stated in such a way as to define what business the company is in or is to be in and the kind of company it is or is to be'. K. R. Andrews, *The Concept of Corporate Strategy* (New York: Dow-Jones Irwin, 1971).

2. See e.g. a study of strategic planning in the oil industry: R. M. Grant, 'Strategic Planning in a Turbulent Environment: Evidence from the Oil Majors', *Strategic Management Journal*, 24 (2003), 491–517.

3. Some studies have found a direct favourable impact of strategic planning on performance. See e.g. J. A. Pearce III, K. D. Robbins, and R. B. Robinson, Jr., 'The Impact of Grand Strategy and Planning Formality on Financial Performance', *Strategic Management Journal*, 8 (1987), 125–34; W. E. Hopkins and S. A. Hopkins, 'Strategic Planning–Financial Performance Relationships in Banks: A Causal Examination', *Strategic Management Journal*, 18/8 (1997), 635–52; and P. J. Brews and M. R. Hunt, 'Learning to Plan and Planning to Learn: Resolving the Planning School/Learning School Debates, *Strategic Management Journal*, 20/10 (1999), 889–913. Other studies have found an unclear or indirect correlation between planning and performance. See e.g. T. C. Powell, 'Untangling the Relationship between Strategic Planning and Performance: The Role of Contingency Factors', *Canadian Journal of Administrative Sciences*, 11/2 (1994), 12–138; and P. R. Rogers, A. Miller, and W. Q. Judge, 'Using Information Processing Theory to Understand Planning/Performance Relationships in the Context of Strategy,' *Strategic Management Journal*, 20/6 (1999), 567–77.

4. G. S. Yip, 'Who Needs Strategic Planning?', *Journal of Business Strategy*, 6/2 (1985), 30–42.

5. A long history of research in industrial organization economics runs from Bain to Scherer. See J. S. Bain, *Barriers to New Competition* (Cambridge, MA: Harvard University Press, 1956); and M. F. Scherer, *Industrial Market Structure and Economic Performance* (Chicago: Rand McNally, 1980). Michael Porter converted the lessons of IO economics to business strategy in his path-breaking book *Competitive Strategy*. See M. E. Porter, *Competitive Strategy: Techniques for Analyzing Industries and Competitors*, (New York: Free Press, 1980).

6. Various studies have argued for the relative contributions of industry, company, and business unit effects on firm performance. See particularly: R. Schmalensee, 'Do Markets Differ Much?', *American Economic Review*, 75/3 (1985), 341–51; R. Rumelt, 'How Much does Industry Matter?', *Strategic Management Journal*, 12/3 (1991), 167–85; and A. M. McGahan and M. E. Porter, 'How Much does Industry Matter, Really?', *Strategic Management Journal*, 18 (special issue) (1997), 15–30. Rumelt's study found that the most important source of economic rent is business-specific (46% of explained variance) and not industry-based (8%), which is opposite to Schmalensee's findings where industry accounted for 20% of variance in business-unit returns. McGahan and Porter found that industry accounts for 19% of the total variance in the profitability of all sectors considered. But business-specific effects account for another 32%. See also: T. C. Powell, 'How Much does Industry Matter? An Alternative Empirical Test', *Strategic Management Journal*, 17/4 (1996), 323–34; A. Mauri and M. P. Max, 'Firm and Industry Effects within Strategic Management: An Empirical Investigation', *Strategic Management Journal*, 19/3 (1998), 211–19; J. Roquebert, R. L. Phillips, and P. A. Westfall, 'Markets vs. Management: What "Drives" Profitability?', *Strategic Management Journal*, 17/8 (1996), 653–64; C. Sea-Jin and S. Harbir, 'Corporate and

Industry Effects on Business Unit Competitive Position', *Strategic Management Journal*, 21/7 (2000), 739–52; E. H. Bowman and C. E. Helfat, 'Does Corporate Strategy Matter?', *Strategic Management Journal*, 22/1 (2001), 1–23; and S. Yannis and L. Spyros, 'An Examination into the Causal Logic of Rent Generation: Contrasting Porter's Competitive Strategy Framework and the Resource-Based Perspective', *Strategic Management Journal*, 22/10 (2001), 907–34.

7. This view is supported by a recent study that found that firm-specific factors prevail over industry factors to influence performance mostly for industry-dominant value creators (leaders) and destroyers (losers). For the rest of the firms, industry factors prevail over firm-specific factors to explain performance. See G. Hawawini, V. Subramanian, and P. Verdin, 'Is Performance Driven by Industry-or Firm-Specific Factors? A New Look at the Evidence', *Strategic Management Journal*, 24/1 (2003), 1–16.

8. Various studies have found that strategic group membership is important to competitive advantage and has a direct effect on performance. See e.g. A. Fiegenbaum and H. Thomas, 'Strategic Groups and Performance: The US Insurance Industry, 1970–1984', *Strategic Management Journal*, 11/3 (1990), 197–216; and A. Nair and S. Kotha, 'Does Group Membership Matter? Evidence from the Japanese Steel Industry', *Strategic Management Journal*, 22/3 (2001), 221–35. But other studies have found that strategic group membership does not create competitive advantage (not important for performance). See M. W. Lawless, D. D. Bergh, and W. D. Wilsted, 'Performance Differences among Strategic Group Members: An Examination of Individual Firm Capabilities', *Journal of Management*, 15/4 (1989), 649–61; and K. O. Cool and D. Schendel, 'Strategic Group Formation and Performance: The Case of the US Pharmaceutical Industry 1963–1982', *Management Science*, 33/9 (1987), 1102–24. Also, some studies found that strategic group membership is important to competitive advantage solely as a mediating factor of the competitive rivalry within an industry. See e.g. K. O. Cool and I. Dierickx, 'Rivalry, Strategic Groups and Firm Profitability', *Strategic Management Journal*, 1/14 (1993), 47–59. An overall problem with strategic group research is that studies generally do not measure intentionally formed groups but post-rationalized groups.

9. This set of generic strategies was proposed by Porter (1980).

10. Academic studies generally do not support the performance effects of generic strategies. Also, the common use of crude surrogate measures for such strategies has compounded the research problem. See C. Campbell-Hunt, 'What have we Learned about Generic Competitive Strategy? A Meta-analysis', *Strategic Management Journal*, 21/2 (2000), 127–54. Or the support is only partial. See G. D. Dess and P. S. Davis, 'Porter's (1980) Generic Strategies as Determinants of Strategic Group Membership and Organizational Performance', *Academy of Management Journal*, 27/3 (1984), 467–88. One study found that highly focused banks did not have higher performance than less focused ones. More focused banks faced less risk. Different strategies generate different risk levels. The risk consideration is as important as the return consideration in decision-making. Risk must be associated with returns to measure overall performance. See D. Jemison, 'Risk

and the Relationship among Strategy, Organizational Processes and Performance', *Management Science,* 33/9 (1987), 1087–1101.

11. This section is based on the discussion in section 7.3.6 of chapter 7 in G. Johnson and K. Scholes, *Exploring Corporate Strategy,* 6th edn. (London: FT/Prentice Hall, 2002).

12. P. J. DiMaggio and W. W. Powell, 'The Iron Cage Revisited: Institutional Isomorphism and Collective Rationality in Organizational Fields', *American Sociological Review,* 48 (1983), 147–60.

13. D. Deephouse, 'To be Different or to be the Same? It's a Question (and Theory) of Strategic Balance', *Strategic Management Journal,* 20/2 (1999), 147–66.

14. E. T. Penrose, *The Theory of Growth of the Firm* (New York: John Wiley, 1959); B. Wernerfelt, 'A Resource-Based View of the Firm', *Strategic Management Journal,* 5 (1984), 171–80; B. Wernerfelt, 'From Critical Resources to Corporate Strategy', *Journal of General Management,* 14/3 (1989), 4–12; J. B. Barney, 'Firm, Resources and Sustained Competitive Advantage', *Journal of Management,* 17/1 (1991), 99–120; J. B. Barney, *Gaining and Sustaining Competitive Advantage* (Boston: Addison-Wesley, 1997); R. M. Grant, 'The Resources-Based Theory of Competitive Advantage: Implications for Strategy Formulation', *California Management Review,* 33/3 (1991), 114–35; R. Amit and P. J. H. Schoemaker, 'Strategic Assets and Organizational Rent', *Strategic Management Journal,* 14/1 (1993), 33–46; R. Henderson and I. Cockburn, 'Measuring Competence? Exploring Firm Effects in Pharmaceutical Research', *Strategic Management Journal,* 15 (1994), 63–84; D. J. Teece, G. Pisano, and A. Shuen, 'Dynamic Capabilities and Strategic Management', *Strategic Management Journal,* 18/7 (1997), 509–33.

15. This is an argument made by R. Priem and J. E. Butler, 'Is the Resource-Based "View" a Useful Perspective for Strategic Management Research', *Academy of Management Review,* 26/1 (2001), 22–40.

16. See the causal ambiguity argument of S. Lippman and R. P. Rumelt, 'Uncertain Imitability: An Analysis of Interfirm Differences in Efficiency under Competition', *Bell Journal of Economics,* 13/2 (1982), 418–38.

17. As argued by M. E. Porter, 'What is Strategy?', *Harvard Business Review,* 96/6 (1996), 61–78.

18. Priem and Butler, 'Resource-Based "View" '.

19. See D. Leonard-Barton, 'Core Capabilities and Core Rigidities: A Paradox in Managing New Product Development', *Strategic Management Journal,* 13 (1992), 11–125.

20. D. Miller, *The Icarus Paradox* (New York: Harper Business, 1990).

21. Richard D'Aveni, *Hypercompetition* (New York: Free Press, 1994).

22. For a focus on tactics see A. Bhide, 'Strategy as Hustle', *Harvard Business Review,* 64/5 (1986), 59–66.

23. See R. E. Hoskisson and M. A. Hitt, 'Antecedents and Performance Outcomes of Diversification: Review and Critique of Theoretical Perspectives', *Journal of Management,* 16/2 (1990), 461–509; R. A. Bettis and W. K. Hall, 'Diversification Strategy, Accounting Determined Risk and Accounting Determined Return', *Academy of Management Journal,* 25/2 (1982), 254–64; R. M. Grant, A. P. Jammine, and H. Thomas, 'Diversity, Diversification and Profitability among British

Manufacturing Companies', *Academy of Management Journal*, 31/4 (1988), 771–801; and M. Mayer and R. Whittington, 'Diversification in Context: A Cross-National and Cross-Temporal Extension', *Strategic Management Journal*, 24/8 (2003), 773–81.

24. This section is based on G. S. Yip, 'Using Strategy to Change your Business Model', *Business Strategy Review*, 15/2 (2004), 17–24.

25. The term 'organizational archetypes' is used by some academics to describe a broader framework for conceiving the 'business model' by including aspects of organization, decision-making, etc. See R. Greenwood and C. R. Hinings, 'Understanding Strategic Change: The Contribution of Archetypes', *Academy of Management Journal*, 36/5 (1993), 1052–81; and 'Understanding Radical Organizational Change: Bringing Together the Old and the New Institutionalism', *Academy of Management Review*, 21/4 (1996), 1022–54.

26. The evidence to support the need for multiple changes in the business model of an organization is also referred to as changes in 'complementarities'. More extensive explanation and evidence for this can be found in, for example, A. Pettigrew, R. Whittington, L. Melin, C. Sanchez-Runde, F. van den Bosch, W. Ruigrok, and T. Numagami (eds.), 'Complementarities in Action: Organizational Change and Performance in BP and Unilever 1985–2002', in *Innovating Forms of Organizing* (London: Sage, 2003).

27. A book by two senior members of a major consulting firm, Gemini Consulting, argues that business transformation is the primary task of chief executives. See F. J. Gouillart and J. N. Kelly, *Transforming the Organization* (New York: McGraw-Hill, 1995).

28. See T. Luehrman, 'Strategy as a Portfolio of Real Options', *Harvard Business Review*, 76/5 (1998), 89–99.

29. On low-cost probes see S. L. Brown and K. M. Eisenhardt, *Competing on the Edge* (Boston: Harvard Business School Press, 1998).

30. Very little is known about transformational strategies and how they are managed over long periods of time. However, at the time of writing, just such a study has commenced with the aim of identifying which UK firms have simultaneously maintained consistent high performance over decades rather than years, in addition to transforming their strategies. Our conjecture is that they will be few in number but will be exceptional businesses from which to learn. This challenge of understanding more about the management of strategic transformation has become one of our research priorities. Study in progress by Timothy Devinney, Gerry Johnson, and George S. Yip.

4

Managing Employment Relations

SUCCESSFUL organizations maximize 'employee contribution and commitment'.[1] UK managers overwhelmingly take the point: when asked about factors influencing competitive advantage, more than half the respondents to the CBI's 2003 employment trends survey stressed 'effective people management' against 14 per cent mentioning R&D and 7 per cent new capital investment.[2] But achieving effective people management is particularly tricky. In the words of the US management scholar David Norton, 'the asset that is the most important is the least understood'.[3]

This chapter has three goals. The first is to explain why 'human capital' is hard to understand and why improving understanding is key to an organization's performance. The core issue is that managers have multiple goals in managing employees, while employees also have their own objectives, which are expressed in ways that may or may not be exact or clear. As with any other input, managers want to minimize the cost of labour. Yet they also need the active enthusiasm and commitment of workers—the willingness to 'go the extra mile'—which is all too easily undermined by cost-cutting. Employees seek interest in their jobs and expect a degree of respect and consideration, expectations that the busy manager (see Chapter 11) may lack the time to address. These issues become even more complex where, as is increasingly common, employees interact with customers. Research shows that they gain satisfaction from the relationship, but that attending to customer wishes can run counter to cost-effectiveness.[4]

Such tensions have to be managed. The issues being messy and often hard to resolve, it is not surprising that understanding sometimes gets lost. Obtaining 'contribution and commitment' is therefore a matter of balancing necessary tensions between different things that firms ask of workers, recognizing and engaging with employee expectations, and being alive to the external pressures that may undermine even well-intentioned efforts to focus on commitment.

The second purpose is to review some key current people-management practices. In line with subsequent chapters on innovation, decision-making, and promising practices in general, we identify the promise but also the limitations of apparently appealing approaches, particularly the increasingly popular High Performance Work (HPW) systems model. As with many other promising management practices, the twin dangers of the HPW model are that managers treat it as a ready-made solution, or conversely as an unattainable benchmark about which nothing much can be done. In reality, however, there are clear policies that firms can adopt, some of them covering basics that still tend to be neglected.

Thirdly, the chapter addresses the opportunities for developing coopera-tive relationships with employees. Other chapters deal with the principles of cooperation within management teams (Chapter 10) and the import-ance of trust in such fields as innovation (Chapter 5). Here we look at applying such ideas to relations with employees and suggest that there are significant opportunities for development as well as constraints.

Note that we use the term 'employment relations' to make an important point. Terms such as 'human capital' or 'human resource management' can imply that employees are simply a resource to be managed at will. An employment-relations perspective stresses that employees have their own expectations, which may or may not coincide with those of senior man-agers. In managing these expectations, moreover, institutions are import-ant, whether in the shape of formal bodies such as consultation committees or informal ones, notably the norms and understandings that any group of people develops over time. The management of employ-ees is thus a two-way process in which individual expectations but also collective rules and understandings are central.[5]

Note also that we focus on people in conventional jobs in long-estab-lished sectors such as manufacturing and banking, retail, and other large-scale services. We do not apologize for this. These sectors continue to dominate employment, and while there has been much publicity about the growth of flexible forms of work, distinctively new working patterns are in practice rare. Four of every five employees are still in 'permanent jobs'. Even in leading-edge organizations, where one might expect the most dramatic changes, a recent study finds little use of practices such as portfolio careers.[6] And some forms of flexible work, notably part-time employment, which is its largest component, are long-established.[7] There has been major change in how employment relations are handled, but this has entailed changing the form of the relationship and not abandoning hierarchy or formal organization. It is of course true that creating commitment and trust is as important for small firms and those in less formal, more fluid sectors like the media and design industries as it is in more traditional businesses, but the processes for doing so are likely to be informal and personal, and they involve rather different issues from those addressed below.[8]

The chapter has five parts. First, we reprise Chapter 2's discussion of the changing institutional context in relation to employment relations. Then we examine the main constraints to change. In the third and fourth sections, we outline some basic improvements in practice that make sense in the light of these constraints and develop them further. Finally, we assess the promise and potential of more advanced High Performance Work systems.

The Emergence of New Models

As we noted in Chapter 2, British employment relations have traditionally been characterized as 'adversarial'. What this meant in practice, however, is often misunderstood. Since references to the past remain important justifications for present attitudes and policies, some comment is in order. The 'winter of discontent' remains engraved in the language as a folk memory of the strikes of 1978 and 1979, suggesting a past of militant and intransigent trade unions, to be contrasted with a present where management has 'freedom to manage' for the common good.

Yet starting with the car and engineering industries that most closely fit the stereotype, a series of studies has shown that shop-floor militancy was not universal. Some firms, even in militant cities, remained oases of calm because they achieved a balance of fairness—a real balance, very different from 'buying industrial peace'. These firms, for example the one-time world-leading machine-tool maker Alfred Herbert, could still collapse in spectacular fashion, but this was not because of poor labour relations. Again, work practices that managers came to define as 'restrictive' were often established on managerial initiative, reliance on trade unions for recruitment purposes being one example. Thirdly, such practices were generally defensive, seen as necessary to counter autocratic management. In contrast to their US counterparts, many UK firms had no developed employment policies at all, relying on authority and assertiveness when they could, and engaging grudgingly with trade unions when they had to.[9]

Engineering, moreover, was far from typical. Other manufacturing sectors such as chemicals and food and drink were much more peaceful. This did not mean, however, that they had carefully developed employment-relations policies. Personnel management was a lowly and poorly resourced function. Payment systems and job evaluation arrangements were rudimentary at best, while issues such as equal opportunities did not arise at all. 'Adversarialism' meant a reliance on settling issues at the level of the workplace, and a distrust of formal arrangements. Under certain conditions, this could develop into overt antagonism between managers and workers. Many firms neglected employment relations, and found that when concrete issues arose they were unprepared to cope, falling back on traditional rights and often making matters worse as a result.

In such a context, much debate turned on the impact of trade unions on productivity. Some research found that union presence was linked to low productivity, but generally only in a few sectors where unions were particularly strong and where other conditions applied—notably a product market that allowed firms to charge high prices and share the returns with employees. Any benefits of reducing union influence were limited to these special cases. They were also, in the words of one expert, 'unrepeatable', one-off changes; sustainable growth depends on 'greater investment in physical and human capital or a change in the rules of the game away from adversarial towards cooperative industrial relations'.[10]

Other scholars question the directness of any link. They note that trade unions have rarely had a formal policy of opposing technical change and that in many heavily unionized industries, such as steel and the railways, major technological changes were introduced from the 1950s onwards with the agreement and sometimes active cooperation of the unions. Finally, being heavily concentrated in a few sectors of the economy, strikes cannot explain generic productivity issues.[11]

Unions may also have been used as a convenient excuse for companies' failure to innovate. 'How is it', ask two scholars, 'that isolated, decentralized, plant-based work groups can impede the advance of management [and] technology?' The evidence was that 'all too often management did not try to innovate'.[12] A striking feature of the Japanese firms arriving in the UK in the 1970s was their focus on the technical organization of production and the structures of management, not worker opposition to change. As a former editor of the *Financial Times* concluded, what appeared to be 'restrictive' practices were often introduced by employers for rational reasons and allowed to continue by employer acquiescence as

much as union insistence, an acquiescence underpinned by 'easy markets': it was the 'labour-relations system' rather than unions as such that
was the problem.[13] It has further been convincingly argued that bad
production organization tended to cause bad industrial relations rather
than the other way round. For example, poor scheduling of work-flow led
to shortages of components and stoppages that encouraged workers to
bargain about payment. The more general effect was to encourage distrust
in management.[14]

The broadest and most persuasive argument is that the real issue was not
overt conflict but managerial style. British managers treated workers at
arm's length, a general neglect of human-resource issues being punctuated
by periodic attempts to crack down on perceived problems, followed by a
retreat to the previous indifference. Up to the 1960s, rights that are now
taken for granted were absent, for example protection against unfair
dismissal and compensation for redundancy; around 90 per cent of firms
had no formal grievance or disciplinary systems. During the 1970s, reform
of industrial relations was the watchword, but in practice change was
patchy and piecemeal, and in the context of generally worsening economic conditions achieved little in the way of positive progress. Crucially,
companies saw employment relations in terms of managing a relatively
free-standing set of issues around pay and conditions, and not as a means
of integrating employees into the positive pursuit of performance.[15]

A central feature was that the search for improved productivity was
almost wholly top-down: managers came up with new schemes that
they attempted to force through often with little or no consultation. Not
surprisingly, workers were sceptical, not least because they could recall
a long history of botched attempts at change. Trust was an inevitable
casualty.

Labour-market reforms of the 1980s and 1990s dismantled the existing
labour-relations system. Trade-union membership and influence fell, and
the proportion of employees whose pay was set by collective bargaining
between unions and employers also declined rapidly. The structures of the
adversarial system were weakened, but they were not replaced with new
institutional arrangements. Two contradictory trends were set in train.

First, employers made widespread use of new technology. Employee
surveys report that levels of skill have been rising consistently and that
workers have considerable autonomy over they way they work. In the
words of one study, there has been a 'very extensive upskilling of the
workforce' combined with a 'significant devolution of responsibilities for
more immediate decisions about the work task'.[16]

More recent surveys report continuing upward trends in skills. According to one, 84 per cent of employees felt that their employer provided them with 'sufficient opportunities for training and development'.[17] Over half of respondents said that their firms made a 'serious attempt to make jobs of people like you as interesting and varied as possible', while approaching half reported the presence of a programme for employee involvement. Moreover, the more of these practices a worker reported, the more likely she was to report a high level of job satisfaction and motivation.

Secondly, however, there were the trends noted in Chapter 2 of increasing work intensity and falling employee satisfaction. Researchers have put these patterns together. Rising work effort could reflect more satisfying jobs and hence a willingness to work harder. On the other hand, since workers report less satisfaction with their jobs, a more promising explanation may lie in declining job security and growing pressures to step up work effort. Other researchers have shown that the growth in performance measurement is reflected in declining commitment.[18] Working harder and working smarter are not necessarily opposed, but under a work-intensification regime workers are likely to lack the time and energy to develop new skills. As we have argued in Chapter 1, and as one key review concluded, 'intensification of effort is hardly viable as a long-term strategy for sustainable growth'. The 'limits', it went on, had been reached in Britain by the late 1990s.[19]

Managers were, in short, developing work practices that called for new skills. But these also created new pressures. The idea of a high-performance model aimed to do two things: link the scattered practices into systems or bundles on the lines discussed in Chapter 7; and resolve or at least minimize the tensions between commitment and autonomy on the one hand and insecurity and work pressures on the other.

Continuing Constraints

There are three main constraints on moves by UK firms towards the high-performance model. The first is long-standing, the second and third more recent.

The long-standing influence is a lack of strategic focus on employment relations. In the US most large firms (both unionized and non-unionized) developed clear and detailed employment policies, supported institutionally by professional human-resource departments. In most of Europe, collective bargaining arrangements at national or industry level, backed up by detailed legal rules, took many employment issues away from the individual firm. In the UK arrangements were never so systematized. This has the benefit of flexibility, but this flexibility tended to mean ignoring issues unless they arose in the shape of a concrete problem or asserting management's right to manage.

In 1992 only 30 per cent of large companies in the UK (i.e. with 1,000 or more UK employees) had an executive member of the main board with full-time responsibility for personnel issues.[20] In 1998 the proportion of workplaces (as distinct from companies) with a personnel specialist was also 30 per cent, while supervisors had low levels of training in personnel responsibilities—in almost one-third of workplaces, none at all.[21]

This links to the second constraint on high performance, the growing pressures over recent years of reorganization, downsizing, and delayering. What do these pressures mean for managers managing employees? One argument was that managers demotivated by uncertainties and insecurity would undermine HPW innovations and other reforms, whether by active resistance or passive indifference. In fact, the issue is a more mundane one. Most managers do not oppose HPW ideas on principle. But delayering means that they have no time to spend on these things, while new responsibilities being heaped on them further limit their ability to put the ideas into practice. Performance-measurement systems tighten the screw. Numerous studies have shown that employee-involvement initiatives have failed not because of specific opposition but because other demands have come first.[22]

This leads directly to the third constraint. Downsizing pressures reflect competitive demands and a growing imperative to create shareholder value. The UK is a liberal market economy in which the pressures for shareholder returns and the threat of takeover are particularly strong. These institutional pressures are familiar in many organizations.

One study found its respondents well aware of them, with competition and shareholder demands being highlighted in the private sector and funding cuts having similar consequences in the public sector.[23] As another review puts it, the fact that firms are struggling with these pressures makes it very hard for them to keep their promises of employee involvement and skill development. This is not, it goes on, 'a question of mendacious exploiters and obstructive middle management', but rather the result of 'shareholder-driven, deregulated and globalizing markets'.[24]

A summary of changing employment strategies is that firms have shifted from 'retain and reinvest' to a policy of 'downsize and distribute'.[25]

Ways Forward: The Basics

While these pressures certainly make the task of managing employees coherently more difficult, in particular by focusing managers' attention on other things, they do not make it impossible. Indeed, managers have many options for fostering employee commitment.

Some basic features of good relations with employees sound obvious. You might take it for granted that any employees who are dismissed should have an explanation of the reasons and the chance to put their case. Yet in more than one-third of cases reaching Employment Tribunals no form of meeting or discussion takes place, despite more than thirty years' experience of unfair dismissal legislation.[26]

Another example is monitoring attendance. Absence from work is widely seen as a large yet controllable cost. But studies repeatedly find that many firms do not measure the costs, that control systems are rudimentary, and that the approach is often one of cracking down on a problem once it has arisen rather than designing arrangements to flag up the issues before they get out of hand.[27]

Or consider the following extract from the field notes of a researcher working in a factory:

> Pat told me that she was 'taken upstairs' recently and told off about her poor attendance.... She said it was the first time in over 30 years at work that she had been told off about this and that it was unfair because people with a much worse record than hers had got away with it. She claimed that she had been ill for one and a half days and also had taken two days off for a bereavement. What's more she had come to work when she was not completely better because she had a week's holiday booked over Easter and she did not want management to think she was skiving. In the five years she had been at [the firm], Pat said every previous attendance grading had been a grade A [the top grade].[28]

Perhaps surprisingly, this was not a small back-street operation but a Japanese-owned firm that paid scrupulous attention to its production systems but that nonetheless treated its employees in ways that they found arbitrary, unfair, and autocratic.

The point of this example is not that the managers were particularly aggressive. Rather, they were under intense pressure to meet delivery and quality targets, and there was little in their experience to lead them to think differently. It was not so much that employee expectations and needs were in principle deemed 'secondary', but that there was no way they could find meaningful expression. Significantly, an employee consultation committee had atrophied because neither managers nor workers could see that it had any point.

Modernizing Employment Relations at 'Truckko'

'Truckko' produces customized commercial vehicles.[29] It is non-union and employs about 150 workers. It had been built on the basis of the abrasive paternalism of the founder, Rob. He loathed challenges to his authority, and was described by workers as 'autocratic' and a 'friendly dictator'. Yet pay was higher than the going rate, and bonuses could be substantial, albeit wholly at Rob's discretion. As a worker saw it, the approach was, 'keep your head down, follow orders and don't think for yourself... but at least you knew they'd take care of you'.

This world began to change as competition from other companies threatened the niche that Truckko had established for itself. Rob recruited Colin from a major company as managing director. Colin set about modernizing Truckko through three linked activities: standardization of the design of the trucks, redesign of the work process, and training and participative systems. He called in two external consultancies to help. Importantly, they adopted a pragmatic, down-to-earth approach that was understood and welcomed by workers.

A key event concerned one of the managers, Aidan, whose approach was increasingly at odds with Colin's participative style. As a production supervisor said, 'It's hard to believe in what Colin says when [Aidan] does the opposite.' Matters eventually came to a head, and Aidan was 'persuaded to leave'. 'Colin meant business, and everyone knew it,' said one worker. Colin also cut the number of team leaders from fifteen to four, demoting those he felt were unable to act as coaches rather than instructors.

A production supervisor, asked how his relationship with Colin differed from that with Rob, commented that 'Colin asks you what you think, and it's hard to get used to'. As another manager revealingly put it, 'It's only now that I can see what being a good manager really means'.

Consider next the example of 'Truckko' in the box. The key points here are that an assertive, indeed autocratic style does not preclude 'fairness', so long as workers respect the style and see what it delivers. Improving employment relations goes along with and helps to reinforce a change of business strategy, and it can be achieved using basic ideas. Sensitivity to the context and what employees expect is key; think in particular of the lessons that shopfloor workers drew from how 'Colin' acted.

The basics of employment relations are fair and consistent behaviour in such core areas as recruitment, pay, and discipline. 'Fair' need not mean achieving exceptional standards. It means fairness in the context of the firm's situation. Addressing these basics is likely to help keep a business performing, and to reduce costly behaviour such as quitting.

Payment systems are a good example. Pay is obviously central to any employment relationship, but individual rewards are particularly salient in countries like the UK where salary is not a matter of national or industry agreements, as in many other countries, and where the structure of jobs within the firm is less formal. With these institutions and norms much weaker, individual pay becomes a key mark of achievement. Does it follow that performance-related pay is the answer? Although the idea of paying according to performance sounds obvious, in many organizations there are major problems with defining what constitutes performance, measuring it, and deciding how to link it to pay. Just how much more should you pay someone for high rather than moderate achievement, and how do you evaluate one kind of contribution against another? The more people take on multiple roles, the harder the calculation gets. The challenges of performance measurement generally are further addressed in Chapter 6.

One substantial review concludes that pay systems can encourage valued behaviour, but only under certain conditions.[30] Individual bonuses may work where workers' own efforts can be identified, where they can attain high performance through their own efforts, and where there are few resource constraints. Sales staff working largely independently would be an example. But where team cooperation is needed or where workers cannot directly influence performance on their own, caution is in order. 'Careful firms', these authors observe, 'ensure that full consultation with the workers and managers concerned is undertaken in any new form of pay system design.'

A manager who is addressing these issues may find it helpful to do so in two ways. First, large parts of a company's policy on recruitment, pay, discipline, and other conditions will be outside the individual manager's control. But this does not mean that they are beyond influence.

One part of the influence of managers concerns how policies are put into effect. The aphorism that strategy 'implementation, rather than strategy content, differentiates successful from unsuccessful firms', has particular relevance here.[31] Schemes to involve employees in decision-making often break down for reasons to do with implementation, notably around time and commitment, rather than principled opposition.[32] How an overall policy is put into effect and how far it respects existing employee expectations will be crucial to the message that employees receive. Is an appraisal scheme, for example, working as intended and does it clash with other parts of the firm's policy?

The other aspect is feedback to policy-makers. Is there a mechanism through which the effectiveness of a policy is evaluated, and can line managers help to shape the formulation of policy? If the elements of the HPW model such as training are being pursued, do they work in practice, and what can be done to help them work better?

Secondly, there is the question of the manager's own practice. A busy manager can easily put off dealing with employee issues in the press of immediate customer needs. And well-intended actions such as resolving an attendance issue can have unintended effects. A key lesson is simply to think through the consequences of one's actions and to be sensitive to the expectations of employees.

Ways Forward: Time at Last for Participation?

To move beyond the basic, but fundamental, themes just discussed turns on the concrete mechanisms that firms have in place to permit meaningful employee involvement, whether in communications exercises, team briefings, or other forms of engagement in the work process. The evidence suggests that these are increasingly common. In a 2001 survey, two-thirds of a random sample of UK employees agreed that 'management hold meetings in which you can express your views about what is happening in the organization', a small rise on 1992.[33] Firms might ask themselves whether they have such arrangements in place and how effective they are.

Information and Consultation

Involvement increasingly refers to 'consultation' with or the 'participation' of employees through the formal means of elected committees. These concepts have never had a very clear meaning in the UK, which lacks a tradition of formally recognized, and often legally defined, works councils that operate in many other countries. This situation may now be changing.

Until relatively recently, many large firms used the trade union as their predominant conduit for engagement with employees. Both managers and unions preferred to keep each other at arm's length, distrusting institutionalized relationships that went beyond bargaining about pay and conditions. But with the waning of their membership and influence, many trade unions have slowly come to embrace ideas of 'partnership' with employers, becoming much readier to engage with agendas around the performance of firms.[34]

At the same time, companies may be taking on board the argument that short-term performance-management approaches square poorly with the long-term development of resources. For example, the HPW debate has consistently highlighted the potential, and necessity, for employee involvement. Acceptance of the broad idea of formal structures for participation has been growing. A good illustration is a joint report by the CBI and the Trades Union Congress (TUC) in 2001, which concluded that 'optimal results are achieved where there is a mix of direct employee involvement *and* indirect participation...through a trade union or works council'.[35] The CBI's 2003 employment trends survey reported that almost half its respondents had in place permanent mechanisms for informing and consulting employees, compared to 35 per cent in 2002.

Finally, firms may have little choice. Since 2005 the EU National Information and Consultation Directive has required firms with at least 150 employees to agree mechanisms for informing employees about business and employment trends, and consulting them 'with a view to reaching agreement' on changes in work organization, including redundancies and business transfers. These requirements are being extended to smaller firms. Legislation requiring companies to consult employees first appeared in the 1970s, initially on redundancies but later on other issues. The novelty of the latest legislation is its general character: instead of being required to consult about specific issues, firms must have a continuing system, provided that 10 per cent of employees request it.[36]

Companies have been used to consulting on specific issues such as redundancy for some time. Early fears of restrictions on managers' freedom to take business decisions have evaporated. Most consultation is about handling the process rather than about the principle. In practice, such discussion can actually make change easier to accept. Dialogue itself reduces the negative, demotivating impact of job losses; and on the positive side employee representatives sometimes make new and constructive suggestions.[37] Moreover, we would argue that stronger constraints on the freedom to hire and fire may be a stimulus to increasing productivity and moving firms up the value chain, preventing managers from falling back on easy options and pressing them to use their workforce more constructively.[38]

Several firms see benefits in formal arrangements of information and consultation. Two examples—particularly interesting in being non-union firms—are B&Q and BP Exploration, described below.[39] Overall conclusions are twofold. Formal representative arrangements can make constructive contributions to decision-making. Representatives can also develop a taste for and skill in involvement—but it follows that firms need to be prepared to allow the time and space for this taste to grow.

B&Q The B&Q DIY chain employs more than 33,000 people in the UK, and also has stores in Taiwan and China. In 1998 it merged with the French firm Castorama to become the largest DIY retailer in Europe. Its 'Grass Roots' consultation framework was introduced in 1998, operating through quarterly meetings at store, regional, divisional, and national levels. Store-level representatives are elected. The company cites a number of benefits, for example the speedy resolution of employee concerns about the safety of a type of delivery trolley, and generally better-quality decisions and easier introduction of changes in procedures. Employee representatives see the formal election of representatives as enhancing the effectiveness and credibility of the system—although they also feel that they could be used more fully on key questions such as work organization and store security.

BP Exploration The company, part of the BP group, conducts oil and gas exploration and field development and production in the North Sea. In January 2004 it employed about 2,100 workers. In 1999 Employee Communications and Consultation Forums were set up in each of thirteen business units, with a further division-wide forum. Each forum has representatives elected by the employees, together with management nominees. The network has dealt with difficult issues, notably redundancies arising from major restructuring exercises. Representatives influenced the redundancy process, for example in defining the criteria to assess people who wish to leave the company. Managers believe trust improved as a result. On the other hand, some employee representatives wanted involvement in key issues such as a new bonus scheme, where they felt there was communication, but not consultation.

Partnership

Partnership arrangements take the principles of involvement a step beyond information and consultation. Although partnership is fundamentally about achieving shared goals, the concept implies that employees are independent partners rather than simply being consulted about arrangements which managers decide. Partnership deals generally involve employee commitments to flexibility in return for managerial efforts to maximize job security and to promote consultation and involvement. Arrangements labelled 'partnership' are very common, running at 700 in one year alone. But there may be only between fifty and eighty more exactly defined deals in the UK, and the main body promoting partnership lists forty-eight cases that meet its 'full' definition. Yet these are often seen as prototypes of new forms of managing employees.[40]

Little research has systematically compared partnership deals with comparable firms. One study that did concluded that 'partnership' can really mean employer dominance: in six out of twenty-two cases, partnership came about when the firm threatened to derecognize the trade union, and in a further three the firm was actively considering the same thing. This matters, since forcing through change is unlikely to promote long-term commitment and hence productivity and innovation, though firms can and do make short-term gains. The study also found that in declining industries partnership firms shed jobs more quickly than average, while in growing sectors they put on more jobs than average.[41]

Another study of three partnership deals offered complementary conclusions. First, it was not the structures and systems that were important but the ways in which arrangements were developed in practice. The deal with the least articulated systems worked the most effectively. Secondly, partnership improved trust and commitment, but this applied most to those immediately involved, with other workers and managers remaining distant. Thirdly, the findings chimed with long-standing evidence on the benefits of information sharing and collaborative approaches.[42]

Partnership is thus the current term for practices with a long history. Those practices have often tended to fade away over time, and managers have found it hard to generalize their impact from the small circle of those directly involved to the organization as a whole. In the present context, the fundamental lesson lies not in the structures or systems themselves, but in how they were made to work.

High Performance Work Systems

Despite this mixed history, many commentators argue that it is possible to go further by integrating the broad ideas of partnership into a fuller system. Current thinking is illustrated by the joint CBI–TUC document cited above. Addressing many of the themes of this book, including investment and best practices, it argued that innovation calls for a 'climate of mutual trust' between firms and employees. 'The research evidence', it went on,

> suggests that new forms of work organization, effective management leadership, a culture that encourages innovation, employee involvement and employee development tailored to organizational needs are all necessary conditions for adaptable, high performance workplaces....Management leadership and employee involvement are complementary features of the high performance/high commitment model.[43]

Yet if this is the case, as two scholars put it, 'the real cause for surprise today is not the message but that so little has been done to put it into effect'.[44] How can we explain this puzzle?

The HPW model is endorsed in many quarters. In addition to the CBI and TUC, leading employers' bodies including the Engineering Employers' Federation and the Chartered Institute of Personnel and Development have presented case study and survey evidence of its benefits.[45] On the basis of thirty case studies, including four in the UK, the European Commission identified a 'revolution' in the way in which work is organized and discerned a set of 'best practices' which entailed strong leadership, clear vision, continuous communication with employees, regular consultation with employees and their representatives, and incremental but continuous change.[46]

The core principles of the HPW model are conceptually simple. Employees need both to be able to contribute to productive improvement, and to have the opportunity and incentives to do so. These principles have been linked to concrete practices as follows:

- the ability of employees to contribute is underpinned by skills and training;
- opportunities to participate in decisions are promoted by autonomy and membership of self-directed teams;
- incentives to participate include a perception of employment security, promotion opportunities, and a sense that pay is fair.[47]

High Commitment and Involvement Practices

- Fair recruitment and selection
- A performance management system with objective-setting, feed-back, and appraisal
- Teamwork wherever relevant
- Direct employee involvement
- Collective voice to develop commitment and trust
- Individual training plans; investment in education and training
- Maximum individual and team autonomy; less hierarchical working methods
- Financial participation/gainsharing and new reward systems

We summarize checklists generated by the CBI and TUC and the European Commission in the box.[48] The present argument is not that such models are wrong. The key point is that employment relations practices need to be connected to organizations' wider strategic goals. And there is a linkage between such high-level ambition and concrete practice. Indeed, a recurring theme of this book is the challenge of linking strategic vision with organizational practice.

But managers should also be aware that employment-relations models are controversial. There is no settled evidence as to how they work. And the great danger is that they will be seen as all-or-nothing solutions.

The first controversial issue is the extent of take-up of the new practices. At first sight, moves towards a HPW model are impressive. For example, the most reliable UK survey, the Workplace Employment Relations Survey (WERS) of 1998, reported that 61 per cent of workplaces used team briefings, and in 38 per cent of workplaces non-managerial employees participated in problem-solving groups.

There are a couple of cautions, however. Notably, individual practices are rarely combined into integrated packages, one of the tenets of HPW. WERS found that, of a list of sixteen 'new' practices, only 2 per cent of workplaces used more than ten. Moreover, the presence of a practice does not indicate its depth. The most sophisticated survey of depth studied 'organizational participation' across ten European countries, measuring the range of tasks on which employees had discretion and also how much say they had over them. It concluded that the HPW model in its fully developed form probably existed in no more than 2 per cent of workplaces.[49]

Reasons for this low take-up reflect the constraints discussed earlier in this chapter. Many firms are not organized to think about the design of work and skills development. As one study based on interviews with CEOs concluded, traditional command-and-control assumptions are widespread; although a 'gradual take-up of more individualized practices such as selection and performance management' might be expected, wider adoption of 'high-performance human-resource management practices' was less likely.[50] Again, the HPW model may not be appropriate in low-skill and routine jobs, which remain remarkably common in the UK; many companies have operated on what is termed the 'low road' of cost minimization with reliance on a low-wage and casual workforce. As we have argued in Chapter 2, the long-term viability of UK firms competing on low cost is increasingly doubtful.

Other issues arise within the HPW model itself. There is now a wealth of research studies reporting links between high-performance practices and various performance outcomes. Yet the nature of causation in such links is extremely unclear—what is cause and what effect? This makes it hard to define precisely what a firm should actually do. Some difficulties thrown up by the research are:[51]

- The components of the model differ in different cases. Training seems to be key in some cases and reward systems in others.
- Although the practices may bring benefits, there are also costs of implementation, notably redesigning work systems and improving training. In addition, benefits take time to emerge, so that promising ideas are sometimes dropped before their value is apparent. This is particularly important given the pressures for short-term results noted in Chapter 2: adopting HPW systems brings parallel changes in ways of operating, improvements in training, and sustained and linked change. Such things do not happen overnight.
- Some of the influences may run the other way: some studies have concluded that it is the successful firms that can afford the practices, rather than the practices leading to success.
- Some sets of practices are not specific to an individual firm. For example, flexible production systems in the clothing industry require changes in ordering and delivery systems across manufacturers, suppliers, and retailers. Benefits emerge only when there is a switch in methods throughout the supply chain, not just in individual firms.

• The reasons why the systems work are not always clear. The general expectation is that they promote employee trust and commitment, which in turn lead to improved motivation and flexibility. But some studies have failed to find these links. For example, teamwork has no overall connection to measures of commitment. The reason for this appears to be that HPW models depend on other conditions for them to work. 'Teams' come in many varieties, and overall they seem to have little effect on employee commitment. Only in certain circumstances do they have more positive impact. These circumstances include a reasonable level of job security for workers and a teamwork design that fits existing practice and expectations. If teams are imposed with little reference to previous experiments or to workers' own views, they tend to fail; where they are consistent with such views and have clear managerial support, on the other hand, they are more likely to succeed.[52]

As explored at length in Chapter 7, the assessment and implementation of management practices is not straightforward. Firms looking at these results on the HPW model may not be able to tell which practices or sets of practices will work for them. Nor will they know whether the practices work only when certain other underpinning conditions exist. And the system may work not because of its own characteristics but because it acts as a symbol or a signal. In the last situation, the HPW elements may be saying to employees that firms now care about them, in which case other mechanisms may be just as effective.

Does this mean that the influential bodies cited above are wrong? No. As they recognize, the HPW model is best seen as a checklist or a benchmark rather than a set of practices that will necessarily deliver returns in all circumstances. They also stress that the specific practices that firms pursue are highly variable. As one review concludes, much of the HPW model is to do with traditional 'good management', which embraces information-sharing, worker discretion, and employment security.[53] The HPW model is a very useful means of encouraging firms to raise their sights, and it has stimulated innovations that might not otherwise have been tried. But it is indeed a framework or stimulus rather than a ready-made solution, and its core aspects apply only under certain, relatively unusual, conditions.

Conclusions

These results illustrate a fundamental theme of this chapter. Much of employment relations is about getting the basics right and responding to what employees expect. Ignoring these needs can create distrust, which is in turn likely to interfere with long-term productive development. In the short run, productive improvement can be attained through the route of work intensification, but this is unlikely to be sustainable. Nor is it desirable for UK companies that need to move away from the low road to high-road strategies favouring innovation and higher-value activities. The HPW approach offers some tools appropriate for a longer-term solution, with the caveat that they need to be applied in a way that is mindful of the specific organizational context.

It used to be said that 'managements get the shop stewards they deserve', meaning that firms managing by arbitrary authority encouraged worker representatives to be equally uncompromising, with trench warfare the result. We can now broaden this statement: managements get the employment relations arrangements they choose or allow to come into existence. The British system is remarkably unprescriptive about the arrangements that firms put in place. There is, of course, a floor of employee rights, but there is no legal requirement as to how these are put into effect; there is no system (such as exists in several countries) for the terms of collective agreements to be extended to all firms within a given sector; and trade unions are rarely strong enough to drive forward their own view of good employment relations. Managements have the power to shape employment relations systems largely as they wish.

In the past many UK firms have assumed that these matters would look after themselves. This option 'worked' for some time, but it is unlikely to be useful in a context of diminishing employee commitment and widespread arguments about the growing importance of skills and knowledge. Firms now have the incentive as well as the opportunity to create employment-relations systems that contribute to their economic performance. In moving towards higher-value-added activities, employment-relations systems will need to contribute to an organizational context that encourages information sharing and collaboration, and supports worker discretion and organizational learning. Such notions provide the foundations for much of what will bring competitive advantage to organizations.

The key constraint is that participative systems rely on trust, which is in turn dependent on a degree of employment security. Firms consciously building employment-relations systems need to be aware of these conditions, and do two things: maximize employment opportunities, and explain clearly why promises can never be certain. But there is also a third issue: working to create active understanding of the economics of the business among employees, rather than explaining at a distance and from on high. 'Trust', one advocate of consultation argues, 'depends on the legitimacy of decisions, and consultation is one of the most tangible ways of expressing legitimacy'. The alternative is giving the impression of having something to hide and obtaining only compliance rather than active commitment in return.[54]

Key overall lessons for companies therefore are:

- No employment-relations system will in itself improve productivity. It needs to be consistent with a firm's strategic direction. And it is unlikely, given the number of other variables and the speed of change, that a clear linkage from an HPW system to productivity will ever be established. The HPW model is undoubtedly promising, but how it delivers its results depends on the context of each individual firm, not on applying a ready-made package.
- Poor employment relations certainly interfere with productivity. Mixed messages, a lack of attention to employee expectations, and poor communications have undermined many well-intentioned efforts. Managers need to recognize that trends towards tighter control of performance may have harmed employee commitment. These things often go in cycles, and loosening the corset of performance measures may now be a sensible means of reversing this damage.
- A good employment-relations system is often built bottom–up, with attention to the basics of how workers are treated. A joint approach, developed by resolving issues as they arise, can give reality and meaning to the language of participation, autonomy, and even empowerment. More strategic approaches can be built on this foundation.
- Time is a key resource. New systems take time to bed down, and have to be given the chance to work.
- Line managers are crucial. They are the people who convey the practical messages about real priorities. Downsizing has put pressure on this group, and the popular policy of devolving responsibility increases the pressure. A key test of a firm is whether its line managers have the space and the training to carry through an increasingly broad employment-relations agenda.

Issues for individual managers to contemplate include the following:

- Think about the problems of acting consistently and fairly; no one is deliberately inconsistent or unfair, but decisions taken in haste are often inconsistent, and what you think is fair may not be fair to others. This leads to:
- Recognize and work with employees' 'collective memory', that is, the expectations that they have developed as a group in the light of history.
- Middle and line managers interpret company policy: filter it downwards in the light of employee expectations, and be prepared to feed issues upwards. (One test of a firm's HR sensitivity is its openness to feedback.)

Finally, there are issues above the level of the individual company. This chapter began by stressing institutions, and it has looked mainly at those within the firm. But in addition, as Chapter 2 showed, collaborative structures between firms can aid the productivity of all national firms. UK employment-relations institutions have always been centred in the firm, with limited collective bargaining at higher levels and weak coordination. International comparative research shows that countries with coordinated arrangements for collective bargaining (generally the Coordinated Market Economic countries identified in Chapter 2) have outperformed others on a range of criteria.[55] There is also growing pressure arising from European integration, which has led to 'multi-level governance' at European, national, and company levels.[56] The challenge for public policy is to find ways to make these institutions work, as opposed to the common assumption, of Labour as much as Conservative governments, that minimizing institutional influence is the solution to labour market issues. This presents a challenge to UK firms, since they have little or no experience of multi-level collaboration in employment relations. However, as we have suggested in the context of the UK institutional framework as a whole, managers actively engaging with such developments will have the opportunity to contribute substantially to the shaping of their employment-relations framework—a critical consideration for the future.

Notes

1. Dave Ulrich, quoted in *People Management*, 19 March 1998. For a leading analysis of the business contribution of human resource management, see B. Becker, M.

Huselid, and D. Ulrich, *The HR Scorecard* (Boston: Harvard Business School Press, 2001).

2. CBI, *Employment Trends Survey 2003* (London: CBI, 2003), 8.

3. In preface to Becker et al., *HR Scorecard*. Norton is best known for his work with Robert Kaplan on the 'balanced scorecard', an approach which the Becker et al. book applies to human resource management.

4. M. Korczynski, *Human Resource Management in Service Work* (Basingstoke: Palgrave, 2002).

5. The nature of an employment-relations perspective is laid out in P. Edwards, 'The Employment Relationship and the Field of Industrial Relations', in P. Edwards (eds.), *Industrial Relations*, 2nd edn. (Oxford: Blackwell, 2003). An alternative excellent introduction is P. Blyton and P. Turnbull, *The Dynamics of Employee Relations*, 3rd edn. (Basingstoke: Palgrave, 2004).

6. L. Gratton et al., *Strategic Human Resource Management* (Oxford: Oxford University Press, 1999), 91, 57.

7. P. Nolan and S. Wood, 'Mapping the Future of Work', *British Journal of Industrial Relations*, 41/2 (2003), 165–74; P. Gregg and J. Wadsworth, 'Job Tenure in Britain, 1975–2000', *Oxford Bulletin of Economics and Statistics*, 64 (2002), 111–34.

8. For a discussion of these issues, see M. Ram, 'Managing Consultants in a Small Firm', *Journal of Management Studies*, 36/6 (1999), 875–97.

9. Studies cited are in M. Terry and P. Edwards (eds.), *Shopfloor Politics and Job Controls* (Oxford: Blackwell, 1988).

10. D. Metcalf, 'Transformation of British Industrial Relations?' in R. Barrell (ed.), *The UK Labour Market* (Cambridge: Cambridge University Press, 1994), 146.

11. A key study remains T. Nichols, *The British Worker Question* (London: Routledge and Kegan Paul, 1986). See also P. Nolan, 'Industrial Relations and Performance since 1945', in I. Beardwell (ed.), *Contemporary Industrial Relations* (Oxford: Oxford University Press, 1996).

12. P. Nolan and K. O'Donnell, 'Industrial Relations, HRM and Performance', in P. Edwards (ed.), *Industrial Relations*, 2nd edn. (Oxford: Blackwell, 2003), 508.

13. G. Owen, *From Empire to Europe* (London: HarperCollins, 1999), 441, 446.

14. E. Batstone, 'Labour and Productivity', *Oxford Review of Economic Policy*, 2/3 (1986), 1–31.

15. J. Storey, *Developments in the Management of Human Resources* (Oxford: Blackwell, 1992).

16. D. Gallie et al., *Restructuring the Employment Relationship* (Oxford: Oxford University Press, 1998), 55, emphasis added.

17. D. Guest, 'Human Resource Management: The Workers' Verdict', *Human Resource Management Journal*, 9/3 (1999), 14.

18. F. Green, 'The Demands of Work', in R. Dickens et al. (eds.), *The Labour Market under New Labour* (Basingstoke: Palgrave, 2003); D. Gallie et al., 'Employer Policies and Organizational Commitment in Britain, 1992–97', *Journal of Management Studies*, 38/8 (2001), 1081–1101.

19. Green, 'The Demands of Work', 145.

20. The figure for UK-owned firms was under 25%, as against 54% of overseas-owned firms: P. Marginson et al., 'Strategy, Structure and Control in the Changing Corporation', *Human Resource Management Journal*, 5 (1995), 3–27.

21. M. Cully et al., *Britain at Work, as Depicted by the 1998 Workplace Employee Relations Survey* (London: Routledge, 1999), 50, 56.

22. M. Fenton-O'Creevy, 'Employee Involvement and the Middle Manager', *Human Resource Management Journal*, 11/1 (2001), 24–40; L. Worrall et al., 'The New Reality for UK Managers', *Work, Employment and Society*, 14/4 (2000), 647–68; A. Wilkinson et al., 'Total Quality Management and Employee Involvement', *Human Resource Management Journal*, 2/4 (1992), 1–20.

23. D. Lapido et al., 'Working Like a Dog, Sick as a Dog', in B. Burchell et al. (eds.), *Systems of Production* (London: Routledge, 2003).

24. P. Thompson, 'Disconnected Capitalism', *Work, Employment and Society*, 17/4 (2003), 359–78 at 366.

25. M. O'Sullivan, *Contests for Corporate Control* (Oxford: Oxford University Press, 2000).

26. Department of Trade and Industry, 'Findings from the 1998 Survey of Employment Tribunal Applications', *DTI Employment Relations Research*, 13 (2002); www.dti.gov.uk/er/inform.

27. For a recent review see P. Edwards, 'Managing Absence from Work', European Industrial Relations Observatory. Available at www.eiro.eurofound.eu.int/2004/04/feature/uk0404103f. This site provides up-to-date information on employment relations across the EU member states plus Norway.

28. G. Palmer, 'Embeddedness and Workplace Relations', Ph.D. thesis, Warwick Business School, University of Warwick (2000).

29. J. O'Mahoney, 'Changing Minds', Ph.D. thesis, Warwick Business School, University of Warwick (2000).

30. P. Boxall and J. Purcell, *Strategy and Human Resource Management* (Basingstoke: Palgrave, 2003), 150.

31. Becker et al., *HR Scorecard*, 39.

32. M. Marchington et al., 'Understanding the Meaning of Participation', *Human Relations*, 47 (1994), 867–94; P. Edwards et al., 'The Determinants of Employee Responses to Total Quality Management', *Organization Studies*, 19/3 (1998), 449–75.

33. D. Gallie et al., 'Changing Patterns of Employee Involvement', SKOPE Research Paper 28 (2002), 10; available at www.eonomics.ox.ac.uk/skope/publications.

34. S. Tailby and D. Winchester, 'Management and Trade Unions', in S. Bach and K. Sisson (eds.), *Personnel Management* (Oxford: Blackwell, 2000).

35. CBI and TUC, Submission to the Productivity Initiative, October 2001, Best Practice section, paragraph 31. Available at www.tuc.org.uk/economy/tuc-3928. They are drawing here on the results of a survey in ten European countries, the Employee Direct Participation in Organisational Change (EPOC) study. For further discussion see P. Edwards et al., 'New Forms of Work Organization in the Workplace', in G. Murray et al. (eds.), *Work and Employment Relations in the High-performance Workplace* (London: Continuum, 2002).

36. Details of these requirements can be found at the European Industrial Relations Observatory; see n. 27. See also the *European Works Councils Bulletin*, 49 (2004).

37. J. Smith et al., 'Redundancy Consultation', *DTI Employment Relations Research*, 5 (1999); www.dti.gov.uk/er/inform.

38. P. Turnbull and V. Wass, 'Job Insecurity and Labour Market Lemons', *Journal of Management Studies*, 34 (1997), 27–51.

39. M. Hall, 'Informing and Consulting your Workforce: Handling Restructuring at BP Exploration' and 'Informing and Consulting Your Workforce: B&Q—Listening to the Grass Roots', IPA Case Studies 4 (3,5) (2003, 2004).

40. See M. Terry, 'Can "Partnership" Reverse the Decline of British Trade Unions?' *Work, Employment and Society*, 17/3 (2003), 459–72. The Involvement and Participation Association promotes partnership. Its website (www.partnership-at-work.com) gives definitions, history, and case studies.

41. J. Kelly, 'Social Partnership Agreements in Britain', *Industrial Relations*, 43/1 (2004), 727–49.

42. G. Dietz, 'Partnership and the Development of Trust in British Workplaces', *Human Resource Management Journal*, 14/1 (2004), 5–24.

43. CBI and TUC, Submission (n. 35), para 25.

44. K. Sisson and J. Storey, *The Realities of Human Resource Management* (Buckingham: Open University Press, 2000), 2; this remains the best short and readable assessment of the issues addressed in this chapter.

45. EEF and CIPD, 'Maximising Employee Potential and Business Performance: the Role of High Performance Working', 2003. Available at www.cipd.co.uk/surveys.

46. European Commission, *New Forms of Work Organisation: Case Studies* (Luxembourg: Office for Official Publications of the European Communities, 1998). The four UK cases were Bonas Machine Company; Leicester Royal Infirmary; Richer Sounds; and Scottish Radio.

47. E. Appelbaum et al., *Manufacturing Advantage* (Ithaca, NY: Cornell University Press, 2000); J. Purcell et al., 'Understanding the People and Performance Link' (London: CIPD, 2003).

48. CBI and TUC, Submission, para. 34; European Commission, *Case Studies*, p. ii.

49. Cully et al., *Britain at Work* (n. 21), 42–4. The second survey is the EPOC study; see J. Geary, 'New Forms of Work Organization', in P. Edwards (ed.) *Industrial Relations* (Oxford: Blackwell, 2003).

50. D. Guest, Z. King, N. Conway, J. Mitchie, and M. Sheehan-Quinn, *Voices from the Boardroom* (London: CIPD, 2001), 77.

51. Key studies include H. Ramsay et al., 'Employees and High-performance Work Systems', *British Journal of Industrial Relations*, 38/4 (2000), 501–31; D. Guest et al., 'Human Resource Management and Corporate Performance in the UK', *British Journal of Industrial Relations*, 41 (2003), 291–314. For critical assessment, see P. Edwards and M. Wright, 'High Involvement Work Systems and Performance Outcomes', *International Journal of Human Resource Management*, 12/4 (2001), 568–85; J.Godard, 'A Critical Assessment of the High-performance Paradigm', *British Journal of Industrial Relations*, 42/2 (2004), 215–39.

52. Marchington et al., 'Participation'; Edwards et al., 'Determinants' (both n. 32).
53. Godard, 'Critical Assessment', 363.
54. K. Sisson, 'Why UK Ministers Should Support an EU Consultation Directive', *European Works Councils Bulletin*, 29 (2000), 8.
55. F. Traxler, S. Blaschke, and B. Kittel, *National Labour Relations in Internationalized Markets* (Oxford: Oxford University Press, 2001). For an accessible development of these ideas, see F. Traxler, 'Co-ordinated Bargaining: A Stocktaking of Its Preconditions, Practices and Performance', *Industrial Relations Journal*, 34 (2003), 194–209.
56. P. Marginson and K. Sisson, *European Integration and Industrial Relations: Multi-level Governance in the Making* (Basingstoke: Palgrave, 2004).

5

Innovating Beyond the Steady State

A CENTRAL component of the shift towards higher-value-added activities is innovation. Innovations take many forms, from new products and processes to new lines of business, and they vary enormously in how radical they are vis-à-vis existing offerings. A recurring theme in the book is that organizations will face challenges that require radical or transformational change. In this chapter we focus our attention on discontinuous innovation—that is, the radical end of the innovation spectrum. The reason for doing this is that incremental or 'steady-state innovation' practices are by now relatively well understood in UK firms. The real test for companies that aspire to leading-edge practice, and to stake a place at the forefront of world competition, is to master the much harder challenge of radical innovation.

Innovation is a key driver of corporate transformation. As noted in Chapter 3, traditional strategies based on distinct market positioning or access to unique resources are no longer sufficient for long-term competitive advantage. Instead, the challenge for today's companies is strategic transformation, which in large part is about identifying and delivering on new sources of customer value.

We saw in Chapter 2 that the UK has a poor record in terms of both investment in, and exploitation of, R&D. Yet innovation is central to most contemporary thinking on national competitiveness. A high and rising standard of living cannot be supported solely by investing in traditional factors of production or creating an attractive business climate: it requires individuals and firms to create new sources of value. In its 2004 Innovation Review, the Department of Trade and Industry (DTI) noted that developments in trade liberalization, falling transport and communication costs, and increasing scientific and technological progress are 'occurring at a speed and on a scale never seen before. In the past many UK-based businesses have prospered even when selling in low value markets, but today British industry faces a new challenge: how to raise its rate of innovation.'[1]

However, while few would question the importance of innovation, there are many sceptics who see the process of developing new products, services, or processes as intrinsically random. Many well-known innovations—from Louis Pasteur's development of the pasteurization process to Pfizer's Viagra—involved a significant element of serendipity and, as any venture capitalist knows, the odds of even a highly impressive business plan delivering its promised growth goals is no more than ten to one.

Our position, based on both research and observation, is that steady-state innovation *can* be effectively managed, even if the outcomes are not entirely predictable.[2] There are some well-established management practices that substantially increase the chances of innovation success. In product development, these include such things as developing close understanding of user needs, strategic portfolio management, early involvement of multiple functions, and systematic risk management and review via some form of 'stage-gate' system. Similarly, successful process innovation requires cross-functional and early involvement of users, policy deployment of key strategic objectives around which continuous improvement can be focused, and emphasis on learning and capture of tacit knowledge. While such practices are not always straightforward to implement and do not guarantee success, they vastly improve the odds that new products and processes will indeed emerge. There will always be an element of chance in innovation, but with good planning firms can make their own luck: fortune, as Pasteur noted, 'favours the prepared mind'.

Yet the ability to manage the innovation process better is not the whole story. The snag is that by getting better at certain approaches to innovation, the firm potentially shuts itself off to others. Thus, Nestlé and Kraft General Foods became so focused on innovating in supermarket coffee that they completely missed out on the upmarket coffee shop concept popularized by Starbucks and Costa.

Why the apparent paradox? The answer lies in the process of learning that develops in firms (particularly large ones). Through a pattern of trial and error, firms develop ways of managing product and process change which work for them and which they refine and elaborate over time, building on what does work and discarding what doesn't. In this way, they develop their own 'routines' of behaviour for managing the elements of the innovation process—and these firm-specific patterns of behaviour give rise to particular structures and procedures for dealing with the

challenge. For example, GlaxoSmithKline has built up a highly sophisticated development pipeline for screening candidate drugs and pushing
them through the phases of clinical trial. Virgin, in contrast, invests in
new businesses with a far less structured process, but nonetheless with a
clear set of criteria and strong biases built up from many years of successful
and failed ventures. In both cases, behavioural routines have emerged that
guide the firm down a particular trajectory of innovation.[3]

So as managers learn, and develop patterns of response born of trial-and-
error, they inadvertently create constraints on employees' ability to continue to be innovative *outside* activities that can be predicted and planned
for. Typically, they become better and better at managing incremental or
steady-state innovations along a particular trajectory, and worse at exploring opportunities beyond that trajectory—which we refer to as radical or
discontinuous innovations.

In this chapter we explore the challenge of managing radical innovation.[4] We first examine the difference between steady-state and radical
innovation, and the reasons why the latter is so much harder to manage.
Then we describe a set of approaches that increase the chances of managing radical innovation effectively.[5] While the principles for managing
steady-state innovation have been developed over time, thinking on discontinuous innovation is still in its infancy. But there are some examples
of successful practice, and rather more cases of poor practice, both of
which offer opportunities for learning.

Steady-state Innovation vs. Radical Innovation

There are many ways of characterizing the different forms of business
innovation. One approach is to focus on the different ways innovation
can take place. The relevant categories here are *product innovation* (the
actual product or service being produced), *process innovation* (how the
product or service is produced), *position innovation* (the context in which
it is offered), and *paradigm* or *business innovation* (which rethinks the
underlying mental models within which the product is being offered).
This typology, and its variants, has been widely used for many years.[6]

A second approach, increasingly popular in recent years, is to consider
the nature of the innovation activity in the light of the existing set of
competencies and networks of the firm. As noted earlier, firms tend to
follow certain trajectories of development that are reinforced through
their existing competencies and through their networks of relationships

with other firms. Such firms often continue to be highly innovative along their existing paths of development (steady-state innovation). However, when the opportunities for product, process, or position innovation are inconsistent with the firm's existing competencies and networks, the managerial challenge in sensing and responding to them is enormous (radical innovation).[7]

Consider a couple of examples to illustrate this distinction. A steady-state product innovation would be the gradual improvement of the Bic ballpoint, which was originally developed in 1950 but remains a strong product today, with daily sales of 14 million. Although the implement is superficially the same shape, close inspection reveals a host of incremental changes that have taken place in materials, inks, ball technology, and safety features. A discontinuous product innovation, in contrast, might be the solid-state white-light-emitting diode technology patented by Nichia Chemical. This product threatens to make the traditional heated-filament light bulb originally developed in the late nineteenth century by Edison and Swan obsolete. It is 85 per cent more energy-efficient, has sixteen times the life of a conventional bulb, is brighter, more flexible in application, and is likely to be subject to the scale economies associated with electronic component production. A similar distinction can be made in process innovation. An example of steady-state process innovation is the widespread adoption of industry standards such as ISO quality standards, which yield efficiency improvements within an existing set of parameters and capabilities.[8] Discontinuous process innovation, in contrast, is an enabling technology that makes the traditional technologies obsolete—for example the Bessemer process for steel-making replaced conventional charcoal smelting, and the Pilkington float-glass process replaced grinding and polishing.

There are, in sum, two important attributes to our definition of radical innovation. First, it involves the development of competencies and network linkages with other firms that take a company out of its existing trajectory of development—'out of its depth' or 'beyond its comfort zone' in those respects. Second, radical innovation assumes some form of abrupt change that makes it necessary or possible for the firm to break out of its existing development path. Such changes are often a combination of technological, social, political, and economic factors.

This distinction between steady-state and radical innovation should make it clear that while they are different, both are necessary elements of a firm's overall innovation strategy. It is important to invest in steady-state innovation, and many new products, from Intel's Pentium 4 processor to Coca-Cola's Lemon Coke, are clearly of this type. The trouble is that such innovations are simply not enough to sustain long-term success; the level of technological, social, and economic change in most industries means that sooner or later an existing trajectory of innovation will run out of steam. For example, McDonald's has dominated the fast-food burger market for forty years, but by 2004 was facing pressure from consumer groups and NGOs, changing diets, and new competitors. If McDonald's is to look forward to another forty years of growth, it will have to get to grips with radical innovation.

Not only is radical innovation a strategic necessity in some industries, it also offers an attractive side-benefit: it takes firms out of the zero-sum game that characterizes many industry battlegrounds. If Lemon Coke succeeds, it is because it is taking market share away from other fizzy drinks, including possibly Coke itself. But if Egg, the online bank, succeeds, it does so at the expense of the big retail banks rather than Prudential's traditional insurance competitors. And Starbucks' reinvention of the coffee shop—a classic example of radical innovation—did not just create value for itself, it generated growth in the entire sector. Firms seeking true competitive advantage are looking for growth levels that are significantly larger than the natural growth of the industry, and radical innovation represents one important way of doing this.[9]

Why is Radical Innovation so Difficult?

Unfortunately, radical innovation is hard to do. By definition, it is an unnatural and uncomfortable activity for most firms, taking them out of their comfort zone into areas that they do not fully understand. It also involves a much higher level of creativity and 'out-of-the-box' thinking than typically goes on in large companies. It should be no surprise that start-ups and new entrants are behind most successful cases of radical innovation—think of Starbucks, Ryanair, Prêt à Manger, Palm, the Smart car, and Innocent fruit juices. This is by no means a new pattern. When disruption occurs, existing industry incumbents tend to do badly and may not survive the transitions involved; the advantage almost invariably passes to the dynamic new entrants.

Why does this happen? And what are the dynamics which cause even well-managed firms to fall down in managing radical innovation? It is clearly not simply a case of firms slowing down and becoming reluctant to look at new things as they age. We know from Chapter 1 that there are many reasons why such inertia occurs. The individual and collective experience of people in organizations tends to privilege certain bases of success and the salience that they attach to signals about particular new developments. The 'not-invented-here' syndrome is not necessarily the response of a stupid firm, but rather that of one which does not—or chooses not to—see the significance and relevance of a new idea being offered to it. It is very difficult for individuals to escape the constraints of past history, industry and organizational norms, and the politics of decision-making, as they must when trying to do things differently.

Equally, managers who do decide to explore radical new directions often find themselves having to manage contradictions and challenges to their existing innovation processes. Portfolio-management and resource-allocation techniques that have enabled them to achieve good fit with the strategic directions and competencies of the firm may be less well suited for reviewing apparently wild and unexpected ideas leading in completely new directions. Likewise, risk-management systems operating with stage-gate reviews over the development life of a new project may not deal well with apparently high-risk projects with raised levels of market and technological uncertainty. Thus the established organizational order constrains the opportunities for change.

The problem is compounded by the networks of relationships the firm has with other firms. Typically, much of the basis for innovation lies at a system level, involving networks of suppliers and partners configuring knowledge and other resources to create a new offering. Radical innovation is often problematic because it involves building and working with a significantly different set of partners than those the firm is used to working with. Whereas 'strong ties'—close and consistent relationships with regular partners in a network—may be important in enabling a steady stream of continuous improvement innovations, evidence suggests that where firms are seeking to do something different they need to exploit much weaker ties across a very different population to gain access to new ideas and different sources of knowledge and expertise.[10]

In sum, managing radical innovation creates managerial challenges that even the most successful firms struggle with. So what should they do, and who can they learn from?

Managing Radical Innovation: Emerging Challenges

There are no clear guidelines for managing the process of radical innovation. Sources of discontinuity vary and involve shifts in technology, market, political, and social conditions in the environments in which firms operate. Not surprisingly, these conditions tend to favour new entrants that can adapt to and exploit the new 'rules of the game'. By contrast, pressures inside and outside the established firm act to reinforce existing development, something that it takes a great deal of energy and imagination to counteract. To put it bluntly, established firms need to find ways of reproducing the entrepreneurial agility of new entrants if they are to cope with discontinuous conditions. There are no easy recipes for doing this; but there are some emerging practices that appear to help, and in the remainder of this chapter we briefly describe some of them.

These practices fall into three categories, according to three principal challenges that the firm faces:

- the cognitive challenge—becoming aware of opportunities and ideas that lie beyond the firm's comfort zone;
- the political challenge—generating support for radical new ideas inside an established and risk-averse organization; and
- the technical challenge—developing the necessary skills and capabilities to commercialize the new innovations.

The Cognitive Challenge

There is an underlying paradox in managing radical innovation. We know that the stimuli we need to respond to lie beyond our ingrained mindset; but that mindset is often so strong that we don't even recognize its boundaries. (This is a subject we return to in more detail in Chapter 9.) The cognitive challenge for would-be innovators, then, is first to recognize that our view of the world is inevitably blinkered and subject to bias and blind spots, and secondly consciously to develop ways of peeling back those barriers to sight.

A good example of the cognitive challenge is Lego's delayed reaction to the emergence of electronic games in the 1990s. When Sega and Nintendo first came on the scene, Lego's executives saw them as an irrelevance—they were selling expensive electronic games to teenagers. But as prices came down, and the target market became younger boys, Lego began to realize that electronic gaming was a serious threat to its core business. By the mid-1990s, Lego was investing heavily in its own electronic games, but in retrospect it was far too late, and the company hit financial difficulties as a result. What could Lego have done differently in the late 1980s to prepare itself for the rise of electronic gaming? We can identify five broad and mutually supportive approaches.

Manage the Idea-generation Process

Innovation needs ideas to fuel the process, whether they come from new technological developments or signals about changes in the marketplace. Combining these 'push' and 'pull' stimuli triggers the process of change. Such stimuli typically emerge in a fairly haphazard way, so managers must be mindful of the organizational conditions that promote such creative and spontaneous activity. Often, top-down management can stifle the bottom-up creativity and risk-taking so vital to meeting the challenge of discontinuity. Nevertheless, it is possible to *manage* idea generation as a process in a way that enables firms to analyse and evaluate ideas systematically.[11] For example, Diageo's new venture division developed a novel form of brainstorming, in which it would bring together groups of twenty people for half-day sessions to generate new drinks concepts. By using particular sequences of prompts and stimuli, they were able to get participants thinking outside their usual constraints, and over the course of a year they generated several hundred ideas for new products. Strategos, the consulting firm, has developed a more sophisticated methodology, using computer technology to integrate insights into market discontinuities, industry orthodoxies, and firm competencies to generate hundreds of possible ideas for subsequent evaluation and prioritization.

Develop an External Scanning Capability

It is widely considered good practice to listen to customers and respond to their feedback. The problem is that customers are often stuck in the same cognitive prison as the supplier: they can see ways of improving on the features of existing products but they cannot imagine an entirely different solution to their needs. In the famous example, no one would have guessed that they would find a Walkman useful before Sony invented it. So an external scanning capability has to take the firm beyond its established relationships with its normal partners. Unilever, for example, has created an externally focused group whose role is to gain access to emerging technologies and to make minority investments in start-up companies with promising ideas. But this approach raises big questions of its own—about which sources to deal with and how to manage the 'targeted hunting' process, for instance.[12]

One important group to watch is the precocious adopters in emerging markets which typically set the tone and pace for others;[13] another is technology labs and science institutes far away from the core expertise of the firm. Consider an example from the motor-sport industry, where leading race-car makers, continually in search of innovation to improve performance, pluck ideas, materials, technology, or products from very different sectors. Indeed, some have people (called 'technological antennae') whose sole responsibility is to search for promising new technologies. For instance, recent developments in the use of titanium components in Formula 1 engines have been significantly advanced by lessons learned about the moulding process from a company producing golf clubs.

Firms develop an external scanning capability in different ways. For some, it is about building closer links on early-stage projects running at universities and research institutes. For others, as in the Shell example in Chapter 9, it is about exploring alternative futures and looking for the fresh combinations which might signal significant opportunities or threats. Others try to make sense of markets which don't yet exist, attempting to pick up weak signals about emerging trends—for example, in the school playground or among the chat-rooms of the Internet.

Tune into Weak Signals Inside the Firm

For many large companies, the challenge is not so much getting hold of information from the external marketplace; it is about making better use of that which already exists inside the organization. Senior executives in a large multinational are typically buffered from the marketplace and the cutting edge of technology by three or four layers of hierarchy. And the channels of information to them are often far from perfect—in fact, they are often filtered in such a way that the only information that gets through is what subordinates think their bosses want to hear. For example, in the months before Marconi's collapse in 2001, it was clear to salespeople and manufacturing employees that the company was nowhere near meeting its sales targets, but this information was withheld from top executives until several months later, at which point they were forced to issue an embarrassing and highly damaging profit warning.

How can senior decision-makers tune into the 'weak signals' that exist inside the firm? The answer is partly cultural—individuals at the firm's periphery have to be able to make their voice heard at the top.[14] One of the reasons Marconi's top executives failed to get the message was that the domineering culture they had created discouraged dissent. There is also a need to put in place mechanisms that actively seek out new approaches and points of view. For example, Nokia set up an 'insight and foresight' group whose role was to look for changes in the marketplace three to five years out.

Typically, it is the peripheral parts of the firm that are the most innovative, because they are least encumbered by rules and traditions. They are also nearest the marketplace. So a good place to look for new ideas is distant foreign subsidiaries, smaller business units, and even affiliated companies that the firm does not wholly own. For example, Diageo's highly successful Smirnoff Ice originated in Australia as a local product, Stolichnya Lemon Russki, before it was picked up by the corporate marketing department as a product with global potential.

Promote a Culture that Tolerates Uncertainty and New Ideas

Unfortunately, most large companies do a good job of killing off the entrepreneurial spirit of employees by a combination of short-term thinking, risk-aversion, and top-down decision-making. But there are a few exceptions. The best-known is 3M, but Virgin, WPP, and Vodafone are also companies that do a decent job of creating a stimulating environment for individual initiative, while still capturing the benefits of size and scope.

Can managers create an innovative culture? Not easily, since it involves systematically influencing the way people behave on a day-to-day basis, and that is driven by a complex set of stimuli—obvious ones such as reward and incentive schemes, as well as subtle ones such as the level of trust and support provided by senior managers.[15] While the evidence on managers 'managing cultural change' is not particularly promising, there is scope for managers to promote behaviours and attitudes that will support innovation.

Innovative cultures are rarely 'strong' cultures that demand conformity to a company way, because innovation relies on diversity, variety, and productive tension. Such norms cannot be dictated nor demanded. However, the evidence does suggest that clear and consistent messages from the top, symbolic promotion, and reward of appropriate behaviour and role-modelling by key managers can help influence and promote certain norms. Yet innovative cultures are inherently fragile—they take years to build, but they can be destroyed very quickly.[16]

Despite its size, Virgin has managed to sustain a highly innovative culture over the years. To some extent, this culture is a reflection of the personality of its founder, Richard Branson, who continues to risk his firm's and his own health in the pursuit of novelty. But Virgin also has a raft of institutionalized systems designed to reinforce its innovative spirit. Similarly, 3M's ability to keep an 'intrapreneurial' spirit alive across a large corporation is not accidental, deriving instead from the interplay of leadership, structures, reward and recognition systems, operating processes, and a climate in which individuals are given 'permission' to explore and challenge.[17]

Foster Divergent Thinking

If the cognitive challenge is about breaking free from the narrow mindsets gained over years of working for the same firm, then one very useful approach is to bring in more outsiders. As chairman, Sir Christopher Bland succeeded in cutting through BT's tangled financial problems in the late 1990s at least in part because as a newcomer to the telecoms business he was able to ask the awkward questions that insiders were oblivious to. Likewise, when Wellington, a Canadian insurance company, embarked on a radical transformation of its business in 1990, the entire management team was brought in from other sectors. The result was a much more daring—and ultimately successful—transformation than would in all probability have been contemplated by industry stalwarts.

The Political Challenge

Even if the firm is successful at opening itself up to new ideas, it faces another formidable difficulty in mobilizing support for those ideas in the corridors of power. The issue here is not whether the ideas are commercially or technically feasible—it is whether the political process can be handled skilfully enough to defuse the critics and the sceptics.

Bear in mind that traditionalists who take a sceptical view of new ideas often have good cause. The fact is that many proposals put forward by mavericks and entrepreneurs are not worth investing in, and the standard evaluation processes do a good job of filtering them out. The risk is that these processes become so effective that they also reject the occasional good idea emanating from an unlikely source. The issue, then, is building some flexibility into the system. Again, there are no simple solutions to this problem, but a number of approaches are worth considering.

Build Pluralism into Decision-making Processes

Decision-making is by nature a highly politicized activity, and it is not uncommon to see an outcome manipulated by the dedicated efforts of one individual. However, steps can be taken to make it more pluralistic (by which we mean open to alternative points of view—an issue we delve into in more detail in Chapter 9).

For example, Intel is well known for having institutionalized a process it calls 'constructive confrontation'—essentially a legitimization of dissent.[18] In many firms, the boss's judgement is effectively unchallengeable; at Intel argument is positively encouraged, because the firm recognizes that many of the critical insights come from those closest to the action and have nothing to do with seniority. As a result, meetings at Intel are often ugly, no-holds-barred arguments, but they are deemed more likely to get to the underlying facts than a more sedate traditional gathering.

We have also seen other experiments in decision-making that are worth considering. Some firms use the analogy of the court of law: every motion has to have an advocate and a detractor, and it is the job of the detractor to be a strong devil's advocate. This process ensures that all relevant information is brought to light before the decision is made, rather than only the information that supports the motion.

Another approach is to create a 'market for judgement'. Gary Hamel has observed that the orange juice futures market provides a better-quality weather forecast than the official one from Florida's Met Office.[19] In other words, the collective point of view of thousands of informed individuals who are each putting their own money on the line is superior to the official judgement of a few experts. This principle can readily be extended into firm decision-making by opening up important investment decisions to large numbers of employees. A number of firms, including Roche, Shell, and Whirlpool, have experimented with such processes.

Decentralize Seed Funding for New Projects

Another way of overcoming political resistance to new ideas is to decentralize the seed-funding process to lower levels in the firm. This serves two purposes—it acts as a clear signal that the firm is keen to promote innovation, and it gives the individuals working on the new idea additional time to work it through before presenting it to senior executives.[20]

For example, in the early 1990s the UK subsidiary of a major German pharmaceutical company developed a new technology for administering therapies transdermally (i.e. through the skin). Initial attempts by the head of UK marketing to convince corporate R&D to take up the project failed, falling foul (he believed) of a 'not invented here' mentality. Instead of giving up, he sounded out marketing managers in other European countries, all of whom were keen on the project, and he ultimately persuaded the European marketing board to come up with the necessary £10 million investment. The project was a success, and the new technology was rolled out across Europe during the late 1990s.

It often happens that an idea seeded by a business unit, having grown into a viable business, is eventually abandoned because it doesn't fit with the rest of the group. Corporate-sponsored development projects therefore provide an important alternative to business-unit-level investments. Consider the case of ABB, the global engineering and technology firm.[21] In the mid-1990s, when it was one of the leading players in its sector, it provided both seed money at the subsidiary level and corporate funding for new ideas that crossed the boundaries of existing business units. In ABB's twelve corporate research centres, located around the world, employees were encouraged to propose 'high-impact' projects—meaning those with broad, cross-business-unit applications—which were then funded from a corporate budget. One such project led to the creation of a state-of-the-art electrical-transformer factory in Athens, Georgia. Dubbed the 'factory of the future', the test factory was fully automated, from ordering through production to the delivery of the finished product.

Build Dual Structures

The third, and most common, approach is to build a 'dual structure' that separates out the new and innovative projects from the existing business. Dual structures exist in many different guises—from the special-project team reporting directly to the chairman; through the incubator, new-venture division or corporate venture unit that has formal responsibility for working with new projects; to the 'skunkworks' which has no formal status. In recent years corporate-venturing units have been particularly popular, with such firms as Diageo, Royal Sun Alliance, Marks & Spencer, Nokia, Intel, and British Airways all creating a venturing arm (and most subsequently closing it down).[22]

The dual-structure approach has one primary advantage—it protects the new and often unpopular new ideas from the mainstream organization until they have achieved a measure of commercial viability. The problem is that venture units and incubators are very hard to manage effectively. Experience suggests that they work best when they have CEO-level support, clear objectives, and their own separate pot of money. They fail horribly when parent-company managers meddle in evaluating and choosing projects, and when they are expected to support multiple (and changing) objectives.

Our belief is that even when they are effective, venture units and incubators are best viewed as temporary vehicles for stimulating change. New ventures can be nicely protected in a specialized venture unit, but most belong in the mainstream businesses. Astute venture managers therefore see their job as far more than just creating some new businesses—they are also a stimulus for change and a source of innovation expertise from which others can learn. Marks & Spencer's venture unit, for example, had a 'brief but merry life', according to its former head, but it 'gave a sense of change at a difficult time in the company, it developed a capability of acting quickly, and it created better links into changes in the outside world'.

The Technical Challenge

The third piece of the innovation puzzle is the skills and capabilities of the firm and its network ties. Are these what are needed to make a success of radical innovation? To return to the Lego example, the company belatedly recognized the need to move into electronic games and mobilized political support among senior managers to fund the new business activities. But ultimately it struggled in the electronic gaming market, because the skill-sets of employees were more suited to developing plastic bricks than software; and its connections were with toyshops, not gaming communities.

The technical challenge has three components—the skills of individual employees, the capabilities of the firm, and the relationships with other firms. In each case, the challenge is to find ways of building, acquiring, or co-investing to gain access to what is missing.

Build Employees' Entrepreneurial Skills

In Lego's case, it was clear what skill-sets its employees were missing, at least once the company had realized the importance of electronic gaming.

The solution was equally clear—recruit new employees with a background in electronic games and software development, and train existing employees in these new areas.

The bigger problem in skills development is that most employees in large firms have never attempted to act entrepreneurially. They have been accustomed to working within traditional boundaries, rather than challenging them; and they have typically developed highly specialized skills around one particular activity, rather than the broader skill-set that is needed to follow through on a new business idea.

Some firms have directly addressed this skill deficiency by putting hundreds, sometimes thousands, of employees through innovation programmes. For example, in 1999 the Swiss pharmaceuticals giant Roche instituted what it called a 'strategic vision process' which generated literally thousands of ideas for new products, markets, or businesses. It formed teams of people around the most promising sets of ideas, put them through 'action labs' to give them the skills to develop business plans, and then after sixty days held an 'idea fair' at which the teams presented their projects to top management. The most promising won seed money to progress to prototype stage, and those that made the next cut were set up as businesses in their own right. While there is a clear expectation that new businesses will emerge from the process, the broader purpose behind the initiative is to get employees across the organization thinking in terms of new ideas and business models. So far, 500 people have been engaged in the programme over four years.

Develop New Technical Capabilities in the Firm

Over and above the skills of employees, firms also have higher-level competencies or capabilities. For example, Lego's capabilities were traditionally in the design and marketing of brick sets, while Diageo won its position in the upmarket drinks sector with well-honed capabilities in global marketing and logistics.

By definition, radical innovation involves a shift away from the firm's traditional areas of strength and a move into domains that require new capabilities. The challenge then is securing the capabilities on which success in the new domain depends. Three generic options exist, each with its own pros and cons. Acquisition involves buying up an entire firm or a team of people with the necessary capabilities. Acquisition is quick, but also risky, because integrating the acquired capabilities is rarely seamless, and people acquired in the deal are apt to leave. For example,

Ericsson bought California-based Raynet in the early 1990s for its networking capabilities, but it managed the acquisition so clumsily that soon almost none of the existing staff was left.

Partnering is a hybrid approach that consists of learning the necessary capabilities from a joint-venture partner. Again, this is a high-risk approach. Research has shown that joint ventures rarely deliver the anticipated learning benefits, and many partnerships end in acrimony because the objectives of the two parties diverge. Lego tried various forms of partnering, including working with a New York software company on its first CD-ROM, Lego Island, and a distribution arrangement with Electronic Arts. But it is not clear how much the company actually learned from these relationships.

Finally, it is always possible to build new capabilities organically. However, the process can take many years—often longer than the firm will tolerate before pulling the plug. In sum (and regardless of the approach taken), the development of new capabilities for managing radical innovation is hazardous. Firms that are successful typically do not stray too far from their core: they leverage certain existing capabilities and build or acquire the few additional ones they are lacking.

Develop New Partner Networks

These days innovation is often a multi-player game. Firms increasingly work in partnerships or through outsourcing arrangements, rather than do everything in-house. So in addition to its own internal capabilities, a vital characteristic of an innovating firm is the quality of its relationships with partner networks. An automotive systems supplier like Robert Bosch, for example, operates within a tight web of relationships with branded car companies like Ford, and to its own tiered suppliers.

These networks are absolutely central to the distinction between steady-state and radical innovation. Maintaining a healthy flow of improvement (steady-state) innovations depends on a rich network of close and mature relationships—but the very strength of these relationships can become a hindrance when the firm tries to branch out into something different. Radical innovation requires the firm to develop new relationships—and typically to break off some of the old ones at the same time. While the close ties of tight networks promote the smooth transfer of resources, they limit exposure to alternative resources and new ideas. This suggests that firms should maintain 'hybrid networks' which consist of a combination of both close long-term partnerships and a large number of looser connections that they can develop as resource needs arise.[23]

Conclusions

In itself, radical innovation is nothing new—major upheavals in technology or markets have occurred throughout history, sometimes (as in the case of the Industrial Revolution) bringing with them massive change across whole societies. For managers, however, discontinuities represent a growing problem because the events that trigger them are on the increase—rapid technological advance, fragmenting markets, and increasing political instability to name but three. Their growing frequency puts a premium on the ability of managers to learn how to deal with it proactively.

One of the key lessons of experience is that when faced with discontinuous shifts, incumbents do badly and new entrepreneurial entrants take up the running. They lead until the next discontinuity, when the process is repeated. This pattern might suggest that the only solution is to keep spinning off or setting up new firms. However, there is no law that prohibits an existing competitor from learning to reinvent itself so that it retains the advantages of experience and accumulated competencies while deploying them more entrepreneurially. As we have demonstrated in this chapter, there are steps that managers can take to deal with the issues across cognitive, political, and operational dimensions. They may not always be able to 'manage' in the sense of controlling and coordinating known elements, but they can shape a context in which new ideas can emerge and be taken forward. As with other areas of management, there is no one size that fits all. But while the themes we have raised need to be considered within the context of each individual situation, the overall message is positive: although hard, radical innovation is not impossible, and there *are* ways in which reflective managers can turn it to advantage.

Notes

1. This report drew together the views of hundreds of practitioners, academics, policy-makers, and other agents concerned with the challenge of innovation and competitiveness. *Competing in the Global Economy: The Innovation Challenge*, http://www.dti.gov.uk.

2. For an overview of the findings on innovation management research see: J. Tidd, J. Bessant, and K. Pavitt, *Managing Innovation* (Chichester: John Wiley and Sons, 2005); M. L. Tushman and W. L. Moore (eds.), *Readings in the Management of Innovation,* 2nd edn. (Boston: Ballinger, 1988); S. Wheelwright and K. B. Clark, *Revolutionizing Product Development* (New York: Free Press, 1992).

3. The idea that firms develop routines of behaviour that become ingrained over time dates back to R. Nelson and S. Winter, *An Evolutionary Theory of Economic Change* (London: Belknap Press of Harvard University, 1982). See also the concept of technological trajectories: G. Dosi, 'Technological Paradigms and Technological Trajectories: A Suggested Interpretation of the Determinants and Directions of Technical Change', *Research Policy,* 11/3 (1982), 147–63.

4. The terms radical and discontinuous change are used interchangeably in this chapter. For background literature on the use of these terms see: M. L. Tushman and P. Anderson, 'Technological Discontinuities and Organizational Environments', *Administrative Science Quarterly,* 31 (1986), 439–65; R. M. Henderson and K. B. Clark, 'Architectural Innovation: The Reconfiguration of Product Technologies and the Failure of Established Firms', *Administrative Science Quarterly,* 35 (1990), 9–30. The term *disruptive* is also used widely in this context, but it is more appropriately used to describe a particular type of technology that often requires discontinuous innovation on the part of the incumbent firm. See C. Christensen, *The Innovator's Dilemma* (Boston: Harvard Business School Press, 1997).

5. One of the important areas of research which is helping throw light on this kind of problem is that of 'complexity theory' where researchers from many different disciplines are looking at the behaviour of systems under what they call 'far from equilibrium' conditions where the rules of managing the steady state break down. There might, for example, be useful lessons which emerge for management through understanding some of the principles of evolutionary biology and how new genetic strains emerge and develop. See e.g. S. L. Brown and K. M. Eisenhardt, 'The Art of Continuous Change: Linking Complexity Theory and Time-Paced Evolution in Relentlessly Shifting Organizations', *Administrative Science Quarterly,* 42/1 (1997), 1–35; B. McKelvey, 'Avoiding Complexity Catastrophe in Co-evolutionary Pockets: Strategies for Rugged Landscapes', *Organization Science,* 10/3 (1999), 294–322.

6. See Wheelwright and Clark, *Revolutionizing Product Development*; and J. Utterback, *Mastering the Dynamics of Innovation* (Boston: Harvard Business School Press, 1996).

7. The challenges in managing innovation processes outside the firm's traditional competencies have been explored in many books. See e.g. Christensen, *Innovator's Dilemma*; C. Markides, *All the Right Moves* (Boston: Harvard Business School Press, 1999); G. Hamel, *Leading the Revolution* (Boston: Harvard Business School Press, 2001).

8. It is important not to underestimate the scope for such steady-state innovation. Much of the dramatic productivity improvement reported across a wide range of manufacturing and service firms as a result of deploying 'lean thinking' is

essentially about driving a waste-reducing innovation agenda within an established product/market envelope. See J. Womack and D. Jones, *Lean Thinking* (New York: Simon and Schuster, 1996), for a full account of these.

9. The concept of developing new sources of value in a given industry setting has attracted considerable attention in recent years. See e.g. C. Kim and R. Mauborgne, 'Value Innovation: The Strategic Logic of High Growth', *Harvard Business Review*, 75/1 (1997), 102–12; Markides, *All the Right Moves*.

10. Collaborative networks have become key features of industries where technology is changing rapidly and the sources of key resources are widely distributed, such as biotechnology: W. Powell, K. Koput, and L. Smith-Doerr, 'Interorganizational Collaboration and the Locus of Innovation: Networks of Learning in Biotechnology', *Administrative Science Quarterly*, 41/1 (1996), 116–45. However, firms with only close partnership relations may become overembedded and suffer from 'collective blindness' (see J. Nahapiet and S. Ghoshal, 'Social Capital, Intellectual Capital and the Organizational Advantage', *Academy of Management Review*, 23 (1998), 242–66). Hence scholars, building on the work of M. Granovetter ('The Strength of Weak Ties', *American Journal of Sociology*, 78 (1973), 1360–80) and R. Burt (*Structural Holes* (Cambridge, MA: Harvard University Press, 1992)), have identified that firms with heterogeneous interorganizational links may benefit from being exposed to different competencies and resources, and thus added opportunities (C. M. Beckman and P. R. Haunschild, 'Network Learning: The Effects of Partners' Heterogeneity of Experience on Corporate Acquisitions', *Administrative Science Quarterly*, 47 (2002), 92–124).

11. For a detailed description of idea generation processes, see W. Buckland, A. Hatcher, and J. Birkinshaw, *Inventuring: Why Big Companies must Think Small* (New York: McGraw-Hill, 2003).

12. For more on P&G's approach and the general problem of building external scanning capability, see L., Huston, 'Mining the Periphery for New Products', *Long Range Planning*, 37 (2004), 191–6.

13. For a detailed discussion of the use of lead users as stimuli for innovation, see E. von Hippel, S. Thomke, and M. Sonnack, 'Creating Breakthroughs at 3M', *Harvard Business Review*, 77/5 (1999), 47–56.

14. There is some emerging literature concerned with the processes by which information on market uncertainties and technological change get incorporated into firm strategy. See S. Kaplan, F. Murray, and R. Henderson, 'Discontinuities and Senior Management: Assessing the Role of Recognition in Pharmaceutical Firm Response to Biotechnology, Industrial and Corporate Change', *Innovation: Management, Policy & Practice*, 12/2 (2003), 203–23.

15. There is a large literature concerned with the development of a culture to support innovation and entrepreneurship. Two recent examples: J. Birkinshaw and C. Gibson, 'Building an Ambidextrous Organization', *Sloan Management Review*, 30/2 (2004), 93–113; C. A. Bartlett and S. Ghoshal, 'Rebuilding Behavioral Context: Turn Process Reengineering into People Rejuvenation', *Sloan Management Review*, 37/2 (1995), 23–37.

16. The whole question of organizational culture and the extent to which its development can be shaped is a key question in organization theory. For more discussion of this see e.g. E. Schein, *Organizational Culture and Leadership* (San Francisco: Jossey-Bass, 1992).

17. For more detail on the 3M approach and its evolution, see E. Gundling, *The 3M Way to Innovation* (New York: Kodansha International, 2000).

18. Further details on Intel's approach to strategy-making can be found in R. Burgelman, *Strategy is Destiny: How Strategy-Making Shapes a Company's Future* (New York: Simon and Schuster, 2001).

19. See G. Hamel, *Leading the Revolution*; also T. Malone, *The Future of Work* (Boston: Harvard Business School Press, 2004).

20. The decentralization of seed money for innovation is discussed in J. Birkinshaw and N. Hood, 'Unleash Innovation in Foreign Subsidiaries', *Harvard Business Review*, 79/3 (2001), 131–8; see also G. Hamel, 'Bringing Silicon Valley Inside', *Harvard Business Review*, 77/5 (1999), 70–85.

21. For more details on this example, see Birkinshaw and Hood, 'Unleash Innovation'.

22. There is a wealth of literature on both the separation of innovative activities, and on the management of corporate venture units per se. For the separation of innovation, see: J. Galbraith, 'Designing the Innovating Organization', *Organizational Dynamics*, 10/3 (1982), 5–25; C. O'Reilly and M. L. Tushman, 'The Ambidextrous Organization', *Harvard Business Review*, 82/4 (2004), 74–86. For corporate venturing, see: Buckland et al., *Inventuring*; H., Chesbrough, 'Making sense of corporate venture capital', *Harvard Business Review*, 80/3 (2002), 90–100; A. Campbell, J. Birkinshaw, A. Morrison, and R. Batenburg, 'The Future of Corporate Venturing', *MIT Sloan Management Review*, 45/1 (2003), 30–42.

23. See B. Uzzi, 'Social Structure and Competition in Inter-firm Networks: The Paradox of Embeddedness', *Administrative Science Quarterly*, 42 (1997), 35–67.

6

Measuring Performance in Innovative Firms

In Chapter 5 we explored some of the challenges of managing innovation, and particularly discontinuous innovation. This chapter investigates the issue of how these challenges can be addressed in a world that appears obsessed with measurement and control.

There is, at least in appearance, a tension here. The core premise of this book is that greater innovation is key to the future competitive success of UK firms. Innovation involves doing things differently—changing products, processes, position, and/or paradigm. Innovation is about exploration. It relies on experimentation, change, and serendipity. Many innovations only see the light of day because of rule-bending or even mistakes, 3M's Post-it notes being the classic example.

By contrast, measurement systems have developed as a form of control, designed to impose structure and order.[1] Measurement systems allow managers to track whether activities and processes are working as planned. They are designed to drive out inefficiency and minimize deviation. Measurement is about exploitation. In that sense, it can be seen as the enemy of innovation. As firms impose tighter measures, and measure more things, they drive out variation and reduce the scope for exploration.

On the one hand, an organization that constantly adopts new technologies and processes can never settle down into a patterned routine, jeopardizing efficiency. On the other, an organization so grooved and measured that it never adopts new processes and technologies will die. What is therefore needed is a balance between exploration and exploitation—an attribute known in the strategic management literature as 'organizational ambidexterity'.[2] Yet while it is relatively easy to see how measurement systems can support exploitation through their control function, it is much less immediately obvious how they can further the more ambiguous and fuzzy processes of exploration.

We argue that one answer is to broaden our conception of performance measurement. Managers should think of measurement as a learning rather than a control system. Collected and analysed suitably, measurement data can provide managers with sharp insight into what is and what is not working around them. This insight can be used to stimulate learning, leading in turn to a search for new and better ways of working. In short, using measurement as a learning tool can help the reflective manager to square the circle, supporting rather than hindering innovation at the same time as yielding a more supple, less constricting form of control.

The Rise of Performance Measurement

In both public and private sectors, performance measurement has become pervasive. In the five years to 2000, around half of all companies attempted to transform their performance measurement systems,[3] while 85 per cent of organizations had performance measurement initiatives under way in 2004.[4] What goes for organizations also goes for individuals. By 1998, workers were subject to formal performance appraisals in 79 per cent of British workplaces.[5] For many, the individual performance management process is a key indicator of the way organizations establish employees' obligations, and hence of how life in organizations is experienced. A graphic illustration of the spread of these ideas comes from a study of a Norwegian hospital, where even the pastor had performance measures that included not only calls made in and out of work hours, but also the number of last rites he performed.[6] Why is this? Why has performance measurement, at both the individual and the organizational level, become so all-embracing? What are the forces—internal and external—that are driving the spread of performance measurement? And even more important for our purposes, how does the tendency to measure everything that walks and moves impact the performance of firms in the area of innovation?

Today's performance obsession is the result of a combination of factors, broadly categorized here as external and internal drivers.

External Drivers

The Rise of the Market for Corporate Control   To an increasing degree, today's firms are judged on their ability to meet externally imposed objectives. Some of these objectives are specified by investors, regulators, and legislators. For investors, the goals are generally financial, with great emphasis placed on the firm's ability to generate cash both now and in the future.[7] The penalty for firms that fail to deliver is being taken over, a fate which befell a sharply increasing number of companies throughout the 1990s.

Regulatory and/or legislative objectives are broader in nature, being designed to influence the way companies behave. For the UK water industry, for example, the regulator has defined a suite of performance indicators (effectively a minimum service standard for consumers) embracing assessed service, interrupted supply, leakage, and resource position, that water companies are expected to deliver on pain of sanctions—in the shape of forced price cuts—if they do not.[8]

There are also significant implications for performance measurement in recent legislation, notably the Company Law Review that requires all UK listed companies to supplement their annual report with an Operating and Financial Review (OFR) from April 2006. Under the OFR, directors have to set out a forward-looking analysis of their business, including an array of key performance indicators to help investors assess the quality of the organization's strategies over time. This legislation effectively obliges more than 1,200 listed companies in the UK to alter their reporting and external disclosure practices, unless they have already done so pre-emptively.[9]

The Changing Nature of Work   It is not just the demands of shareholders, regulators, and legislators that have moved measurement up the management agenda. Broader societal and organizational trends have also had an impact. Of particular significance is the shift towards the 'knowledge economy'. As Peter Drucker wrote in 1999:

> The most important, and indeed the truly unique, contribution of management in the 20th century was the 50-fold increase in the productivity of the manual worker in manufacturing. The most important contribution management needs to make in the 21st century is to increase the productivity of knowledge work and of the knowledge worker. The most valuable assets of the 20th-century company are its production equipment. The most valuable asset of a 21st-century institution, whether business or nonbusiness, will be its knowledge workers and their productivity ... [But] work on the productivity of the knowledge worker has barely begun. In terms of actual work on knowledge worker productivity we are, in the year 2000, roughly where we were in the year 1900, a century ago, in terms of productivity of the manual worker.[10]

Implicit in Drucker's observation is the question of how knowledge workers can be managed. Consider, for example, the highly skilled and specialized research scientists who work in GlaxoSmithKline's pharmaceutical labs. They operate in an inherently unstructured and uncertain environment in which no one can be sure who is working on the next blockbuster drug, or if indeed any of them is. It may be that the next best-selling drug originates outside the organization. As each development project comes to an end, researchers move to a new one which may or may not bear a close resemblance to the previous project, but in any event is unlikely to follow the same development path. How in these circumstance can controls be established and performance be measured? How can progress be tracked and communicated? Paradoxically, even the planned end result—a compound delivered on time and within budget— is irrelevant if the drug becomes a blockbuster, as then profits will outweigh normal concerns about budget and time overruns.

The Changing Basis of Value   A further contributor to the obsession with performance management is the changing basis of value. The investment community needs to be able to value firms to assess whether its investments are paying dividends appropriate to the risk it is exposed to. But how can firms be valued when most of their assets are intangible? This is becoming an ever more important issue.[11]

A study called 'Measures that Matter' by Ernst & Young found that US investors increasingly take non-financial measures into account in their valuations. E&Y has calculated that on average 35 per cent of an investment decision is driven by non-financial criteria, the most important being strategy execution, management credibility, quality of strategy, innovation, ability to attract talent, market share, management experience, quality of executive compensation, quality of major processes, and research leadership. When E&Y replicated this study in the UK three years later, it generated an almost identical list of the ten most important non-financial measures, albeit in a slightly different order of priority.[12]

Internal Drivers

Evolving Organizational Forms   A number of internal organizational factors have also helped to push measurement up management's priority list. Many of today's accounting measures were devised around 1900, when industrial structures were fundamentally different. In economic terms, there was much more focus on manufacturing, direct labour generally constituted the highest proportion of product costs, and the past was a reasonable guide to the future.[13] By the mid-1980s, none of these things was true, and influential voices began to question whether traditional measurement systems had outlived their usefulness. For example, in the early part of the twentieth century, it made sense to allocate overhead on the basis of direct-labour costs. By the 1980s, when the latter had shrunk to 1–10 per cent of total product costs, continuing to allocate overhead on this basis was giving rise to significant errors in product costings.[14]

In addition, managers were starting to realize that narrowly defined accounting definitions of performance were driving some highly undesirable behaviours. In an article provocatively entitled 'Managing our Way to Economic Decline', Steven Wheelwright argued that one of the reasons for the apparently terminal decline of US manufacturing industry was the obsession of senior managers with short-term performance gains at the expense of long-term investments in superior customer service and competitiveness.[15] Why, he wondered, would managers sanction investment in long-term, high-risk product-development projects when they could sweat the assets for a couple of years, deliver superior short-term performance, and move on to another job before the long-term consequences of underinvestment emerged for all to see.

Novel Methods of Work   Another reason for the growing practitioner interest in measurement is the larger process of organizational improvement and renewal. What programmes such as Total Quality Management, Lean Production, World Class Manufacturing, the Deming Plan–Do–Check–Act cycle, and more recently Six Sigma have in common is that they rely on performance data. This is hardly surprising: before any organization can determine what it needs to improve, it has to establish where and why its current performance falls short. Hence the need for performance measures.

The widespread business interest in benchmarking has been another important driver. The rapid emergence of benchmarking clubs and a number of high-profile research studies have also heightened industrial interest.[16] In essence, benchmarking studies—especially those which compare performance rather than practice—are effectively structured applications of business-performance measurement. Such studies are valuable precisely to the extent that they provide rich performance insights.

Technological Developments   The final driver of performance measurement is IT, which has enabled the capture and analysis of vast quantities of data both within firms and across entire supply chains. Throughout the late 1990s, companies were replacing their existing information systems with so-called 'enterprise-wide solutions', most of which contained performance-measurement modules offering an integrated view of performance across the firm. Firms that did not adopt enterprise-wide systems could always buy stand-alone executive information systems as an alternative—in 2004 there were sixty vendors selling IT reporting systems for the balanced scorecard, for example.[17]

A major selling feature of these systems is their capability to drill down into performance details. Emblematic is the sales pitch of one major software vendor featuring a mythical chief executive of a shoe retailer who discovers that his chain is losing orders because of stock shortfalls. In the demonstration, he delves down through layers of data, identifies the culprits, and demands that they sort out the problem before the end of the day. Although this kind of management by remote control was discredited years ago, software vendors today are still trying—and appear still able—to sell it to senior managers desperate to retain an impression of control over their disparate empires.[18] This is a stark example of how measurement systems backed by sophisticated information technologies can be grossly misused. Sadly, potential abuses of power are not the only challenge that measurement systems offer.

The Enduring Challenges of Performance Measurement

Measurement has figured as a challenge in the academic and practitioner literatures for at least 100 years. Initially, debates centred primarily on financial measures and practical questions such as how to develop accurate product costs or allocate capital investment. As we shall see, these issues remain pertinent today, particularly in the context of innovation. The particularity of innovation is that it is impossible to know in advance which initiatives will come to fruition and generate significant returns, and which will fail. But all the costs of R&D still have to be borne. To whom or to which budgets should the costs of failed innovations be booked, and who will be held accountable? Over-rigid frameworks of allocation and accountability can simply stifle innovation, encouraging managers to avoid risk, and instead favour safe bets with more predictable returns.

Practical Challenges of Measurement

By the mid-1950s, as organizations grew in size, scale, and complexity, attention in the academic literature shifted to non-financial as well as financial measures. Writing in the first issue of *Administrative Science Quarterly*, Ridgway bemoaned the 'strong tendency to state numerically as many as possible of the variables with which management must deal'. Ridgway rehearsed debates that still rage today. Harvard's Michael Jensen and Robert Kaplan, for example, have a long-running disagreement over the relative merits of single versus multiple objectives. Ridgway pre-empted this debate by pointing out that single measures of performance could easily result in optimizing the wrong variable. Multiple measures present problems of prioritization and focus, while composite measures, which are inherently difficult to understand and interpret, can simply result in confusion, employee stress, and conflict.[19]

Now roll forward to today's economic environment. As we have seen, organizations are increasingly subject to multiple and sometimes conflicting measures of performance. Investors wish to understand current and predicted cashflows. Managers want to track efficiency and effectiveness. Regulatory and legislative concern about corporate accountability has grown rapidly in the wake of corporate-governance scandals and high-profile company collapses. At a more detailed level, in the much more technical literature on organizational performance measurement, authors debate practical issues such as choosing the right measures, accessing appropriate data, and setting meaningful targets. Throughout the 1980s and 1990s, the research community paid significant attention to the technical issues of designing and deploying performance-measurement systems.[20] The challenge was to identify processes that could be used to select from among the myriad possible measures available. These processes not only had to be coherent, they also needed to recognize the plurality of organizations and provide scope for the engagement of individuals in what was inevitably a political process.[21]

Once companies had chosen *what* to measure, the next challenge was to decide *how*. A manager might decide that she wanted to measure the effectiveness of the new-product development (NPD) process—but what does effectiveness in NPD mean in practice? Is it completion on time and within budget? What about a product that is completed on time and within budget but subsequently misses its sales targets? Or the converse, already mentioned: the product that runs over time and budget but becomes a blockbuster. Has the NPD process still been effective?

The Problems of Multiple Measures

Answering questions such as these is fundamental. If there is no clarity about definitions, organizations end up measuring the same thing in different ways. It is not unusual to find managers heatedly arguing over some performance dimension only to discover later that the root cause of disagreement was the imprecise definition of a measure. Often this fuzziness results in paralysis. This is what happened at Sanford Berol, a leading European manufacturers of pens and markers, where a review uncovered two different reports on current work-in-progress. Both documents had the same date, but in one the WIP figure was 25 per cent higher than in the other. When asked why, the management team was perplexed—the immediate response was, 'We never noticed that before'. To find out the cause of the discrepancy, Sanford Berol had to return to the original computer code and look up the basis of the inventory calculation. It emerged that the value in both reports was correct—the organization had more than one way of defining work-in-progress.

The Data Overload Problem

A consequence of failing to be precise about measurement is that managers end up drowning in data. Modern information systems capture vast amounts of data in the blink of an eye. For example, by linking purchase data captured by electronic point of sale (EPOS) systems, retail managers can analyse the shopping habits of individuals and households. A sudden purchase of nappies suggests that a new baby has arrived or is about to arrive, and hence gives clues on potential future purchases. The opportunities for analysis are endless—and therein lies the problem. Most managers receive too many performance reports containing too much data. Indeed, the author recently witnessed the production manager of a small manufacturing business toss a freshly delivered 200-page performance report into the wastepaper basket without a glance. He explained: 'All it contains is last week's absenteeism figures. I need up-to-date information to manage production, not spurious figures from the accounting department.' He recounted that the company had had a problem with absenteeism in the past, which was why the measures had been introduced. But that had long ago been dealt with. He concluded, 'I don't need weekly figures any more. I only need that report on a by-exception basis. On a weekly basis it is useless to me.'

Work grounded in the accounting, operations-management, and organizational-behaviour schools of thought further expose the potentially dysfunctional nature of performance management.[22] These literatures suggest that performance measures can:

- lack strategic focus and fail to provide data on quality, responsiveness, and flexibility;[23]
- encourage local optimization, for example 'manufacturing' inventory to keep people and machines busy;[24]
- encourage managers to minimize variances from standard rather than seek to improve continually;[25]
- fail to provide information on what customers want and how competitors are performing.[26]

Another reproach is that the measures are historically focused. Sales turnover simply reports what happened last week, last month, or last year, whereas most managers want predictive measures that indicate what will happen next week, next month, or next year.[27] As this literature consistently demonstrates, each of these seemingly simple activities results in nested and knotty challenges of performance measurement that are political as well as practical.

Political Challenges: The Perverse Incentives Problem

The well-known adage, 'You get what you inspect, not what you expect', lies at the heart of the problem of perverse incentives, especially when performance measures are linked to recognition and reward systems.[28] In many organizations, the measures used to judge success define the rules of the game that people play. Responding to the measures, in the worst case people act to make the measures look good even at the expense of the wider interests of the firm. Take a widely used measure of innovation—annual spend on R&D. It is easy to make this measure look good—just spend more: pay R&D staff higher wages; spend more on projects, even if they are known to be blind alleys. In itself, none of these benefits the firm, but any of them makes the figures look better. This is a simple example, but perverse incentives are extremely common.

Measuring Profit, Destroying Value

WF Electrical, a leading UK electrical components wholesaler, grew at 30 per cent a year throughout the 1990s. By 2000 it had a network of more than 140 branches across the UK. The board strategy emphasized national coverage and consistent service. The intention was that customers should be able to walk into any branch and receive the same high-quality service. The measure of success was branch profitability: each branch was a profit centre, and the branch manager's bonus depended on the profits it generated.

The behavioural consequences were fascinating to behold. Branch managers regularly competed for orders. Aware that the manager who booked the sale earned the profit generated on the order, customers would phone three different branches and provoke a bidding war. As well as undercutting each other on price, branch managers pursued even more extreme tactics to retain orders. Electricians are mobile entrepreneurs, often working the length and breadth of the country. A Newcastle electrician, for example, might have a job to do in central London. However, he would still order components from his local branch, typically phoning to request delivery to site the next day. In turn the Newcastle manager would order the components by overnight express delivery from the central distribution warehouse, which happened to be in north London, and promptly load them in a van for transport back to central London.

Clearly the 600-mile round trip not only adds no value, it actively destroys it. Yet it was common practice at WF, because people's bonuses depended on it. The measurement and incentive schemes encouraged perverse behaviour. This is a simple but by no means extreme example. Even in organizations that think themselves to be rational and sophisticated, the rules of the game often provoke significantly counterproductive behaviour.

Focusing on Measurement in Innovative Firms

We have seen why measurement has become so pervasive and discussed the political and practical challenges traditionally associated with it. It is now time to step back from the broad debate and turn to the context of innovation. As noted elsewhere, innovative organizations can be expected to display a high degree of creativity, an open and inclusive culture, and a desire for exploration as well as exploitation.[29] Larger organizations are increasingly moving to a paradigm of open innovation, seeking to acquire knowledge and ideas from many different sources across the globe.[30] They are also adopting loosely-coupled control structures, with distributed leadership.[31] How does measurement sit within such an environment?

We need to start by considering how the measurement drivers we have already identified apply to innovative organizations. For both internal and external reasons, the move to more innovative organizational forms is likely to increase rather than reduce the demand for measurement. As organizations rely more and more on innovation to compete, they move to a world that requires more knowledge work, and where intangible assets are increasingly important. To assess future rates of innovative output, investors will demand more information about the firm's investment in intangible assets. Clearly, this issue poses a major research challenge, since by definition intangible assets are hard to identify, let alone measure and value. Addressing this question is a major concern for the investment and accounting communities globally.

Similar arguments apply to the internal factors. As organizations move to open innovation models, with increasing reliance on networks and geographically dispersed teams, the requirement for new forms of coordination and measurement will increase. Co-location makes it far easier to understand what others are doing and how they are performing. As organizations shift to dispersed and/or networked forms, the centre will seek to impose mechanisms for coordination, if not control. Whatever the level of autonomy permitted, it will require information to flow from local units and teams to those who are ultimately accountable for the investment being made in them. Thus, as organizations adopt more innovative forms, the pressures to measure are likely to grow rather than shrink. It is highly unlikely that they will abandon measurement, even if it is difficult. What, then, are the dilemmas and challenges that they will need to understand and overcome to make measurement a friend of innovation rather than a foe?

The Dilemmas of Measurement in Innovative Environments

At the heart of innovation is the need to experiment, to vary the approach, and to take advantage of emergent opportunities. Take 3M, a company that prides itself on its capacities for innovation. It was established by five businessmen who set out to mine a mineral deposit for grinding-wheel abrasives in 1902. It soon transpired that although the mineral deposits were worth little, the sand produced in the mining process could be used to make sandpaper. Today 3M encourages all employees to spend up to 15 per cent of their time working on personal and potentially innovative projects. Richard Branson launched the Virgin empire in 1968 by publishing a student magazine. He then moved on to making and selling records by mail order and retail, before diversifying into air and rail travel, mobile phones, and several other areas. Simon Woodroffe, founder of the Yo Sushi chain, explains how the idea arose from a conversation with a Japanese acquaintance, who suggested that he open a Japanese sushi conveyor-belt restaurant populated by young women wearing black PVC mini-skirts. James Dyson, the UK entrepreneur, tells how he made 5,127 prototypes of his revolutionary bagless vacuum cleaner over five years before it was ready to be launched on the market.

Each of these examples illustrates the role that uncertainty, creativity, and chance play in the innovation process, elements that formal measurement systems struggle to make sense of. Conventionally speaking, the original 3M investment was a mistake; in efficiency terms, the 15 per cent of people's time spent on personal projects is waste; the development of 5,127 prototypes is hopelessly inefficient, while the nature of the inspiration for Yo Sushi and Virgin is simply unquantifiable. As these examples show, it is hard to reduce innovation to numbers, and this gives rise to a number of dilemmas.

Process-related Dilemmas of Innovation Measurement

The first set of dilemmas relate to the nature of the measurement and innovation processes. Innovation is inherently uncontrollable. Ideas emerge through chance conversations. Failed activities give rise to new opportunities. Measurement systems have difficulty coping with such conditions. If the organization is constantly in flux, the basis of measurement has to change with it. But this means that it is impossible to compare progress over time, and hence to establish any means of control. As we have seen, control systems work best with structured, repetitive processes, where history and previous experience provide a reasonable basis on which to form views of the future. The less structured and repetitive the process, the more difficult it becomes to establish systematic controls. Hence the first dilemma—measurement systems seek to provide control, but innovative environments may be inherently uncontrollable.

A second dilemma results from the nature of the innovations themselves. Frequently these are unquantifiable and intangible. For example, how can the idea that resulted in the Dyson bagless vacuum cleaner be quantified? How can the idea that resulted in a product and/or service being developed be pinned down? Was it a single idea delivered by an individual—Woodroffe's chance conversation—or one that was built cumulatively through a process of trial and error, as in Dyson's prototypes? The intangible nature of innovation gives rise to dilemma number two—measurement systems require quantifiable and tangible constructs, yet innovations are typically unquantifiable and intangible.

The third dilemma derives from the first two—measurement systems require targets, but innovative environments make these difficult to specify. Without targets, control systems founder. It becomes impossible to ascertain whether performance is acceptable and hence whether corrective action needs to be taken. Yet how can acceptable performance be defined in an environment that is inherently uncontrollable and revolves around the unquantifiable and intangible?

The Challenge of Measuring Inspiration

Implicit in the previously discussed dilemmas is that it is important to think about the source of inspiration for an innovation. Where do ideas that lead to innovation come from? Companies are increasingly acknowledging their need for open search processes that span functional, organizational, and geographic boundaries. Within the firm, the philosophy of *kaizen* or continuous improvement, for example, recognizes that employees at all levels are liable to have excellent ideas for product or process improvement and that a key role of management is to encourage people to share them.[32] In a broader context, there is growing awareness of the need for open and global innovation, and more specifically of the importance of clusters and national systems of innovation. The point is that the source of inspiration for new ideas is rarely an individual. Instead, innovations usually arise from interactions between different groups of people. Yet, as the case of WF Electrical illustrates, ill-adapted measurement systems often constrain opportunities for such interactions by encouraging groups to compete rather than collaborate, giving rise to the fourth dilemma: measurement systems can hinder cooperation and result in suboptimization (through internal competition), yet innovative environments require knowledge-sharing and cooperation.

As we have noted, an increasing number of organizations are searching outside their traditional boundaries for new ideas, whether for products, services, or ways of working.[33] Yet most measurement systems are internally orientated. This is dilemma number five: measurement systems tend to be internally orientated and focused, whereas innovative environments require an organization to look outwards for ideas beyond its own boundaries.

Creating an Innovative Environment

The environment within which innovations occur also needs to be considered. If freedom and the ability to take controlled risks inspire creativity in organizations, as is often proposed, how does that freedom sit in relation to control? If control constrains freedom and creativity and promotes risk aversion rather than risk-taking, then what role does control play in innovative environments? Hence the sixth dilemma—measurement systems can constrain creativity and increase risk aversion, yet innovative environments require managed risk and creativity.

Behind the invocation of freedom as an aid to innovation is the need to loosen traditional efficiency controls to allow for experimentation and exploration as well as exploitation—the concept of ambidextrousness mentioned earlier. But it is often hard to reconcile the two sides of the equation. Experimentation and exploration are anathema to a control system that focuses on efficiency and optimization—the most efficient means of delivery. Hence the seventh dilemma: measurement systems are orientated towards efficiency and productivity (the best/most effective route to a solution), yet innovative environments need to embrace search, exploration, experimentation, and iteration.

Measuring Innovative Outputs

A further set of dilemmas concern the output—the results of innovation. Innovation often goes together with adaptability. Organizations that have learned to cope with innovation tend to be highly fluid, able to adapt rapidly in response to new and emerging opportunities.[34] But measurement systems can lock organizations into rigid structures and forms, as in the case of the Western manufacturers that were held back from adopting Japanese just-in-time manufacturing models by outdated accounting measurement methods.[35] This observation leads to the eighth dilemma: measurement systems can lock organizations into particular structures and processes, yet innovation requires rapid response to emerging opportunities.

Measurement gives rise to an even more extreme dilemma in the face of market innovation. Market innovation occurs when an organization introduces an innovation that fundamentally changes the market—for example, the low-cost airline model originated by Southwest and extended by easyJet and Ryanair; online bookselling (Amazon.com); Starbucks' reinvention of the coffee house. Innovation requires organizations to break or at least reframe conventional industry rules, while measurement systems require companies to remain within them. Hence the ninth dilemma: measurement systems encourage repetition and structure, yet innovative environments require idea generation. Measurement systems provide a framework for people to operate in. Innovation requires companies to devise a new framework.

The final dilemma again relates to innovation output, but this time in terms of time horizon. Measurement systems are invariably concerned with the relatively short term (this month, next month, this year). Innovations, however, can involve much longer periods, depending on the clock-speed of the industry concerned.[36] For example, developing a new drug can take ten years or more. Measurement systems that concentrate on the short term often fail to take into account the potential future value of such long-term investments, and this is the tenth dilemma—measurement systems are focused on the short term, while innovation can provide a long-term payback.

The Fundamental Dilemma: Measurement is Inevitable, yet Measurement is Flawed

The preceding analyses raise a fundamental issue. Measurement is fraught with practical and political challenges in all environments. It poses particular challenges in innovative environments, where we have identified a series of dilemmas. Yet at the same time, measurement is unavoidable. The internal and external pressures on managers to measure and report are growing and will continue to do so. So managers, particularly those systematically attempting to innovate, are faced with a situation in which measurement is inevitable, yet measurement is flawed. How then is the reflective manager to react? Given its inevitability, how can measurement be made more useful in such contexts?

Much of the preceding analysis reflects the traditional assumption, derived from the engineering-control school of thought, that a measurement system is a means of control. Managers set a target, monitor performance, observe deviation from the desired outcome, and take corrective action. Using measurement systems in this way is one of the reasons why organizations encounter the practical and political problems that they do. Measurement systems used as controls set up gaming and manipulation, as the measures become the de facto purpose. Individuals worry about how to deliver predetermined performance levels, particularly when they cannot influence the system in which they operate. The result is endless negotiations about the validity of the measures, the 'right' targets, and the quality of the data. Junior managers try to negotiate targets down, senior managers to put them up. Information and even pots of resources are hidden from the rest of the organization to serve 'for a rainy day'. Inevitably, the process becomes politicized, and those who can't do so any other way manage the system by 'cheating'—delivering the numbers at the expense of the broader interests of the organization.

In the context of innovative organizations, it is the notion of control that underlies many of the dilemmas identified previously:

- the desire to control the inherently uncontrollable (dilemma 1);
- the need to quantify the unquantifiable (dilemma 2);
- the requirement of tangible targets for intangible processes (dilemma 3);
- the need for knowledge sharing and cooperation, not competition driven by the desire to optimize locally (dilemma 4);
- the need to search for ideas outside the organization's boundaries hindered by the internal focus of control (dilemma 5);
- the need for managed risk and creativity stifled by the fear of failing to deliver (dilemma 6);
- the need for search, exploration, experimentation, and iteration, not a continual focus on efficiency and optimization (dilemma 7);
- the need to break the rules, not simply conform to them (dilemma 9).

An alternative conceptualization is to think of measurement not as a control but as a learning system. Innovative organizations require exploitation—they have to deliver current products and services efficiently and effectively—and for this they require controls. But innovative organizations also have to explore—they have to search for new products and services, and identify more efficient and effective ways of delivering them. Exploration requires learning. It requires managers to legitimize processes of experimentation and reflection. Measurement systems can facilitate these processes in several ways.

What to Measure and What Not to Measure; and Where?

As this chapter has shown, there is a natural tendency of managers to wish to control; and, in controlling, to measure. What this chapter has also demonstrated is that that may not always be for the good, especially where innovation is a prime concern. Measurement may actually get in the way of helping create a context for innovation. However, it is just not practical, or desirable, to give up on measurement. Managers do need to know what is going on. So a key question is: what do managers at different levels really need to measure, and what do they not need to measure? It is much easier to err on the side of measuring more rather than less. This is always a problem, but even more so where innovation matters.

In innovative contexts, two challenges become really crucial. First, to understand what needs measuring and what does not. Second, to manage effectively without complex and extensive measurement systems. This is not easy, and research done so far provides glimpses of solutions rather than prescriptions. But these glimpses are useful.

Top managers need to keep it simple

In her work on the management of fast-moving hi-tech industries, Kathy Eisenhardt found that in the most successful organizations the top management excelled at discerning what the critical measures needed to be, but they did not crowd the measurement arena.[37] Typically they focused on some key but essential 'simple rules'. The argument of Eisenhardt and her colleagues is not that these are the correct ones, but that managers need to focus on deciding which are the most appropriate ones given the circumstances. They then ensure that these yardsticks are absolute. After that they allow latitude to front-line managers. In effect, they are saying, you get on and manage, especially you get on and innovate, but ensure you deliver against these absolutes. At one and the same time that determines: (1) the focus of front-line managers; (2) the focus of top management on what they need to be primarily concerned about; and (3) what they need to measure. The difficulty, of course, is precisely in distinguishing between what really does and does not matter. This focuses the issue, in turn, on the strategy of the organization to achieve the sort of innovation required. It also focuses attention on what top management can expect to be able to control and what it cannot.

The Implications for Strategic Management of Innovative Organizations

We have already established that top managers are not well placed to manage the front line of innovation. That must be left to those closest to the markets or to the technologies. But if they are to become experts in devising the 'simple rules' discussed above, what is their role in managing the process of innovation? The feedback they will get will be against the key measures that they have established. Their responsibility is, then, to allocate resources at their disposal to ensure that these key objectives are met. Eisenhardt has collaborated with other researchers to try to understand how top management administers its available portfolio of resources.[38] Their conclusion is that in allocating and reallocating resources strategically amongst the portfolio of businesses, or business activities, at their disposal, top managers need to be able to discern which parts—or modules—of their organization are most likely to be able to take advantage of opportunities that arise.

If they are to focus the activities of business units on a particular market or technological area of innovation, they also need to be aware that, across their portfolio, they need to balance such resources in such a way that they can retain organizational units at an optimum size and dynamism to take advantage of the competences they have. While they should avoid becoming over-involved in the management and control of those units, they need to understand them well enough to spot where resources for new innovative opportunities can be allocated. Their job is not the day-to-day control of these units, but the strategic allocation of resources.

So here we come back full-circle to the need for simple rules. How is it likely that they can decide on which resources match which modular opportunities? It is not likely to be on the basis of detailed reporting criteria. It is much more likely to be on the basis of understanding just what matters most in ensuring the firm can take advantage of the opportunities afforded by the matching of the changes in their dynamic environment and the competencies of each business unit. The upshot of this logic is that in innovative organizations, organizing for innovation may mean establishing a modular organization where resources can be moved around rapidly to take advantage of the opportunities. And to do so, top management needs to be critically aware of the relatively few key measures that matter to gauge this.

However, measurement for innovation does not just take place at the top level. It also needs to take place at the front line of management. And here, maybe, some other lessons need to be learned.

Reconceptualizing Measurement as a Learning System

Any measurement process has two separate phases—designing the system, and operating it. The design phase offers an opportunity to debate and identify what matters most to people in the organization. Recognizing the plurality of organizations, and encouraging those who do the work to help decide what should be measured, and how, is an important means of developing shared understanding of organizational priorities. That it constitutes a valuable learning process in itself is well recognized; many practitioners comment that the process of devising a measurement system is at least as valuable as the system that results.[39]

A fundamental aspect of design is identifying measures that encourage appropriate behaviour—effectively reversing the problem of perverse incentives. In all but the exceptional firms managers tend to revert to the easy to measure—as Ansoff put it, 'Corporate managers start off trying to manage what they want, and finish up wanting what they can measure.' A classic measure for innovation is the percentage of revenue deriving from new products. At first sight this seems a sensible indicator of innovativeness, at least in terms of product innovation. New product revenues appear easy to measure. However, this is where the doubts set in. In practice, firms often struggle to define a new product. Should variants of existing products be classified as new? Should old products in new packaging count? Are old products sold in new markets innovations? For how long should products be classified as new? The problem does not end there, for 'simple' counts such as new product revenues ignore other important dimensions of innovation performance such as process and organizational innovation.

An alternative is to measure factor inputs. This is the basis of the DTI's R&D scoreboard,[40] which measures percentage of revenue invested in research and development. As we have seen, however, as a measure this has the disadvantage of ignoring qualitative aspects. It simply assumes that more is better.

This is not to say that measuring new-product revenues or R&D spending as a percentage of revenue is necessarily wrong. The essential point is that measures are context-specific, and in devising them managers need to bear in mind both the context and the nature of the signals they wish to send to the organization. If their perception is that people are not bringing forward enough risky projects, they may want to measure the percentage of projects that fail, thus legitimizing project failure, at least to some extent. Conversely, if the aim is to stimulate more collaboration with suppliers, a measure of the proportion of projects co-developed with suppliers might be more appropriate. Suitably chosen and designed performance measures can encourage and legitimize desired behaviours, just as bad measures generate unwanted ones. If the right people are involved in selecting and designing the measures, the shared learning can be significant.

Managing through Measurement

For many managers, someone else will handle the design phase of the measurement process. Once decisions have been made and measures put in place, however, managers will receive reports on a host of different performance dimensions—profitability, budgets, revenues, costs, customer and employee satisfaction, operational efficiency, health and safety, environmental performance, quality levels, supplier service, market share, lead times—for both NPD and manufacturing. Potentially, the list is endless. The problem is that many of these reports contain data that do not readily facilitate learning. How can they be converted into insight that does?

By Thinking in Terms of Performance Planning, not Performance Review   In most organizations, measurement forms the basis of performance reviews, which are historic or backward-looking and—either implicitly or explicitly—designed to put people on the defensive. Often, performance reviews involve people justifying why performance is as it is rather than how it can be improved. This is even embedded in the language: a 'review' explores the reasons why something is as it is.

It is more productive to think in terms of planning sessions to explore how performance might be improved. Take the example of a health and safety manager at an oil major who had prepared an update on health and safety for the board. Having been allotted a thirty-minute slot on the agenda, he had put together twenty slides showing there were no outstanding problems. Taking an exception-reporting stance, he could have delivered his steady-as-she-goes message in three minutes rather than thirty and freed up valuable time. Why didn't he? The manager replied that he couldn't make a statement like that without providing the background data. His superiors would demand the information anyway, so he might as well present it at the start.

Why should this be the case? Why do organizations appoint people to positions of responsibility and then expect them to provide data to justify statements that clearly fall within their area of competence? Of course, data are important to form views and opinions about issues, but as Power notes in his work on the 'audit society',[41] there is a related issue of trust. In this case senior executives were apparently unwilling to trust the manager without seeing the underlying data. The compulsion to use data to micro-manage from on high is strong in many organizations, often with extremely damaging consequences. If the approach emanates from the board, there is a real danger that it will colour the working of the entire organization.

By Asking for Answers, not Data   Why do people get sucked into performance reviews rather than performance-planning sessions? Very often, because that is how the meetings are structured. Rather than information, most performance reports consist of large amounts of raw data that executives are expected to analyse during meetings. Today's sophisticated information infrastructures only compound the problem. While it is easy, and tempting, to develop new performance reports drawing on the copious data amassed in a data warehouse, they are often as short on analysis as they are long on numbers.

By Building the Capability of Performance Analysts   Many companies are appointing performance analysts, increasingly not just to manipulate performance data but also to interpret and present the numbers in a way that engages and provides insight to others. A useful analogy in this context is journalism. When presenting a story, the journalist carefully identifies the 'hook' or headline that will capture the reader's attention and then flushes out the detail in the small print. So with performance reports: being clear about the headline—the main message behind the story—makes them much more valuable to readers. To continue the analogy, as in journalism, the individual analyst will need to work within clear 'editorial guidelines' set by the board.

By Thinking in Terms of Systems   Recent literature on measurement frameworks such as the balanced scorecard and the performance prism highlights the importance of thinking in terms of systems.[42] Systems thinking in management is not new, but these frameworks put

Solving the Performance Puzzle: Numerical Crosswords

Data overload, said David Coles, former managing director of DHL UK, is like 'numerical crosswords'. He described how his board spent a significant part of its meetings trying to solve the clues by linking up data contained in separate performance reports. Directors would search for meaning in the data and then suggest relationships between, say, new service introductions and subsequent sales volumes.

Uncomfortably aware that these were too often personal opinions rather than systematic analysis, however, the board decided that a more productive way of running its meetings was to focus on reviewing answers to questions central to the welfare of the business instead of raw performance data. Directors drew up a list of a dozen questions that they agreed they needed answers to by the end of each meeting—are we going to meet our financial targets, how are our customers feeling, how are our people feeling, are we building sufficient capacity today to ensure we can operate tomorrow? Once the questions were formulated, performance analysts were tasked with recasting DHL's performance data as answers to the questions rather than raw data. The board's role then became one of critiquing the quality of the analysis and debating its implications for the business. This approach enabled directors to move away from using measures as controls and instead stimulate shared learning between them about the challenges and issues facing the business.

fresh emphasis on the links between the measures of performance that companies use in different functions and departments. Clearly, functions rely on each another. Marketing relies on operations, operations on human resources, HR on finance, and so on. Yet when it comes to measurement, these interdependencies are often ignored. Each function concentrates on its own data. But this functionalization of measurement is a mistake. Everyone intuitively understands that a downturn in employee satisfaction is likely to affect customer service, or that an operational blip will damage financial results. Making the most of measurement data requires recognizing these interactions. Rather than operating in functional silos, managers need to use measurement data to understand the big picture. Thinking in terms of systems is an essential guide to understanding this complexity.

Conclusion

Innovation is essential to the long-term competitive success of both firms and the UK as a whole.

Yet it also poses important challenges. Insofar as the processes of innovation differ largely from the processes of optimizing present efficiencies, managing innovation through traditional measurement approaches is problematic if not counterproductive. As Chapter 5 illustrates, innovation is difficult to control, and many of its determinants are unquantifiable. Yet measurement systems are expressly designed to control and quantify. Innovation requires search and cooperation. Yet poorly designed measurement systems often result in dysfunctional behaviour that promotes competition and destroys cooperation. Innovation requires experimentation and the legitimization of failure to encourage learning. Yet measurement seeks to reduce variation, maximize efficiency, and (in essence) to punish failure.

On the other hand, abandoning measurement is not an option. The necessity to measure is not going to go away. If anything, internal and external pressures on organizations to measure and report are growing, not least in the light of recent regulation and legislation. The challenge for managers therefore is to find a way of squaring the circle. At the heart of this chapter is the suggestion that we need to reconceptualize measurement as a learning rather than a control system. Four simple principles—think in terms of performance planning, not reviews; ask for answers, not for data; build the capability of performance analysts; and think in terms of systems—go a long way towards resolving the innovation dilemmas. Measurement data used and analysed in this way can provide valuable insights into what is and what is not working, thereby provoking the search for new and better ways of operating. Appropriately designed and deployed measurement systems can thus facilitate and support innovation rather than stifle it.

Notes

1. Various authors have used the terminology associated with control theory to describe the functioning of a performance measurement system. Amongst the most notable are: R. Anthony, *Planning and Control Systems: A Framework for Analysis* (Boston Harvard University Press, 1965); J. Dixon, A. Nanni, and T. Vollmann, *The New Performance Challenge* (Burr Ridge, IL: Business One Irwin, 1990). Others have argued that cybernetic control is too narrow as a concept

and suggested that one has to recognize pluralism in organizations. Measures are defined and targets set only through processes of negotiation involving multiple parties, often with different levels of power and authority. Hence even the simplistic notion of cybernetic control is problematic—see e.g. C. Emmanuel and D. Otley, *Readings in Accounting for Management Control* (London: Chapman and Hall, 1995).

2. The notion of the ambidextrous organization has been introduced into the strategy literature. Underpinning this is the idea that organizations have to be able to exploit and explore simultaneously. The question, from an organizational design perspective, is whether this simultaneous exploitation and exploration is feasible and, if so, what organizational forms best support it. If you accept the notion that a performance measurement system is a control system, then it can clearly be argued that performance measurement can facilitate exploitation, but may hinder exploration. For a more detailed description see C. A. O'Reilly and M. L. Tushman, 'The Ambidextrous Organization', *Harvard Business Review*, 4 (2004), 74–81; J. Birkinshaw and C. Gibson, 'Building Ambidexterity into Organizations', *Sloan Management Review*, 45/4 (2004), 47–55.

3. Mark Frigo and colleagues have been running a series of surveys on the uptake of new measurement methodologies such as the balanced scorecard. See e.g. M. L. Frigo and K. R. Krumwiede, 'Balanced Scorecards: A Rising Trend in Strategic Performance Measurement', *Journal of Strategic Performance Measurement* 3/1 (1999), 42–8.

4. B. Marr, A. Neely, M. Franco, M. Wilcox, C. Adams, and S. Manson, 'Business Performance Measurements: What is the State of the Art?' *Conference Proceedings from Performance Measurement Association* (Edinburgh, 2004); D. Rigby, 'Management Tools and Techniques: A Survey', *California Management Review* 43/2 (2001), 139–60; S. Silk, 'Automating the Balanced Scorecard', *Management Accounting*, 79/11 (1998), 38–44; G. Speckbacher, J. Bischof, and T. Pfeiffer, 'A Descriptive Analysis on the Implementation of Balanced Scorecards in German-speaking Countries', *Management Accounting Research*, 14 (2003), 361–87; M. S. Williams, 'Are Intellectual Capital Performance and Disclosure Practices Related?' *Journal of Intellectual Capital*, 2/3 (2001), 192–203.

5. M. Cully et al., *Britain at Work* (See Ch. 4, n. 21).

6. S. Modell, 'Performance measurement and Institutional processes', *Management Accounting Research*, 12 (2001), 437–64. Modell, 2001—ref. Chapter 4.

7. This point has been argued by many commentators—see e.g. A. Rappaport, *Creating Shareholder Value* (New York: Free Press, 1986).

8. Neely argues that this form of measurement is effectively one that requires compliance in his book *Measuring Business Performance* (London: Economist Books, 1998).

9. Recent publications on the Operating and Financial Review have been released by the Department of Trade and Industry (www.dti.gov.uk) and the Accounting Standards Board (www.frc.org.uk/asb). The latter published its Exposure Draft on the OFR for public comment on 30 November 2004.

10. P. F. Drucker, *Management Challenges for the 21st Century* (Washington, DC: Harper Business, 1999), 135.

11. B. Lev, *Intangibles Management, Measurement and Reporting* (Washington, DC: Brookings Institution, 2001).

12. These two studies were carried out by members of Ernst and Young's Centre for Business Innovation in collaboration with academics from INSEAD and Wharton. Further details on the studies can be found in P. Bierbusse and T. Siesfeld, 'Measures that Matter', *Journal of Strategic Performance Measurement*, 1/2 (1996), 6–11; and Anon., *Measures that Matter: An Outside-in Perspective on Shareholder Recognition* (Ernst and Young, UK Study, 1999).

13. It is widely recognized that measures such as return on capital employed were developed specifically in response to the growth of multi-divisional firms and strategic business units. Alfred Chandler, for example, traces the development of the accounting measure return on capital employed to three DuPont cousins and their efforts to manage multiple business units at the start of the 20th century. See A. Chandler, *The Visible Hand: Managerial Revolution in American Business* (Boston: Harvard University Press, 1977); H. T. Johnson and R. S. Kaplan, *Relevance Lost: The Rise and Fall of Management Accounting* (Boston: Harvard Business School Press, 1988).

14. Harvard Professor Robert Kaplan wrote a series of provocative papers in the early to mid-1980s setting out new challenges for the accounting community. See e.g. R. S. Kaplan, 'Measuring Manufacturing Performance: A New Challenge for Managerial Accounting Research', *Accounting Review*, 58/4 (1983), 686–705; R. S. Kaplan, 'Yesterday's Accounting Undermines Production', *Harvard Business Review*, 62 (1984), 95–101. Interestingly Kaplan acknowledges that many of the problems he points out are not new. In his paper 'Yesterday's Accounting Undermines Production', for example, he quotes A. Hamilton Church, who wrote in 1908: 'Shop charges (overhead) frequently amount to 100 percent, 125 percent, and even much more of the direct wages. It is therefore actually more important that they should be correct than that the actual wage costs should be correct.'

15. Various authors have commented on the potential dysfunctional consequences of measurement and their link to short-termist behaviour. See e.g. R. L. Banks and S. C. Wheelwright, 'Operations versus Strategy: Trading Tomorrow for Today', *Harvard Business Review* (May–June 1979), 112–20; W. Skinner, 'The Anachronistic Factory', *Harvard Business Review* (January–February 1971), 61–70.

16. See e.g. studies such as Andersen Consulting, *The Lean Enterprise Benchmarking Project* (London, February 1993); Andersen Consulting, *World-wide Manufacturing Competitiveness Study: The Second Lean Enterprise Report* (London, 1994); IBM Consulting and London Business School, *Made in Britain: The True State of Britain's Manufacturing Industry* (London, 1993); IBM Consulting and London Business School, *Made in Europe: A Four Nations Best Practice Study* (London, 1994); J. P. Womack, D. T. Jones, and D. Roos, *The Machine that Changed the World* (New York: Rawson Associates, 1990).

17. For a comprehensive review of these software applications see B. Marr and A. D. Neely, *Balanced Scorecard Software Report* (Stamford, CT: Gartner, 2003).

18. The phrase 'management by remote control' was coined by H. Thomas Johnson in his book *Relevance Regained: From Top–Down Control to Bottom–Up Empowerment*. Johnson uses Plato's analogy of shadows dancing on the walls of caves to illustrate graphically the point that many measurement systems simply provide shadows of organizational reality. See H. T. Johnson, *Relevance Regained: From Top–Down Control to Bottom–Up Empowerment* (New York: Free Press, 1992).

19. V. F. Ridgway, 'Dysfunctional Consequences of Performance Measurements', *Administrative Science Quarterly*, 1/2 (1956), 240–7.

20. Important contributions to the debate on how to design and deploy performance measurement systems have been made by numerous authors. Amongst the best-known contributors are Dixon, Nanni, and Vollmann, *The New Performance Challenge* (n. 1); R. S. Kaplan and D. P. Norton, *The Balanced Scorecard: Translating Strategy into Action* (Boston: Harvard Business School Press, 1996); A. D. Neely, J. F. Mills, K. W. Platts, A. H. Richards, M. J. Gregory, M. C. S. Bourne, and M. P. Kennerley, 'Performance Measurement Systems Design: Developing and Testing a Process Based Approach', *International Journal of Operations and Production Management*, 20/10 (2000), 1119–46.

21. Critics of some of the early work on processes, most notably Nørreklit, argue that many authors did not recognize the importance of plurality in their work and hence specified top-down dictatorial processes that could never work in practice. For a fuller discussion and critique of the balanced scorecard approach, see H. Nørreklit, 'The Balance on the Balanced Scorecard: A Critical Analysis of Some of Its Assumptions', *Management Accounting Research*, 11 (2000), 65–88.

22. See e.g. Anthony, *Planning and Control Systems* (n. 1); C. Argyris, 'The Dilemma of Implementing Controls; The Case of Managerial Accounting', *Accounting, Organizations and Society*, 15/6 (1990), 503–11; A. G. Hopwood, *Accounting and Human Behaviour* (Englewood Cliffs: Prentice Hall, 1974); S. Kerr, 'The Folly of Hoping for A While Rewarding B', *Academy of Management Executive*, 9/1 (1995), 7–14; K. A. Merchant, *Control in Business Organizations* (Marshfield, MA: Pitman, 1985); and Ridgway, 'Dysfunctional Consequences of Performance Measurements', (n. 19).

23. W. Skinner, 'The Decline, Fall and Renewal of Manufacturing', *Industrial Engineering* (October 1974), 32–8.

24. E. M. Goldratt and J. Cox, *The Goal: Beating the Competition* (Hounslow: Creative Output, 1986); R. W. Hall, *Zero Inventories* (Homewood, IL: Dow-Jones Irwin, 1983).

25. R. W. Schmenner, 'Escaping the Black Holes of Cost Accounting', *Business Horizons* (January–February 1988), 66–72; P. B. B. Turney and B. Anderson, 'Accounting for Continuous Improvement', *Sloan Management Review*, 30/2 (1989), 37–48.

26. R. C. Camp, *Benchmarking: The Search for Industry Best Practices that Lead to Superior Performance* (Milwaukee: ASQS Quality Press, 1989); R. S. Kaplan and

D. P. Norton, 'The Balanced Scorecard: Measures that Drive Performance', *Harvard Business Review* (January–February 1992), 71–9.

27. Dixon, Nanni, and Vollmann, *The New Performance Challenge* (n. 1); A. D. Neely, 'The Performance Measurement Revolution: Why Now and What Next?', *International Journal of Operations and Production Management*, 19/2 (1999), 205–28.

28. The impact of measurement systems on behaviour are widely discussed in several streams of literature. Important contributions include Steven Kerr's paper entitled 'The Folly of Rewarding A While Hoping for B', originally published in the *Academy of Management Review* in 1975 (n. 22) and updated recently to appear in the *Academy of Management Executive*. Agency theorists and their critics make important contributions to this debate—e.g. K. Eisenhardt, 'Agency Theory: An Assessment and Review', *Academy of Management Review*, 14/1 (1989), 57–74; M. C. Jensen and W. H. Meckling, 'Theory of the Firm: Managerial Behaviour, Agency Cost and Ownership Structure', *Journal of Financial Economics*, 3 (1976), 305–60.

29. The notion that innovative organizations have to be able simultaneously to explore and exploit has given rise to the concepts of the ambidextrous organization. For a fuller discussion of this concept and the related literature, see C. A. O'Reilly and M. L. Tushman, 'The Ambidextrous Organization', *Harvard Business Review* (April 2004), 74–81; and J. Birkinshaw and C. Gibson, 'Building Ambidexterity into Organizations', *Sloan Management Review* (Summer 2004), 47–55.

30. The trend towards open and networked innovation is discussed extensively in the works of several authors—see e.g. H. Chesbrough, *Open Innovation* (Boston: Harvard Business School Press, 2003) and J. Santos, Y. Dos, and P. Williamson, 'Is your Innovation Process Global?', *Sloan Management Review* (Summer 2004), 31–7.

31. For a discussion of this literature see N. Munshi, A. Oke, P. Puranam, M. Stafylarakis, K. Möslein, and A. D. Neely, 'Leadership for Innovation', summary of AIM/CMI Management Research Forum, 2005.

32. *Kaizen* or continuous improvement has been linked to the quality and lean movements in the Operations Management literature—see e.g. the work of M. Imai, *Gemba Kaizen: A Commonsense Low Cost Approach to Management* (London: McGraw-Hill, 1997) and J. P. Womack, D. T. Jones, and D. Roos, *The Machine that Changed the World: The Story of Lean Production* (New York: Harper Business, 1991). Similar points, however, could be made for the literatures on Six Sigma and Knowledge Management—see e.g. P. Pande and L. Holpp, *What Is Six Sigma* (London: McGraw-Hill, 2001).

33. Clayton Christensen highlighted the importance of this externally orientated search process in his classic book *The Innovator's Dilemma* (Boston: Harvard Business School Press, 2003).

34. See e.g. K. Eisenhardt and D. Sull, 'Strategy as Simple Rules', *Harvard Business Review* (January 2001), 107–16.

35. An excellent illustration of this point is provided by Turney and Andersen's widely cited article that argued that the accounting systems used in their case

study firm significantly hindered its progress in adopting new working methods—see P. B. B. Turney and B. Anderson, 'Accounting for Continuous Improvement', *Sloan Management Review*, 30/2 (1989), 37–48.

36. The concept of industry clock-speeds was explored in Charles Fine's book *Clockspeed: Winning Industry Control in an Age of Temporary Advantage* (Boston: Perseus, 1999).

37. Eisenhardt and Sull, 'Strategy as Simple rules' (n. 34).

38. C. E. Helfat and K. M. Eisenhardt, 'Inter-Temporal Economies of Scope, Organizational Modularity, and the Dynamics of Diversification', *Strategic Management Journal*, 25/13 (2004), 1217–33.

39. Tony Singarayar, formerly director of process redesign at McNeil Consumer Products, part of Johnson and Johnson Inc., emphasized the importance of the process when he said: 'There are few today that know how to do this [build a balanced measurement system]. And fewer still that do it well. I'm not sure which is more proprietary in a scorecard—the data it contains, or the management process that went into creating it' (B. McWilliams, 'The Measure of Success', *Across the Board* (1996), 16–20). For a fuller review of the academic aspects of this debate see R. S. Kaplan and D. P. Norton, *The Strategy Focused Organization: How Balanced Scorecard Companies Thrive in the New Business Environment* (Boston: Harvard Business School Press, 2000); A. D. Neely, *Measuring Business Performance* (London: Economist Books, 1998); Nørreklit, 'The Balance on the Balanced Scorecard' (n. 21), 65–88.

40. For details on the R&D Scoreboard see www.dti.gov.uk

41. There is significant evidence that recent years have seen a shift towards the 'Audit Society'. Increasing numbers of organizations—in both the public and the private sectors—are deciding or being forced to implement ever more comprehensive and formal performance measurement systems. Some of these measures are used for internal purposes, but there also appears to be increasing demands for external disclosure. For a fuller discussion of these trends, see M. Power, *The Audit Society: Rituals of Verification* (Oxford: Oxford University Press, 1997).

42. For an overview of these frameworks and methodologies see Neely, *Measuring Business Performance* (n. 39). For detailed descriptions, see: R. S. Kaplan and R. Cooper, *Cost and Effect: Using Integrated Cost Systems to Drive Profitability and Performance* (Boston: Harvard Business School Press, 1998); Kaplan and Norton, *The Balanced Scorecard: Translating Strategy into Action* (n. 20); M. Meyer, *Rethinking Performance Measurement: Beyond the Balanced Scorecard* (Cambridge: Cambridge University Press, 2002); A. D. Neely, C. Adams, and M. Kennerley, *The Performance Prism: The Scorecard for Measuring and Managing Stakeholder Relationships* (London: FT/Prentice Hall, 2003); A. Rappaport, *Creating Shareholder Value* (New York: Free Press, 1986).

PART III

The Reflective Practitioner

7

Adopting Promising Practices

IN Chapter 4 we discussed the potential importance of high-performance work systems and questioned why organizations so often fail to exploit such apparently successful practices. In this chapter, we argue that identifying and choosing practices to adopt is deceptively unstraightforward. For managers to be successful, they must be both reflective about the issues of applying management practices in general, and mindful of the key elements of the particular practice. They must also understand the specific local organizational context and how it affects processes of adoption and implementation.

Many of the insights about 'best practice' may at first sight appear obvious. However, we have found that in reality there are many pitfalls in the path of managers seeking to import advanced new practices into their business—witness the high proportion of change initiatives that are ultimately judged disappointing. Potential pitfalls in the successful integration of promising practices include:

- adopting practices simply because everyone else is doing so (the danger of following fads);
- adopting only the easy elements of practices rather than the difficult and crucial core (the danger of 'picking only the low-hanging fruit');
- the tendency constantly to introduce new practices without successfully following through on implementation (the danger of becoming a 'flavour-of-the-month' organization).

Furthermore, many initially successful initiatives run out of steam as people slide back into old habits before change has been fully integrated into the routines and systems of the organization and become part of the taken-for-granted norms.

Still, while there are numerous challenges and dilemmas in adopting new practices, there are also dangers in failing to recognize the need for change. In an earlier chapter, we noted that although the UK possesses some excellent firms and managers, there are too many poor performers, while national levels of productivity and innovation lag those of comparable national economies. One potential cause of this underperformance is complacency. Senior managers' perception of their organizational capability is often strikingly at odds with what a visitor sees on a tour of the shop floor. It is not uncommon to be told that an organization is approaching best in class, and then to find standard good practices missing or incompletely deployed, and the resulting performance well off the competitive pace. The problem may be particularly acute in the UK. Compared with their actual competitive performance, UK managers are far more likely to overestimate their capabilities than counterparts in the US or Germany.[1] Moreover, managers seeking to make a difference to the performance of their organization cannot allow the difficulties of practice adoption to stifle needed improvement.

Our purpose in this chapter is to articulate a series of questions that the thoughtful manager needs to reflect on when confronted with the need or opportunity for change. Among the fundamental challenges surfaced are:

- initial identification of promising practices for attention;
- evaluation of potentially significant practices for their core characteristics;
- the need proactively to review organizational requirements and confront complacency;
- difficulties in assessing the prospects for putting the practice into operation;
- the fundamental issue of sustaining and embedding new practices so that they become part of the organization's day-to-day routines.

In most organizations, new ideas are constantly bubbling to the surface. Confronted with all the possibilities, managers can all too easily feel either paranoid about the need to jump on the latest bandwagon or inadequate for having missed it. Managers are faced with ideas with important-sounding abbreviations or acronyms (MBO, CRM, BPR, IJVs, TQM, 6σ, JIT, MRP, MRPII, ERP, HPW, CSR, and 360° to name a few from recent years) or in the shape of specially constructed '-ing' words (downsizing, offshoring, outsourcing, benchmarking, decentralizing, partnering, and organizational learning)—labels that say little about the real content of the practice or its effectiveness in the context of their business.

Research on the how management practices are adopted suggests that new ideas tend to go through a period of enthusiasm and glorification before falling from grace and being relegated to the status of 'management fad', to be replaced by the next 'big thing'. 'Fads' become common currency for a while, but then lose their potency as perceived 'best' practice and fall out of fashion.[2] The impression given is that the idea is based on weak underlying logic and so has little lasting value.

However, the fact that a practice label ceases to be used does not necessarily mean that the ideas were, or are, worthless.[3] When practices that work effectively become embedded in organizations, they become part of the day-to-day routines and the style and culture of management. The branding or labelling of the practice becomes less important, to the point where it often disappears. A case in point is Business Process Re-engineering (BPR), which was taken up by many organizations in the 1990s. Today, few companies are explicitly re-engineering their processes. Over time, organizations have drawn on the initial ideas of BPR, adapted them, learned what parts of it are relevant to their day-to-day business, and incorporated them into 'the way we work around here'. While some of these practices have brought longer-term value, others have failed to live up to their initial promise. So how does a manager go about distinguishing between the two?

We believe that while the rationale behind some practices is weak, others do have the potential to make a positive difference. Studies have found a broadly positive relationship between the use of some practices and operating and business performance.[4] Practices that have led to major benefits when properly implemented include high-performance work practices, scenario planning, collaborative practices, lean manufacture, service recovery, and six sigma, to name a few.

We argue that by identifying and developing promising practices, and once developed and adopted, by embedding, sustaining, and renewing them, companies can gain significant advantage. One of the best (and best-known) examples has been the transformation of Toyota through lean production. After the Second World War, Toyota set out to transform itself through a journey that is still continuing. It built on practices developed elsewhere. For example, managers studied American production methods, in particular Ford's mass-production systems, and the statistical quality control practices of Ishikawa, W. Edwards Deming, and Joseph Juran. The attention to operations was complemented by equal care for how work was organized and managed. Over a period of twenty years, managers developed and continually refined a complex web of new practices, tools, and techniques that became known as the Toyota Production System (TPS). Toyota's interlocking management practices have provided a significant advantage to the company in areas such as product quality, production efficiencies, and bringing new models to market.

The principles of TPS have been generalized under the label 'lean production'. Companies all over the world, initially in manufacturing and more recently in services, have adopted lean-production practices. However, this does not mean that Toyota has lost its substantial advantage over competitors—far from it. First, the company continues to hone its practices through continuous improvement. Secondly, it has aggressively deployed TPS, not just in its own plants worldwide, but across its entire supply chain.[5]

Toyota illustrates powerfully not only how one company can gain leadership by developing new practice, but also how it can sustain its position by deploying and embedding them across the extended organization, and by continuous development.

That's the good news. The less good news is that there are no short cuts or off-the-shelf formulas for practice adoption—after all, Toyota has been developing lean production for forty years. The essence of introducing and managing new practices, therefore, is a highly reflective and mindful approach. In the next section, we examine what this means.

Reflective and Mindful Management

The complexity of identifying and developing promising practices is well illustrated by the area of collaboration, one that is highly relevant to UK competitive performance. Collaborative relationships (alliances, partnerships, joint ventures, and networks) have become increasingly common over the last decade and a half as managers seek new ways of accessing resources or expertise, promoting learning, or gaining strategic advantage over rivals: high-profile examples include airline alliances such as Oneworld and the Star Alliance. Governments and institutions such as the European Union have also seen the advantage of collaboration, sometimes promoting partnerships by making membership a condition of funding schemes and contracts, or sponsoring regional and industry-specific networks: the Scotland-wide Creative Entrepreneurs Club for very small businesses in the creative industries, and the North West (England) Automotive Alliance are two examples. However, by no means all collaborative relationships live up to expectations. According to follow-up studies, it is often the context of the companies that prevents collaboration from paying off. Contextual issues include differences between partners in terms of goals, cultures, decision-making structures, and power, as well as logistical complications and internal changes among partners.[6]

Not surprisingly, both managers and policy-makers have been eager to establish the nature of good practice in alliance and network management, with a view to developing practical guidance on 'how to do it'. A typical government approach has been to support research to identify and document successful partnerships. There are also many 'how to' guides published by government agencies and consultants. However, studies show that while best-practice descriptions are useful in generating ideas, managers are frustrated by their lack of direct applicability to the complexity of their own situation. This complexity leads to difficulties in understanding what really makes for good management practice. What success means can differ between partners—a good outcome for one may be disappointing for another. Pinpointing the reasons for success and establishing whether they can be replicated are also problematic. The conclusion is that the passive sharing of stories and use of simple practice guides are unlikely to lead to significant steps forward in developing practices for collaboration.

The challenges organizations face in the complex process of identifying, assessing, choosing, and implementing promising practices can lead to ambiguity, uncertainty, and apparent internal contradiction.[7] To make matters worse, managers have to address these ambiguities in an organizational context in which strategic shifts can happen imperceptibly, and limited resource, bias, collective culture, and pressures to conform inevitably militate against reaching fully rational decisions.

Making progress in these circumstances brings into play two themes that form a central thread of this book. The first is what it means to be an exceptional manager, that is, one that makes a difference; the second is being mindful in considering new ideas rather than just following the crowd. 'Making a difference' in this context means actively managing and making judgements based on thoughtful, reflective practice. In turn, reflective management is a three-pronged exercise in understanding and reflecting on the general issues involved in applying management practices; considering management practices in their specific local context; and taking action based on considered managerial judgement.

Reflecting on the general issues and considering the local context are essentially ways of *rehearsing* what happens when a practice is put into operation.[8] It is possible to rehearse at various levels of depth depending on the situation, ranging from very detailed formal analyses in cases where heavy investment is needed at one extreme, to cultivating a general awareness of issues at the other. As we shall see in Chapter 9, managers need to approach the decision-making process with a combination of intuition and insight, judgement, and rationality, and there are various techniques to support this end.

The idea of 'mindfulness' throws light on what reflective management might achieve.[9] Mindfulness is a state of awareness characterized by openness to new information and an appreciation of multiple perspectives. Mindfulness requires resistance to oversimplification, resilience (bouncing back from failure), and open-minded enquiry about new practices, including the proactive search for alternative views. Mindful managers are able to make a distinction between the practices themselves and the situation in which they are applied. A healthy scepticism about simplistic solutions and conclusions is essential, since, as we shall see, even the most clearly defined technical practice cannot normally be considered in isolation. On the other hand, the ability to simplify temporarily is also necessary in order to make particular issues manageable.

In the remainder of the chapter we highlight a set of issues that managers need to consider as they evaluate emerging ideas and practices.

Key Issues in Adopting Practices

Understanding Practices as Bundles

Even the simplest practice rarely stands in isolation from others. Usually, there is strong complementarity between several practices that combine in a practice 'bundle'. For example, as we saw in Chapter 4, the high-performance work (HPW) model includes a bundle of human-resource management (HRM) practices that are in turn composed of a number of individual activities. In operations management, lean production can be seen as four broad bundles—just-in-time (JIT), total quality management (TQM), total productive maintenance (TPM), and HRM—each of which itself comprises many practices and tools. Bundles tend to be made up not only of hard, measurable practices, but also of the less measurable values and philosophy that underpin them. Practices within and between such bundles often support each other, so the benefits of each are realized only when all, or a significant set of them, are in place.

The challenge here is to go further than simply 'picking the low-hanging fruit'—the easiest elements to adopt. Picking and choosing among parts of the set may well do more harm than good, incurring costs without benefits. For example, to be successful many new-technology practices require parallel changes in human-resource and work practices. JIT demands changes in work organization and practice alongside concurrent implementation of operations and logistical techniques. Thus, smoothed production requires process quality management and small batch sizes; and the latter in turn requires progressive reduction in set-up times.

A growing body of experience suggests that certain 'foundation practices' must be in place before other parts of a bundle can take effect. Typically, these are associated with quality and people management: hence the emphasis in Chapter 4 on the crucial importance of an organization's employment-relations context. For example, in adopting the complex bundle of practices that make up lean production, the willingness of employees to embrace change and the quality and stability of processes are essential foundations. Without them, changes in both physical and organizational practice may fail, and companies may have to abandon their programmes or start them all over again from the beginning. A key challenge for managers is thus to understand how practices work together so that they can put in place the full set in the right sequence.

In broad areas of management such as innovation, organizational learning, or strategic transformation, however, managers may sometimes need to take the opposite approach. Where initiatives cover a multitude of different and often hidden activities, incorporating tools and techniques such as innovation programmes, company-based courses, or scenario planning, it is important to understand how to *unpack* the bundle. One way to do this is to think of an area of management concern as a combination of overlapping sub-practices or themes;[10] each of these may be complex and challenging in its own right, but is more manageable both conceptually and practically than the whole. So, to return to the earlier example of building collaboration, managers might break up the process into the overlapping sub-practices of choosing a partner, forming goals, building trust, and so on. Of course, being a means to a larger end, none of these can be operationalized in isolation, but in implementation planning it may prove helpful temporarily to consider them separately.[11]

It is important to understand the systemic implications of the bundles, and to explore from both the bottom up (building up the bundle) and the top down (unpacking the bundle). There are complex interactions among even seemingly well-defined technical practices, and breaking down broad areas of managerial practice into simpler and more manageable chunks can help here. Where practices are interconnected and interdependent, managers should beware the pitfalls of partial or selective implementation of the bundle, and in particular of neglecting the parallel changes needed in organization and work practices. In particular, many bundles are built on foundation practices that are a prerequisite for the successful adoption of the rest of the set.

Identifying Practices

In the field of medicine, identifying promising new practices is a well-defined exercise. For many conditions, a clinical need gives rise to research in an industry or university setting, which eventually yields a product or technique that can be developed, tested, and if successful widely adopted. Alternatively, when a piece of fundamental research is recognized as holding potential for practical development, the process starts from the other end. In the field of management, practices frequently result from processes of emergence and gradual recognition, which are generally much harder to see. Often discoveries are serendipitous rather than deliberate. Practice frequently precedes theory, rather than the other way around, so organizations seeking innovative practices need to search in a variety of different places.

New practices often develop inside organizations. However, their emergent property sometimes means that even managers already using them fail to recognize them for what they are until they are obliged formally to articulate the process for external consumption. This was the case for executives at Robert Wiseman's Dairies and Scottish & Newcastle Breweries when their companies were shortlisted for a corporate citizenship award. Senior managers from both companies interviewed during the assessment process remarked that they had only become fully aware of what practices and how much of their company's activity could be viewed as corporate citizenship as a result of preparing for the interview.

Most companies will have good and promising practices within their organization. Recognizing them provides the opportunity for developing them further, and to formalize and make effective ones more explicit. In the above example, senior managers became aware opportunistically of their good practice in corporate citizenship. Even better is active scanning for internal good practice with the potential for development and wider deployment. Isolating promising practices within the firm is a first step to evaluating, developing, codifying, and finally deploying them across the organization.

Promising new practices may also emerge directly from consultancies or academia. Many new approaches to operations management have derived from innovative attempts by companies to solve particular problems, sometimes relying on third parties such as academics or consultants to 'codify' and disseminate them. For example, the first major codification of lean production was an academic study of a Japanese motorcycle factory in the US.[12] As with lean production, once practices are articulated and codified, they can be experimented with and developed further. As they become established, knowledge about them is often readily available from a variety of sources, ranging from consultants to industry associations.

Looking to the future, an interesting example of an emerging practice may be 'social capital'. In Chapter 10 we describe the way in which Nokia created strong relationship ties across its internal boundaries in order to foster the flow of knowledge around the company. These ties are a form of social capital. As yet the concept has not been widely understood or adopted by managers, but it is increasingly attracting research attention. If it can be adequately formulated and generalized for operational use, social capital management may come to be an important practice for the future.

Identifying new and promising practices is a key challenge. It requires active internal and external search for good practices, readiness to spot opportunities in a company's operational issues, wide but critical reading, and competitive intelligence.

Recognizing Promise

Knowing whether a practice has promise means being able to identify what aspects of practices make the difference, understanding what it has achieved in different settings in the past and what an organization wants it to achieve in a new setting.

Understanding the causality between managerial action and practical outcomes, as discussed in Chapter 1, is central to singling out the practices and the aspects of practices that have made—or have potential to make—a difference. In some areas of management practice, models of cause and effect are well established and accepted. For example, in service

Figure 7.1.   The service–profit chain

management the 'service profit chain' (see Figure 7.1) is often used as a
model. Although simple, in many organizations this model has served as a
basis for exploring and evaluating the practices and their impact on outcomes.[13] In particular, some organizations have used the model as a basis
for collecting data to enable them to assess the practices they have put in
place and their deployment across the organization.

However, even with established models and tangible practices, what causes
successful outcomes is not always obvious.[14] For instance, are successful outcomes from high-performance work practices the result of the practice itself,
or the particular circumstances of its implementation (see Chapter 4)? Research has still not been able to clarify whether it is HPW practices that cause
good performance or the other way round—high-performing companies have
the resources and willingness to implement advanced HR practices.

An interesting example concerns ISO 9000 quality certification and its
relationship to total quality management. Research shows that adopting
ISO 9000 seems to be associated with improved quality outcomes. However, it is usually implemented alongside TQM. When this is so, the
quality improvements seem to be almost entirely linked to TQM, with
ISO 9000 having little extra impact.[15] The distinctive benefits of ISO 9000
may be more to do with the market benefits of certification than quality.
What the ISO 9000 and TQM experience tells us is that it is important to
identify the real impact of individual practices.

As we have seen in an earlier chapter, however, measuring performance
is itself often problematic. In most areas of practice, success is a deceptively slippery concept. For example, success can be measured in terms of
the substantive outcomes as in Figure 7.1, whether the practice is adopted
and whether it works, or a combination of both. While performance
measures are fairly well established for some of the more mature practices,
there is little agreement about evaluation methodologies for many others.
Judgements about success may also be subject to qualifications. It is important to look for unintended negative outcomes as well as the expected
positive ones. In addition, outcomes may differ from stakeholder to stakeholder. Thus, collaboration practices may have different impacts for different parties; many have intended and unintended outcomes for the

Kwik-Fit Financial Services

In 2003 Kwik-Fit Financial Services offshored part of its call-centre operations to a company in India. Although cost savings were part of the rationale, Kwik-Fit's main aim was to 'dip a toe in the water' of the offshoring market, following many of its competitors. A successful pilot would also allow it to pursue other business goals, such as removing the need for unsociable shifts. After a three-month pilot, managers found that offshoring had indeed cut costs, but much less than expected. Nevertheless, they judged the initiative worth pursuing because it had delivered other benefits—for example, releasing space at its Glasgow premises that could be put to good alternative use. A year later, however, Kwik-Fit cancelled the deal, managers deciding that demonstrable success on a number of dimensions was more than outweighed by the sheer managerial energy needed to keep it going.

workforce and organization. Different yardsticks for evaluation may be required. The Kwik-Fit example (see box) highlights how a dilemma can arise when the benefits, while positive, turn out to be different from those expected.

As this case illustrates, apparently successful practices can have unexpected negative consequences, objectives can change with circumstances, and short-term success does not automatically continue into the long term. In such cases, it is important to ask whether 'success' is aligned with the company's objectives and contributes to overall competitiveness.

As with offshoring, for many practices 'promise' is hard to evaluate in any clear-cut fashion; to understand the potentially complex benefits of practices, managers need to 'triangulate' data from a variety of sources. As we have seen, success depends crucially on perspective. Another caveat is that people often report what they sense others want to hear—or what they want them to hear—quietly suppressing the bad news or overemphasizing short-term gains. In addition, it is important to determine whether short-term success is a reliable indicator of long-term promise, and to be sensitive to unintended outcomes. Having a model of the intended cause and effect (or underlying logic) of practices can help in evaluation. Finally, managers must establish whether operational success is worth the effort— that is, it is aligned with the organization's overall business aims.

Fit, Adaptation, and a Firm Foundation

Having decided to introduce a new practice, managers need to consider the related issues of organizational fit and adaptation. One influential view is that, particularly for well-established practices, this requires a two-stage approach. The first stage is to choose the appropriate best fit or configuration of the practice for the particular context. For example, it has been found that the best fit or configuration of an enterprise resource planning (ERP) system will depend on a number of factors, including the complexity of the business and the stability or otherwise of its environment.[16] Another example is TQM, where some people practices have been found to fit well across a wide set of manufacturing contexts, while others such as zero defects or in-process feedback are more appropriate to contexts of high product variety and customization, and relatively low product volumes.[17] In addition, small firms will find some aspects of large-company practice quite inappropriate. For new and emergent practices, finding 'best fit' may be difficult, for, as we have noted, it is not always easy to isolate the aspects of practice—or the combinations of practices—that make the difference.

The second stage is adapting practices to the company circumstances. Here there is a strong contrast between new and mature practices. Not surprisingly, when a new practice is emerging, organizations may adjust them extensively as they go along. In this case, adaptation is as much a process of learning about, and improving, the practice as of fitting it to its environment. How far a practice can be adjusted while still remaining the same practice, and how far it can be adapted before the characteristics that made it look promising in the first place are lost, is often a matter of fine judgement.

With mature practices, it is tempting to start by adapting the practices to the organization's context. However, there are number of dangers here. The first is overconfidence—trying to run before you can walk. In addition, adapting too quickly can mean that core elements of the practices are changed or dropped, endangering overall success. The final danger, as noted above, is picking only the low-hanging fruit, ignoring more difficult elements that are vital to success. This is what happened to early UK adopters of just-in-time (JIT) processes, who learned the hard way that because of the systemic nature of the activities, applying them partially yielded insignificant or even negative results.[18] Thus, it may be better to begin by adopting the practices in full and only adapt them later in the light of experience.

In implementing as in evaluating complex bundles of practices, it is often necessary to identify 'foundation practices'. At any one time, a company only has the resource to address so many new practices. The expression 'death by a thousand initiatives' well describes what happens when organizations dissipate their energies trying to do too many things at once. There is a trade-off between the need to implement a complete bundle of practices and the inability to get to grips with all of them at the same time. Managers therefore need to consider the sequence in which to put them into practice. Foundation practices are those that need to be in place before others are tackled. These are often associated with gaining process stability and workforce involvement. Identifying these is a critical part of the process adoption and adaptation.

Addressing fit—what elements of the bundles of practices should we use in this context—and adaptation—how much should we adapt individual practices to match the organization—is vital. On the one hand, one size does not always fit all. Since each organization is unique, practices may have to be adapted to fit the organization's context. On the other hand, too much or impulsive adaptation may put the core of the practice at risk. Moreover, adaptation needs to be handled differently between new and emergent practices and mature well-defined ones.

Harnessing Wisdom

A theme of this book is that there are few short cuts to successful management. Sensitivity to context, learning, and imagination are central to the exercise of critical judgement that is its essence. Nowhere is this truer than in adopting and adapting promising new practices. Some knowledge is both difficult and expensive to transfer.[19] In other areas the choice is huge.

Take for example lean production, a bundle of practices, tools, and behaviours that is increasingly well defined, with readily available and effective supporting material. Yet companies still find it difficult to adopt and implement. Part of the reason is lack of knowledge of what is best fit and the tacit knowledge needed for implementation. Companies use a wide range of knowledge-transfer mechanisms to get over this hurdle.

One important source of knowledge is visits to exemplar organizations, often in Japan. Visits provide validation and a valuable source of ideas. They do not, however, equip managers with enough knowledge for implementation. Diagnostic benchmarking has played a role both in highlighting weaknesses that might be addressed by lean production and in pinpointing the core practices.

Another widespread source of knowledge is industry groups, in which companies share knowledge and experience of practice in operation. The UK government has promoted industry forums to spread manufacturing good practice across a range of industries. In some cases, companies at the top of the supply chain introduce suppliers to the techniques and coach them in their application. Continuous improvement (an important element of lean practice) can then operate across company boundaries—sometimes to great effect, as the Toyota example shows. As we shall see in Chapter 8, networks uniting practitioners across one or several organizations have been successfully used to build on experience and develop the body of knowledge of a practice.[20] In an influential early documentation of the operation of communities of practice, managers found that repair technicians working on complex IT equipment had better results when they had the opportunity to meet and informally discuss issues than when they operated individually, with recourse only to the official repair manual. When managers tried to ban the meetings around the water cooler in the name of efficiency, the results fell off, since the technicians were unable to tap into the collective experience of dealing with complex problems that were not codified in the manuals. More formal communities of learning can be a way of systematizing knowledge and improvements that often remain tacit. They work best, as in the above case, where the focus is fairly tight and, crucially, where the incentives to share knowledge are strong.

The complexity and degree of tacit knowledge required to introduce new practices has led organizations to make use of experts in a number of ways. One is as a direct source of support and help, as with consultants or experts from within similar industries. For example, the Society of Motor Manufacturers and Traders invited Japanese 'guest engineers' to the UK to support the transfer of knowledge within the industry. Another is using them to challenge the company and act as stimulators for further adoption and implementation. The process is iterative, practices being constantly refined and new ones added. For example, total productive maintenance has increasingly become associated with lean production in recent years. With necessary adaptations, lean practices are being progressively extended to service organizations.

However, while knowledge about best practice can be transferred in a number of ways, success is not a foregone conclusion. According to a recent study,[21] learning can be derailed by, for example, uncooperative sources (guardians of an existing practice refusing to help others), strained personal relationships between experts and managers, competition between source and receiver, overemphasis on innovation ('not invented here'), and inadequate copiers, where the managers charged with implementing a best practice are temperamentally unsuited to absorbing new knowledge, afraid to change, or excessively focused on preserving their own status.

An organization can't necessarily control all these factors, but being aware of them and finding ways to respond may make the difference between being able to access the buried wisdom or not. Moreover, these barriers affect not only transfers of knowledge between organizations, but also within them—an area where management can have a direct influence.

The challenge is to recognize that paper understanding and even technical knowledge are rarely enough on their own to equip managers for effective adoption and adaptation of new practices. There is no avoiding the need to draw on the wisdom and knowledge of others. Learning is a key element of adoption of promising practices. Being able to demonstrate that they work is vital for winning buy-in; the knowledge of how the practice can be made to work in context is a vital part of learning, and being challenged drives good implementation.

Making it Happen—from Promising Practice to 'the Way we Work'

The crucial significance of practices is how they impact the way the organization actually works. When looking to make things happen, it is important to address the issues of deployment, embeddedness, and sustainability.

Deployment

Companies often pilot new practices in one part of the organization before rolling out more widely. However, too often they fail to complete the process. Yet deployment is an essential step on the way to long-term success. Once new practices have been identified, piloted, and suitably adapted, a step that is often missed is codification. Codifying practices makes it easier make sure they are adopted throughout the organization. It also facilitates the equally important step of embedding.

Embedding

To be effective, a practice needs to mutate from something externally imposed to an ingrained part of routines and culture. Otherwise it risks being diluted or rejected. Codification and incorporation in everyday routines and processes is one part of embedding; more difficult is integrating into it the values and culture of the organization. Embeddedness is the combined result of involvement, communication, training, commitment, and leading by example. As practices are embedded, they become part of the 'way we work'. Indeed, as noted earlier, good practices often seem to disappear in name as they are absorbed into the fabric of the organization—paradoxically, disappearance is thus a sign of embeddedness rather than the opposite. Embedding is a function of leadership. The signature practices at RBS described in an earlier chapter are a good example of practices that have been fully embedded in the organization.

Sustaining

A practice once in place is not static but dynamic. As new people join the firm and priorities change, managers need to subject practices to renewal, reinforcement, and review. Some practices evolve and are refined and developed. Others, for example quality circles, have a life-cycle, so managers need to spot when a practice has served its useful life and how it may or may not be modified or replaced. It is important, too, not to lose sight of the practices' original purpose. A cautionary tale is the US aerospace industry's botched adoption of strategic sourcing. A central plank of strategic sourcing is the opportunity to benefit from close working relationships and trust. But during implementation, managers at the top of the supply chain forgot the longer-term objectives and reverted to the previous focus on short-term cost reduction. The result was that much of the benefit from strategic sourcing never materialized. Worse, disgruntled smaller suppliers started bypassing the large manufacturers and selling spare parts direct to airline end users, disrupting the supply chain and depriving the aerospace giants of their lucrative aftermarket.[22]

Conclusion

Adopting and refining good business practice is a key management responsibility. But, as we have seen, it is less straightforward than it might first appear. Interrelating issues of complementarity, fit, context, causality, implementation, and indeed what constitutes success all help to explain why even well-established practices often yield disappointing results on the ground. Success in harnessing all these elements puts a premium on reflective, mindful management. Reflective management is not a passive activity. On the contrary, it is purposeful: as indicated earlier, *taking action* is a critical—indeed the most critical—aspect of it. Mindfulness is particularly important in the processes of identifying and evaluating new practices, in resisting the temptation to follow the herd, and in challenging complacency.

Notes

1. Complacency was measured in both the Made in Europe (C. Voss, P. Hanson, K. Blackmon, and B. Oak, *Made in Europe: A Four Nations Study* (London Business School/IBM, 1994)), and the Service in Britain studies (C. A. Voss, K. Blackmon, R. B. Chase, E. Rose, and A. V. Roth, *Competitiveness of UK Service: An Anglo-US Benchmark Comparison of Service Practice and Performance* (London Business School, 1996)). In both studies UK organizations were found to be more complacent than manufacturing companies in Germany and service companies in the USA.

2. Abrahamson has written extensively on the development of management fads, most notably in E. Abrahamson, 'Managerial Fads and Fashions: The Diffusion and Rejection of Innovations', *Academy of Management Review*, 16 (1991), 586–612. Fads and fashions extend beyond practices, but in this chapter we confine ourselves to managerial practices.

3. We would thus regard as problematic research such as that by Miller and colleagues which distinguishes 'fad' from 'classic' on the basis of longevity of the usage of the label (particularly if, as in their case, this is measured in terms of appearances of the label in published articles): D. Miller, J. Hartwick, and I. L. Breton-Miller, 'How to Detect a Management Fad—and Distinguish it from a Classic', *Business Horizons*, 47/4 (2004), 7–16.

4. Two extensive studies of management practices in manufacturing (Made in Britain) and service (Service in Britain) found strong correlations between use of established 'good' managerial practices and operational and business performance. See C. A. Voss, K. Blackmon, P. Hanson, and B. Oak, 'The competitiveness of European Manufacturing: A Four Country Study', *Business Strategy Review*, 6/1 (1995), 1–25; and A. Meyer, A. V. Roth, R. Chase, C. A. Voss, K. U. Sperl, L. Menor, and K. Blackmon, 'Service Competitiveness: An International Benchmarking Comparison of Service Practice and Performance in Germany, UK and USA', *International Journal of Service Industry Management*, 10/4 (1999), 369–79.

5. The evolution of Toyota Production System is well described in J. P. Womack, D. T. Jones, and D. Roos, *The Machine that Changed the World* (New York: Harper Perennial, 1990).

6. A full account of issues in managing collaborations and the theory of collaborative advantage can be found in C. Huxham and S. Vangen, *Managing to Collaborate: The Theory and Practice of Collaborative Advantage* (London: Routledge, 2005).

7. The notion of 'tensions' between alternative, sometimes diametrically opposed notions of good practice has been elaborated in C. Huxham and N. Beech, 'Contrary Prescriptions: Recognizing Good Practice Tensions in Management', *Organization Studies*, 24/1 (2003), 69–94.

8. This idea of 'rehearsing' is similar to that which underlies the use of Scenario Planning to consider the implications of alternative conceivable futures: P. Schwarz, *The Art of the Long View* (Chichester: Wiley, 1997). Antonacopoulou introduced the term in the context of rehearsal of general management situations: E. P. Antonacopoulou, 'The Virtues of Practising Scholarship: A Tribute to Chris Argyris a "Timeless Learner" '. Special Issue 'From Chris Argyris and Beyond in Organizational Learning Research', *Management Learning*, 35/4 (2004), 381–95.

9. The concept of mindfulness was developed by Langer (J. E. Langer, *The Power of Mindful Learning* (Reading, MA: Addison Wesley, 1997)) and is further developed by Fiol and O'Connor (M. Fiol and E. J. O'Connor, 'Waking Up! Mindfulness in the Face of Bandwagons', *Academy of Management Review*, 28/1 (2003), 54–70).

10. The idea of building theory around themes that managers see as significant is the basis of the theory of collaborative advantage. An overview of themes relating to alliance management can be found in C. Huxham and S. Vangen, 'Doing Things Collaboratively: Realizing the Advantage or Succumbing to Inertia?' *Organizational Dynamics*, 33/2 (2004), 190–201.

11. The principle of considering parts of practice in isolation of the whole is discussed in C. Huxham and N. Beech, 'How to—Turn Theory into Practice', *People Management,* 12 February 2004, 46–7. The argument is made in more depth in Huxham and Beech, 'Contrary Prescriptions' (n. 7).

12. Richard Schonberger studied the practices at a Japanese motorcycle factory in Nebraska. He codified the practices that he observed and published them in an influential book—*Japanese Manufacturing Techniques: Nine Hidden Lessons in Simplicity.* (New York: Free Press, 1982).

13. The service profit chain was proposed by J. L. Heskett, T. O. Jones, G. W. Loveman, W. E. Sasser Jr. and L. A. Schlesinger, 'Putting the Service–Profit Chain to Work', *Harvard Business Review*, 72 (1994), 164–74. It is widely used by UK and US companies as an underlying model for service management.

14. Students of early HRM practices will-remember the classic studies of the Hawthorne plant in the USA in the 1920s and 1930s, which demonstrated that the process of implementing well-defined work practices can be more significant than the practices themselves (F. Roethlisbergr and W. Dickson, *Management and the Worker* (Cambridge, MA: Harvard University Press, 1939)).

15. These results were based on comparing the impact of ISO 9000 and TQM practices on quality and business outcomes; see K. Blackmon and C. A. Voss, 'Is ISO 9000 Good for Business? Institutional and Efficiency Perspectives on Quality Management', *Academy of Management Best Paper Proceedings*, San Diego Conference, 1988. It is fair to note that in recent years ISO 9000 has been updated to include more of the content of TQM to increase its effectiveness.

16. In an extensive study of ERP implementation, Masini found different configurations were appropriate in different contexts (A. Masini, 'Knowledge Integration and the Development of IT Capabilities: Configurations of ERP Adopters in the European and US Manufacturing Sector', London Business School Working Paper, OTM 03–012).

17. R. Sousa, and C. A. Voss, 'Quality Management: Universal or Context Dependent. An Empirical Investigation across the Manufacturing Strategy Spectrum', *Production and Operations Management*, 1/4 (2001), 383–404.

18. Voss and Robinson found that the early adopters of just-in-time practices tended to adopt the practices that were seen as easy and ignore those that were difficult, leading to limited or no effect—C. A. Voss and S. Robinson, 'Application of Just-In-Time Manufacturing Practices in the UK', *International Journal of Operations and Production Management*, 7/4 (1987), 46–51.

19. This is sometimes known as 'sticky knowledge'—see e.g. G. Szulanski *Sticky Knowledge: Barriers to Knowing in the firm* (London: Sage, 2003).

20. The idea of communities of practice was developed by J. S. Brown and P. Duguid, 'Organizational Learning and Communities of Practice: Toward a Unifying View of Working, Learning and Innovation', *Organization Science*, 2 (1991), 40–57. Their role in one particular practice area has been well described by J. Swan, H. Scarborough, and M. Robertson, 'The Construction of "Communities of Practice" in the Management of Innovation', *Management Learning*, 33/4 (2002), 477–97.

21. These barriers come from the work of Szulanski, who studied internal transfer of practices in firms: G. Szulanski, 'Exploring Internal Stickiness: Impediments to the Transfer of Best Practice within the Firm', *Strategic Management Journal*, 17 (1996), 27–43.

22. A study of US aerospace found problems and negative outcomes in seven sourcing practices: C. Rosetti and T. Choi, 'On the Dark Side of Strategic Sourcing: Experiences from the Aerospace Industry', *Academy of Management Executive*, 19/1 (2005), 46–60.

8

Learning in Organizations

THE capacity of exceptional managers to learn rapidly is crucial to their ability to deal with the many challenges we have considered in this book. Yet, while individual learning is indeed a key building block of organizational effectiveness, it is not sufficient. Over the last fifty years, we have built a deeper understanding of how the dynamics of groups and the structures of organizations can create a context in which learning may flourish, or indeed where it may decline. In this chapter we take a closer look at what we know about these contexts for learning, and at how organizations succeed or fail to use learning and knowledge as key resources for innovation, productivity, and ultimately competitiveness.

From the outset, we must critically consider the widely held assumption that alignment between individual and collective development is a key to competitiveness. Experience shows that alignment is hard to achieve in practice: personal agendas and organizational contexts constrain the ability and willingness of individuals to show and share what they know. The methods and techniques designed to capture the knowledge and experience of individuals often fail because they do not resolve the tension between the organizational need for control (and systematization) and the basic unmanageability of learning processes. Firms are often incapable of responding to radical changes in the business environment because the political agendas that underpin learning and knowing are such that the insights and experiences of managers and other employees are not fully engaged and benefited from. An acknowledgement of the political nature of organizational knowledge is crucial if managers are successfully to manage these processes.

Our central premise is that learning is an important bridging concept which links the firm with its external environment; the strategic with operational levels of the organization; and past experience with current practice. Yet to realize the potential of learning, it is necessary to decide whose knowledge is most important, how individual knowledge can best be translated into organizational knowledge (and vice versa), whether the most useful forms of knowledge can be managed in systematized ways, and what weightings should be given to knowledge derived from the top or bottom of the organization. These are essentially political issues, and the theories and examples put forward in this chapter are intended to help managers to recognize and resolve the challenges arising from them.

We believe that a critical way for managers to make a difference is to maximize the potential of individual and organizational knowledge. To see how this can be done, we examine three concepts that have gained currency since 1990—organizational learning, knowledge management, and the development of dynamic capabilities. In each case, we look briefly at the underlying principles, give examples of how the practice has developed, and summarize the lessons that can be learned from them.

There are close links between this chapter and several other parts of the book. It draws on the need for organizations to adjust to external competition, often involving major strategic change (Chapter 3); it looks at some of the sources and implications of innovation (Chapter 5); it challenges managers to be discerning about apparently 'promising practices' (Chapter 7); and it flags issues of both horizontal and vertical communication which are developed further in Chapter 10.

Organizational Learning

In the early 1960s the idea first surfaced that organizations might learn in ways that were similar to, yet independent of, individual learning. Researchers noted that organizations adopted routines and operating procedures that evolved over time in response to cumulative experience and crises, and that these could embody both history and complexity which were beyond the awareness, or intentionality, of any individual.[1] Other academics began a debate about whether the most valuable learning comes from incremental improvements or as radical response to major crises, a debate that is still reflected in the literature on corporate strategy and innovation (see Chapters 3 and 5).

The next major contribution came from the work of Chris Argyris and Donald Schön in the late 1970s.[2] They, too, highlighted the difference between incremental and radical forms of learning, arguing that organizations needed to develop greater capacity for the latter. They called this 'double-loop' learning, involving the detection and correction of error resulting in modification of an organization's underlying norms, policies, and objectives.[3] They suggested that organizations generally fail to grasp the challenge of 'double-loop' learning because managers are unwilling to acknowledge the nature and consequences of bad news, poor performance, or organizational shortcomings. Instead, they set up 'defensive routines' to protect themselves, resulting in a gap between their espoused views and what they actually do in practice. For example, senior managers may espouse radical and critical thinking, but then punish subordinates whose suggestions are too radical or critical of current practice.

Although well-known, the theories of Argyris and Schön are often criticized for being naive and impractical because they neglect the impact of wider organizational systems. These issues were tackled a decade later in Peter Senge's 1990 book, *The Fifth Discipline*, which popularizd the idea of the 'learning organization'. Senge argued that learning had to be organization-wide and not just based around the behaviour of enlightened top managers. His model included five elements:

- personal mastery—all employees need to develop their own skills through training and education;
- mental models—following Argyris and Schön, managers must examine their own assumptions for potential discrepancies between theory and practice;
- team learning, stressing greater awareness of how teams and groups work and the behaviours that can support or undermine collective learning;
- shared vision—encouraging creative ideas that can inspire the organization and its members;
- 'the fifth discipline', or systems thinking, which says that all the above elements need to be present, because the different parts reciprocally reinforce each other.

Senge was not the first person to use the term 'learning organization',[4] but his work had a major impact for several reasons: his ideas were neatly packaged; he explicitly built on the work of Argyris and Schön, and on the systems-dynamics arguments of Jay Forrester; his book was packed with practical examples from US companies; and he was supported by a network of consultants and companies, many of which were mentioned in the book. In the next few years, many companies followed the trail of the 'learning organization', although some seemed to be more interested in using the label for public-relations purposes. Below are three examples from the 1990s showing what can go right or wrong under the name of the learning organization.

Individual Learning without Organizational Learning at Rover

Rover has been the subject of many case studies showing how its decline and final downfall was a product of poor strategy, decision-making, industrial relations, and so on.[5] But part of its reputation that has survived is of being one of the UK's pioneer learning organizations. In 1990, Rover established an independent company called the Rover Learning Business, with the aim of spreading learning principles across the group. A highly visible feature of this business was the provision of learning opportunities for all 35,000 employees through personal development plans (affectionately referred to as 'pizza boxes' because of the shape and size of the containers), supported by an allocation of £100 to spend on any aspect of personal development.

By 1994 senior managers were claiming significant benefits. According to one manager:

> Every year we spend over £30 million on learning and development. Many competitors ask why? The answer is obvious when our business gains are examined: if we look at shareholder value, profitability and revenue per car sold—all have shown a dramatic improvement; the same is also true of revenue per employee, breakeven levels and vehicle pipeline stocks. Of course the judgment of our business success lies with satisfying our customers. This is demonstrated by our sales growth and customer satisfaction levels.[6]

At the time of the group's sale to BMW in 1994, it was estimated that people-development initiatives had improved shareholder value overall by some £650 million. Rover had also won a Global Learning Organization Award for 'being a global leader in the development of learning organizations, and [its] commitment to continuous learning'. The subsequent trajectory of Rover is well documented: sold to BMW for £800 million, it failed to prosper and in 2000 was bought by the Phoenix consortium, headed by the previous chief executive, John Towers, for £10. Ultimately, this deal failed too.

Rover's reputation as a learning organization survived the company's demise. In an interview, consultant Ian Rose described what Rover did as 'a beacon for all aspiring learning organizations'. But a new study[7] shows that much of the reputation was based on rhetoric. The research found no systematic calculations of the financial benefits of the initiative, most of the figures appearing in the press apparently being based on a 'back of the envelope' calculation by a senior manager on his way to a conference where he was giving a presentation. Also, the focus was on employees, and certainly did not reach as high as the board. When Towers was asked what the 'learning organization' meant for senior managers, he admitted that he had 'a group of board directors who were all working in the same old way'.

On the positive side, the initiative provided substantial benefits for individuals, and many remained highly enthusiastic throughout. Even employees who left in subsequent downsizings were still very enthusiastic about the learning initiatives to which they were exposed. However, it had very little impact on the company as a whole, for two main reasons. First, it did not get beyond the first of Senge's five principles to address the systemic aspects of the organization. Secondly, it was used by senior managers mainly as a PR story, and was not actively supported by their own behaviour. In short, learning served as a tool to enhance company reputation without fundamentally transforming anything.

The Success of Organizational Learning at Chaparral Steel in the 1990s

The US firm Chaparral Steel applied the principles of the learning organization more comprehensively than Rover, and its reputation stands up to greater examination. The differences are marked, both in terms of the way learning was integrated and institutionalized, and by the company's sustained profitability during a difficult period when it beat US and Japanese records for productivity and quality. Chaparral's method emphasized the quality of collective learning and information on four dimensions: gathering information about the environment; disseminating it widely around the company; establishing procedures to make collective sense of it; and encouraging members to take action and conduct experiments on the basis of the information thus gathered (see Figure 8.1)

Examples of the initiatives employed for each of these four phases at Chaparral are:

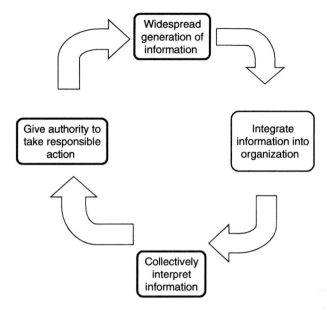

Figure 8.1.   Four phases of the learning models adopted at Chaparral Steel

- Generation of information
  - ▶ operatives sent on regular visits to suppliers and competitors;
  - ▶ supervisors encouraged to take (paid) sabbaticals;
  - ▶ new process experiments conducted on the line, not in the labs.
- Integration of information into organization
  - ▶ regular shift rotation;
  - ▶ new process teams dispersed around the factory as processes introduced;
  - ▶ all staff multi-skilled.
- Collective interpretation of information
  - ▶ building designed to encourage informal interaction;
  - ▶ no more than 1000 employees per plant;
  - ▶ egalitarian culture.
- Authority to take responsible action
  - ▶ supervisors given a budget with which to conduct experiments;
  - ▶ mistakes expected as the basis for learning;
  - ▶ bonus and reward system dependent primarily on group performance.

Chaparral appears to have benefited from its implementation of 'learning-organization' principles, continuing to be one of the most profitable steel producers.[8] According to vice president of administration Dennis E. Beach, 'When you're looking at a learning organization, you have to take a holistic approach.' This is a critical point, clearly differentiating Chaparral from Rover, and reflecting how learning as a bridging concept can make the connections supplying the holistic approach that Beach refers to. Such approaches are not apolitical. The phases of the learning model adopted at Chaparral Steel allow for personal development and responsibility, encourage informal interaction and discussion, establish processes of collaborative activity, and reward on the basis of collective performance. Managing in a politically astute manner is central to the business. It creates consistency and clarity in the communication processes, thus encouraging a cultural identity that guides action-taking at all levels.

... and in BP in the New Millennium

The previous examples were drawn from the 1990s, when the idea of the learning organization was most in vogue. The same principles are still being applied in the first decade of the twenty-first century, although without the original packaging. As Lord Browne, the chief executive of BP, strikingly puts it: 'A company has to learn better than its competitors and apply that knowledge throughout its business faster than they do.' BP has taken a number of steps to introduce learning principles and mechanisms across the company (we discuss some of them further in Chapter 10). They parallel the elements of Senge's model and are strongly supported by the words and action of top managers.[9] All five of Senge's elements are evident in the structures and processes employed:

- Personal learning and development: strong emphasis on building human capital by means of intranet-based training and career development, with development programmes, mentoring, and shadowing schemes for high flyers.
- Mental models: a tradition among the top team of challenging each other's assumptions. Deputy CEO Rodney Chase says: 'We are a deeply questioning team; we constantly inspect what we do to find out whether it is in fact the exercise of laziness or prejudice.' This intellectual rigour runs through the company.
- Team learning: following the example of top management, teams are encouraged to combine openness to ideas with rigorous challenge. According to a senior manager, 'We are experimenting with a new learning model based on reflection ... meetings [can involve] deep, meaningful dialogue.'

- Shared vision: employees at all levels are encouraged to help develop the corporate vision. This is reinforced by the performance-management system, which requires people to link their personal goals to corporate objectives.
- Systems approach: a concerted approach to generate learning through training, IT, personal communication, teamwork, and experience. Horizontal communications are encouraged through reward systems that reinforce cooperative behaviour and the 'Peer Assist' framework where managers are expected to ask for, and provide, help right across the company.

The management team that introduced these learning systems led the successful turnaround of the company from the mid-1990s on. Obviously, BP's continuing success is not solely the product of a strong learning culture, but those close to the company are convinced that organizational learning gives an underlying coherence to other factors (good strategic decisions, effective structures and systems, even luck) that have also played a part.

From these three examples, we can see two important patterns that distinguish the more from the less successful cases:

First, companies like BP and Chaparral, that seriously seek to become learning organizations, introduce a wide range of initiatives to encourage learning. Fundamentally, however, they seek to integrate these initiatives so that the message remains clear and consistent. In contrast, at Rover the single initiative (successful so far as it went) focused solely on individual development and was not supported at a wider level by performance-management and reward systems.

Secondly, there is a difference between BP and Rover in the role of senior managers. At BP the chief executive and his immediate team were directly involved in leading the learning initiatives—some of them were products of the high-flyer system. Conversely, in Rover the initiative was, in effect, outsourced to a separate business, which meant that senior managers were neither seen to be in the lead nor likely to be affected personally.

To some extent the lessons from these cases are obvious: organizational learning only 'works' if it involves a comprehensive range of learning and development mechanisms (formal and informal) which support each other, and it needs to be actively driven by organizational systems and the example of top management. Both patterns highlight the significance of sensitivity to the political agendas that underpin learning in organizations. People do not learn in a vacuum. They learn in response to the signals the organization sends about what it values. Failing to integrate individual learning into organizational systems suggests such initiatives will be of limited significance. Senior managers play a key role in providing political support for learning processes, and this includes being willing to accept personal feedback, to match their own behaviour to the rhetoric, and to resist the temptation to use the 'learning-organization' label for PR purposes or to gain compliance from employees.[10] Exceptional managers will be prepared to listen and learn from their employees, to debate objectives and practices, and to build collaborative commitment to the success of the organization.

One of the main lessons is that efforts to support and 'manage' learning in companies involve challenge and risk. It appears that the more managers seek to control learning to maximize organizational performance, the greater the risk of damaging it by limiting learning to a form of political games-playing. Supporting collective learning therefore calls for a delicate balancing act between formal and informal learning modes. If they rely solely on formal modes, organizations limit the body of knowledge to current operational priorities and fail to develop the learning capability to respond to unexpected challenges. For learning to become the connecting force between strategic intent and operational reality, it must be part of the business bloodstream. Similar issues apply in the efforts to support learning through knowledge management, as we will see below.

Knowledge Creation and Management

The next idea to attract strong attention was that it might be possible to 'manage' knowledge. For some time, economists had been suggesting that knowledge was a crucial determinant of competitiveness.[11] But two other factors came together in the mid-1990s. The first was developments in IT and the Internet. For example, the International Knowledge Management Network (IKMN) started in Europe in 1989, went online in 1994, and was soon joined by the US-based Knowledge Management Forum and related groups and publications. At the same time, international consulting firms such as Arthur Andersen and Booz-Allen & Hamilton began to realize that knowledge-management systems might offer a desirable alternative to what were increasingly being seen as failed TQM and business-process re-engineering initiatives. The result was that knowledge, and its management, became big business. The second key influence was the publication of a prominent book by Nonaka and Takeuchi called *The Knowledge-Creating Company*.

In essence, Nonaka argues that organizational knowledge is created by the direct experience of individuals and then needs to be spread by various means across the organization. His model includes four main processes:

- 'Socialization': individuals learning through direct experience, within organizational contexts;
- 'Externalization': making this personal knowledge public so that others can understand it;
- 'Combination': linking this knowledge to other formal knowledge to create innovations;
- 'Internalization': absorbing the knowledge into the normal operating procedures of individuals and teams.[12]

Nonaka also suggests that knowledge can be converted from tacit to explicit and from individual to collective levels, and vice versa. This is illustrated in the book by examples of product innovations such as Matsushita's domestic bread-making machine and Honda's 'Tall Boy' car which captured the imagination of many readers and seemed to substantiate their explanatory model. From there it was a short step to the idea that knowledge could be 'managed' by converting what people know and learn into codified organizational knowledge, and again to the use of technical tools able to cope with large volumes of data.

Consequently, the knowledge-management systems developed by consultants generally rely on IT implementations such as intranets, data warehousing, collaborative software, 'Yellow Pages' of internal expertise, and virtual knowledge-worker networks. Some are highly automated. For example, Ernst & Young's consultancy arm used IT to standardize solutions for typical small-business problems. Its Center for Business Knowledge employs more than 200 people to collate the experiences of consultants handling typical problems and codifying them into 'knowledge objects'. This process of externalization, in Nonaka's terms, is valuable to a business looking to solve many similar (technical) problems at high speed. Computer manufacturer Dell uses a similar highly centralized and codified system to link the supply chain elements, from order to delivery, in such a way that buyers can customize their orders in more than 40,000 different configurations.

Despite these successes, it is now widely recognized that IT cannot deliver 'knowledge management' on its own.[13] Useful though formalized systems were in some circumstances, they had difficulty handling complex processes. Companies specializing in complex problems or unique processes increasingly turned to more interactive and informal modes of managing knowledge. Consultancies such as Bain and McKinsey, which specialize in strategic problems, use IT as a means of supporting human networks. Informal modes of interaction supported by formal means of knowledge exchange assume that knowledge is created and transferred through discussions and brainstorming sessions between individuals. And client projects often require the lead consultant to assemble a virtual team, which draws on different experience and expertise from within the firm. Similarly, computer maker Hewlett-Packard, which builds its competitive advantage around the development of innovative products, makes much less use of IT support for knowledge management because it regards knowledge as too complex to be codified. It concentrates on knowledge transfer through personal exchanges, travel, face-to-face meetings, and conferences.

The basic issue is whether to rely on IT or people processes to transfer knowledge around organizations.[14] The former concentrates on explicit knowledge, while the latter is better suited to tacit knowledge. The examples above suggest that at the basic level the choice depends on whether the primary task can be standardized, or whether each instance is unique, as summarized in Figure 8.2.

That knowledge-management procedures can contribute significantly to the bottom line has been documented at companies such as Dow Chemical and Xerox.[15] But they also throw up a number of problems. At their heart is the politics of organizational knowledge. Knowledge-management systems are often charged with naivety for assuming that people will willingly share information in the general interests of the company. But studies have shown that knowledge is more likely to flow between people if reciprocal relationships exist, and if there are incentives to do so. For example, a study of knowledge exchange between scientists showed that they used different criteria for seeking or offering knowledge: they would offer knowledge only to those they trusted, but they would seek information from people whose scientific expertise they respected.[16]

This point highlights a less discussed aspect of knowledge management: the responsibility that knowing entails. There is a powerful connection between knowledge and what people do with it. To be knowledgeable is not so much to *have* information as it is to know how to *use* it in action and interaction with others. In short, knowledge reflects the way individuals and groups balance the inherent conflicts embedded in what is expected of them, what they expect, and consequently what they do in the context of the communities of which they

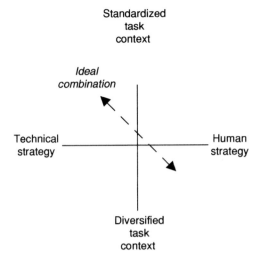

Figure 8.2. Knowledge-management strategies and context

are members.[17] The social and collective nature of knowledge has become a primary focus for recent research.

Researchers have shown how practical knowledge is often developed and disseminated within 'communities of practice'—naturally occurring groups of people tackling similar issues, whose task-based bond is often supplemented by social ties. This informally based knowledge is often quite different from the formal systems and manuals that provide instructions on, for example, how to repair complex machinery or how to navigate an aircraft carrier.[18]

In the case of field technicians servicing Xerox photocopiers, managers noticed that the technicians usually ignored the detailed official manual. In practice, 'identical' models could have very different operating characteristics, depending on how the machines were being used and by whom. To keep the machines running, the technicians needed to find out about the people who used them, and they would regularly gather for lunch to swap stories and information about clients and operatives. In this way, they built up a stock of local knowledge and shared experience which was quite outside the purview of the technical manuals, but which was essential for solving their practical problems in the field.

A similar story concerns a bakery company where senior managers hired an external market-research company to help it anticipate changing consumer tastes. Ironically, all the necessary knowledge already existed inside the company—among distribution drivers who talked daily to shopkeepers about what was selling or not and shared the information informally among themselves. But the information failed to trickle upstairs, because the drivers were of low status and peripheral to decision-making.[19]

These two stories well illustrate how organizations tend to undervalue the knowledge and expertise of junior and less powerful staff. Senior managers have the power to determine which kinds of knowledge are significant, and this is essentially a political process. But some of the most significant knowledge is local, built up in social interaction between employees who are in daily contact with customers, far from the gaze and direct control of managers.

As the importance of the social and local dimensions of knowledge have become clearer, consultants and practitioners have been quick to seize on the ideas to remedy the weaknesses of IT-based forms of knowledge management. By the end of the 1990s, a wide range of companies, including BP, Microsoft, Monsanto, and DaimlerChrysler, were trying to leverage local knowledge by fostering communities of practice among groups of professionals and scientists, often distributed across the world, to share insights and problems.[20] Peer Assist, described more fully in Chapter 10, has evidently created a highly effective lateral community of scientists and managers for BP.

On the face of it, the lesson is that informal interaction between individuals can be more significant than formal systems for capturing knowledge, a finding that builds on the lessons of organizational learning. But although communities of practice overcome some of the limitations of IT-based knowledge management, they have also been criticized for failing to take sufficient account of the political, systemic, and structural aspects of organizations. In practice, communities can be even more coercive than formal organizations, and enormous pressure can be placed on individuals to conform to the group mindset. Such homogeneity can severely reduce the creativity and openness to ideas that are supposed to be the virtue of natural communities.

The foregoing underlines the need for exceptional managers to create contexts in which the social and technical dimensions of knowledge management can coexist. It also bridges into the next section of this chapter, which focuses on the importance of greater integration between knowledge, learning systems, and structural changes in developing dynamic capabilities to underpin the organization's competitiveness.

Dynamic Capabilities

In response to the ongoing challenge of sustaining competitiveness in unpredictable markets, the resource-based view (RBV) of the firm highlighted the importance of routines, systems, and procedures that not only distinguish them from competitors, but which are also hard for competitors to imitate.[21] By extension of that argument, as markets and technologies evolve, internal routines need to evolve with them; and it is the ability to change internal routines and procedures regularly which constitutes a dynamic capability.[22] However, the term 'dynamic capabilities' has come to be used in different ways. For example, within this book it is used with reference to the ability to change strategic capabilities (Chapter 3), and also the ability to innovate and learn (Chapter 5).

One reason for these differences is that the term has been adopted by researchers who use different methods to examine different phenomena. Evolutionary economists seek to understand the performance of organizations in terms of linear, cause-and-effect relationships, and therefore focus on organizational-level processes and routines that can be observed or identified across large samples of companies. One strand of this research examines how strategic routines can be established and modified to maintain competitive advantage within strategic alliances and through takeovers.[23] Interestingly, the research shows that past experience in managing alliances does not transfer well to new ones, unless the partners have worked together before. This suggests that the quality of relationships between partners affects their ability to adapt individual routines appropriately, and this can have a direct bearing on subsequent economic success.

But to understand how and why such relationships work, it is necessary to examine the inner workings of organizations, and this has led to a different research tradition based on detailed case studies, for example comparing highly innovative with less innovative firms. One researcher looks at the structuring of everyday work in product-development teams through shared responsibility, valuing knowledge and expertise, and encouraging people to search for, and exploit, the unexpected.[24] The insights from such research highlight the importance of institutionalizing close links with customers, the need to create space and time within which innovation can flourish, the need to provide flexibility in organizational structure and roles, and the importance of nurturing attitudes that encourage teamwork and creativity.

A similar list of principles emerges from a case study of the innovative Danish hearing-aid firm, Oticon. The company had been a global leader in hearing aids until the late 1980s, when its market share fell from 14 per cent to 9 per cent in the space of eighteen months. This triggered a major restructuring, which involved abolishing departments, positions, titles, and job descriptions, and replacing the previous functional structure with a project-based organization. During the next few years, Oticon doubled its innovation rate,[25] and forged ahead of rivals with a series of new products combining technical advances with new market appeal, for example using colours and designs aimed at hard-of-hearing children.

Oticon's innovation programme was supported by many measures, including a panel of 950 users with whom the R&D department maintained close links, the introduction of cross-functional project teams in charge of single development projects, and the establishment of a senior group with sufficient political clout to ensure that knowledge was shared between projects. As a result, the company was able simultaneously to create, absorb, and integrate knowledge—an attribute that is critical to dynamic capability in a business that relies on technical innovation.[26]

Exceptional cases such as Oticon are usefully for flagging underlying principles, but, as we noted in Chapter 7, good practice is context-specific: what works in one context can't necessarily be transferred to another. Several unique organizational characteristics combine to create promising practices that support the ongoing renewal of organizations through their dynamic capabilities. Our own research concentrates on 'live' case studies of organizations in the process of transformation. Early findings already show great diversity within companies: some parts of the firm are highly dynamic, others much less so, meaning that it is unwise to generalize to whole companies. Also, there is an important time dimension, because the success of companies and projects can vary greatly over time. This is shown by the examples below, which further add to our current understanding of the complexity of dynamic capabilities.

Ciba Speciality Chemicals, a global leader in industrial chemicals, like many multinationals has restructured around market segments instead of the previous product divisions. Over the years, it had built up a large body of proprietary technical know-how, which had been carefully guarded as the source of the company's competitive advantage. But a new strategic focus on customers has led Ciba radically to rethink of the role of knowledge, which Ciba has now decided to sell to its erstwhile rivals in the form of consultancy services. Drawing on this expertise and its experience of supporting customer industries, Ciba has started to offer knowledge-based services to other chemical companies on a global basis. The creation of this new business, although relatively small in relation to the whole company, is significant because the establishment of new marketing routines and customer relationships demonstrates dynamic capability. It also highlights a trend, first identified by Gary Hamel and colleagues, of simultaneous collaboration and competition between modern firms.[27]

Although conceived at a strategic level, the decision to develop the expert services business had major implications for the company's existing skills and competency base. Employees who had previously relied on technical and scientific innovation within their own communities of practice suddenly needed additional customer-relations skills, leading to a major training programme for existing staff, and changed recruitment criteria for new hires. The change was not universally welcomed: some scientists resented being obliged to move outside their natural competency range, and other observers had wider misgivings about the principle of selling core expertise to competitors. Nevertheless, the initiative went ahead and is still evolving at the time of writing. Following the research model, the case demonstrates how a fresh strategic routine (switching from selling products to selling services) has to interface with a range of new operational routines (organizational structure, training, recruitment). Change at both levels is necessary for dynamic capability. The integration of strategic and operational practices is at the core of connecting knowledge and learning with action. Dynamic capability emerges from the connections created as learning redefines new practices and expands the current body of knowledge through new insights and modes of working, and in a complex network of interacting players within and outside the organization. These networks provide a platform for rethinking core competencies and constantly updating them through an agile and flexible approach to managing. This point is in evidence in our second example, set in a much smaller company, which focuses on innovation driven by internal processes linking strategic and operational processes.

Business Serve, founded in 1998, delivers Internet services to businesses—it is an ISP, optimizes web services, and provides enhanced connectivity. It has prospered during the post-dotcom IT downturn, maintaining rapid growth and remaining substantially profitable. In early 2003 the company developed a new product called Netsuite, which combined its three core services into one package. The bundled product was conceived by middle managers and offered as a service to new customers. But initial sales were disappointing, and managers worried whether they would make the sales target of twenty packages in the first month. Meanwhile, a manager dealing with existing accounts heard about the product and realized that it exactly matched the needs of an existing customer. That afternoon he took orders for six packages. Quickly alerted, senior managers overhauled the initial strategy and authorized sales to existing customers, selling 1,400 packages in two months as a result. The unanticipated alteration naturally triggered a cascade of further changes through the organization—to structure and departmental boundaries, training and development programmes, reward systems, and recruitment, particularly in the area of web design. The initial sales plan was completely overturned as a new strategy emerged for selling the product.

The Business Serve case highlights some important aspects of dynamic capabilities—first, the need for flexible strategy to match fast-changing markets (i.e. strategic changes can be driven by operational concerns); secondly, a key principle, that employees can find opportunities in unexpected areas; and thirdly, the crucial role played by senior management in appreciating and then legitimizing knowledge originating from an employee who was effectively operating on the firm's periphery.

The lesson is that dynamic capabilities require and comprise flexibility at individual, collective, and organizational levels, and in the interface with the environment. Individual flexibility is helped by the development of learning capability such that a broad skill base is maintained. Moreover, valuing and involving individuals in shaping strategic and operational practices is vital as a means of encouraging identities and careers which do not depend on maintaining the status quo. Collective flexibility can be supported by development processes that enable teams to form quickly and disband when no longer needed. Tolerating and even encouraging internal diversity is key, coupled with the proactive support of top management to drive and steer the collaborative activities and actively connect strategic and operational routines. Organizational flexibility can be supported by paring down structures and hierarchies, by generating processes and information systems that support flexibility elsewhere, and that can themselves be reconfigured easily. Flexibility in relation to the environment demands close contact with customers and alliance partners, and anticipating the moves of competitors.

Clearly, the idea of dynamic capabilities, as we have developed it here, builds on the insights of organizational learning and knowledge management. In particular, it draws on the need for systematic support for, and integration of, learning, and the key role of senior managers. Overall, it emphasizes the importance of the interaction between and within organizational structures, systems, and human behaviour. In our view, dynamic capability has considerable potential as an idea. On the other hand, its relative newness means that it is not well understood and still so far experimental in application.

Conclusion

Learning and knowledge are key underpinnings for the dynamics of organizational competitiveness, not just as organizational resources but also as central practices and routines. As a means of connecting individual and organizational development, learning is a critical process for supporting flexibility and renewal, a bridge between operational and strategic priorities, present and future, known and unknown.

But, as we have seen from our examples, knowledge management and learning are not easy to manage, or at least not easy to manage in ways that produce lasting results. For example, it is clear that at Rover the 'learning organization' label was a misnomer, the changes being cosmetic rather than transformational and failing to include those with the formal power at the top of the organization.

This example underlines another important lesson: the social and political nature of learning and knowing. They are not tangible assets that can be measured and controlled. Instead, as intangible assets, the power of learning and knowledge is based on the way they are employed in flexible but systematic ways to build formal and informal mechanisms for connecting the internal and external environment. The alignment of individual and organizational goals in relation to development remains a key challenge.

The exceptional manager as a leader, therefore, needs to be politically astute, particularly in recognizing and deploying power coupled with responsibility and accountability to support organization learning and capability development. The exceptional manager is the one who has sufficient political skill and awareness to configure both formal and informal power in support of organization learning and renewal.

The key messages for managers therefore are:

- For learning to make a serious contribution to corporate development, managers need to be sensitive to the politics that underpin learning and knowledge, mindful of both the positive and negative implications of politically driven learning agendas.
- Fostering learning and knowing from both external and internal sources, and providing consistency between operational and strategic practices, are critical. Formal and informal systems and structures must facilitate rather than hinder the flow of ideas and information.

- To support collective learning, managers need to pay special attention to legitimizing the ideas and experiences that come from the operational levels, which again requires an awareness of organizational power and politics. These ideas may be vital in gaining or maintaining competitive edge.
- Learning from both successes and failures is essential. Success is often seized on, and winning formulae regularly repeated. Failure is a better teacher, but since no one wants to be associated with it, its learning potential is mostly lost—until it turns into catastrophe.[28] A learning culture needs to combine aggressive, and rigorous, search for new ideas with encouragement to learn from and make sense of failure. This is where the exceptional manager can really make a difference.

Notes

1. The first two publications that deliberately used the term 'organizational learning' were R. M. Cyert and J. G. March, *A Behavioral Theory of the Firm* (Englewood Cliffs, NJ: Prentice Hall, 1963); and V. E. Cangelosi and W. R. Dill, 'Organizational Learning: Observations toward a Theory', *Administrative Science Quarterly*, 10/2 (1965), 175–203.
2. This theme underlies most of the writings of C. Argyris and D. A. Schön, and is developed most fully in their classic book *Organizational Learning: A Theory of Action Perspective* (Reading, MA: Addison-Wesley, 1978). Also see M. Easterby-Smith and M. Lyles, 'Re-reading Organizational Learning: Selective Memory, Forgetting and Adaptation', *Academy of Management Executive*, 17/2 (2003), 51–5, for a review of the long-term impact of this book.
3. This definition is from Argyris and Schön, *Organizational Learning*.
4. See B. Garratt, *The Learning Organization* (London: Fontana, 1987). Also Arie De Geus used a similar concept but labelled it as 'institutional learning', in 'Planning as Learning', *Harvard Business Review*, 66/2 (1988), 70–4.
5. I. Rose, *Creating the Learning Organization* (West Vancouver: IBR Consulting Services, 1994); M. J. Marquardt and M. Sashkin, *Building the Learning Organization: A Systems Approach to Quantum Improvement and Global Success* (New York: McGraw-Hill, 1996); A. Lorenz, 'BMW Finds £271m Cash Pile at Rover', *Sunday Times*, 27 February 1994, pp. 1–2; F. Mueller, 'The Role of Know-How in Corporate Rejuvenation: The Case of Rover', *Business Strategy Review*, 4 (1993), 15–24.
6. Shareholder value is defined as £650m, being the difference between the recent two purchase prices of the company, i.e. that paid by BAe in 1988 (£150m) when sold by the UK government and that paid by BMW (£800m) during the subsequent acquisition. Profit is based on PBIT (profit before interest and taxation), which was minus £52m for the year ended 1991 and £56m for 1993. Revenue per car sold was quoted as being £6,800 in 1989 with the

equivalent figure for 1993 rising to £10,200. Revenue per employee was calcu-lated at £31,000 and £122,000 for the years 1989 and 1993, respectively. Break-even levels were reduced from 480,000 units (cars) in 1990 to 413,000 for 1993. Vehicle pipeline stocks were decreased by a total of 60,000 cars. The 1990 level was quoted as 164,000 with a corresponding figure of 104,000 units for 1993. Customer satisfaction levels were interpreted as 'warranty costs as %age of net sales revenue', the improvement being a reduction from 1.63% (in 1990) to 1.10% (by 1993).

7. We are grateful to David Simm for insights into the Rover case. For further information, see D. Simon, *Organizational Learning and Performance Enhance-ment: The Case of Rover*, Ph.D. thesis, Lancaster University (2006). For more insights about learning, see D. Leonard-Barton, 'The factory as a learning laboratory', *Sloan Management Review*, 34/1 (1992), 23–38; and N. Dixon, *The Organizational Learning Cycle: How We can Learn Collectively*, 2nd edn. (Alder-shot: Gower Press, 1999).

8. Record profits were posted in July 2004 by TXI Chaparral.

9. These observations on British Petroleum are based on the insightful case study by M. Rogan, L. Gratton, and S. Ghoshal, *The Transformation of BP* (London Business School, 2004). We are very grateful for permission to reproduce quotes and principles from this study.

10. See T. B. Lawrence, M. K. Mauws, B. Dyck, and R. F. Kleysen, 'The Politics of Organizational Learning: Integrating Power into the 4I Framework', *Acad-emy of Management Review*, 30/1 (2005), 180–91; J. Coopey, 'The Learning Organization: Power, Politics and Ideology', *Management Learning*, 26/2 (1995), 193–213. See the debate between Adler and Berggren about whether the group-based methods of Volvo or the systems-based learning processes of the GM-Toyota joint-venture, NUMMI, were superior for achieving or-ganizational learning: P. S. Adler and R. E. Cole, 'Designed for Learning: A Tale of Two Auto Plants', *Sloan Management Review*, 34/3 (1993), 85–94; C. Berggren, 'NUMMI vs. Uddevalla', *Sloan Management Review*, 35/2 (1994), 37–45.

11. F. A. Hayek, 'The Use of Knowledge in Society', in F. A. Hayek (ed.), *Individualism and Economic Order* (London: Routledge, 1945); R. R. Nelson and S. G. Winter, *An Evolutionary Theory of Economic Change* (Cambridge, MA: Harvard University Press, 1982); E. T. Penrose, *The Theory of the Growth of the Firm* (Oxford: Blackwell, 1959).

12. See I. Nonaka, 'A Dynamic Theory of Organizational Knowledge Creation', *Organization Science*, 5/1 (1994), 14–37; and I. Nonaka and H. Takeuchi, *The Knowledge-Creating Company: How Japanese Companies Create the Dynamics of Innovation* (Oxford: Oxford University Press, 1995).

13. With acknowledgements to Richard McDermott, 'Why Information Inspired but Cannot Deliver Knowledge Management', *California Management Review*, 41/4 (1999), 103–17.

14. For further discussion of this strategic dilemma, see M. T. Hansen et al., 'What's your Strategy for Managing Knowledge?' *Harvard Business Review*, 2 (1999),

106–16; and M. Martiny, 'Knowledge Management at HP Consulting', *Organizational Dynamics*, 27/2 (1998), 71–7.

15. See for further details J. S. Brown and P. Duguid, 'Balancing Act: How to Capture Knowledge without Killing it', *Harvard Business Review*, 78/3 (2000), 73–80.

16. See K. M. Andrews and B. L. Delahaye, 'Influences on Knowledge Processes in Organizational Learning: The Psychosocial filter', *Journal of Management Studies*, 37/6 (2000), 797–810.

17. See E. P. Antonacopoulou, 'Modes of Knowing in Practice: The Relationship between Learning and Knowledge Revisited', in B. Renzl, K. Matzler, and H. H. Hinterhuber (eds.), *The Future of Knowledge Management* (London: Palgrave, 2005); E. P. Antonacopoulou, 'The Paradoxical Nature of the Relationship between Training and Learning', *Journal of Management Studies*, 38/3 (2001), 327–50.

18. See S. D. N. Cook and D. Yanow, 'Culture and Organizational Learning', *Journal of Management Inquiry*, 2/4 (1993), 373–90; and K. E. Weick and K. H. Roberts, 'Collective Mind in Organizations: Heedful Interrelating on Flight Decks', in M. D. Cohen and L. S. Sproull (eds.), *Organizational Learning* (London: Sage, 1996).

19. For these and other examples, see D. Yanow, 'Translating Local Knowledge at Organizational Peripheries', *British Journal of Management*, 15 (2004), 9–25.

20. See E. Wenger and W. M. Snyder, 'Communities of Practice', *Harvard Business Review*, 78/1 (2000), 139–45; J. Storck and P. Hill, 'Knowledge Diffusion through Strategic Communities', *Sloan Management Review*, 41 (2000), 63–74; T. H. Davenport and L. Prusak, *Working Knowledge: How Organizations Manage what they Know* (Boston: Harvard Business School Press, 2000); J. S. Brown and P. Duguid, *The Social Life of Information* (Boston: Harvard Business School Press, 2000).

21. The concept of resource-based strategies was introduced by B. Wernerfelt, 'A Resource-Based View of the Firm', *Strategic Management Journal*, 5/2 (1984), 171–80. There are now many books and papers that explain and summarize the approach. See e.g. the beginning of D. J. Teece, G. Pisano, and A. Shuen, 'Dynamic Capabilities and Strategic Management', *Strategic Management Journal*, 18/7 (1997), 509–34, and the introductory paper by D. Hoopes, T. Madsen, and G. Walker, 'Why there is a Resource Based View', *Strategic Management Journal*, 24/10 (2003), 889–902.

22. David Teece has written about dynamic capabilities in the paper referred to in n. 21 above. See also K. Eisenhardt and J. Martin, 'Dynamic Capabilities; What are They?', *Strategic Management Journal*, 21 (2000), 105–21; M. Zollo and S. Winter, 'Deliberate Learning and the Evolution of Dynamic Capabilities', *Organization Science*, 13/3 (2002), 339–51.

23. See Zollo and Winter, 'Deliberate Learning'; M. Zollo, J. J. Reuer, and H. Singh, 'Interorganizational Routines and Performance in Strategic Alliances', *Organization Science*, 13/6 (2003), 701–13.

24. D. Dougherty, H. Barnard, and D. Dunne, 'Exploring the Everyday Dynamics of Dynamic Capabilities', CRITO, 2004.

25. Innovation rate is defined as the proportion of sales in one year accounted for by products introduced in the previous two years.

26. See G. Verona and D. Ravasi, 'Unbundling Dynamic Capabilities: An Exploratory Study of Continuous Product Innovation', *Industrial and Corporate Change*, 12/3 (2003), 577–606. Another study which looks at the development of dynamic capabilities in a midwifery practice is provided by L. P. Wooten and P. Crane, 'Generating Dynamic Capabilities Through Humanistic Work Ideology: The Case of a Certified Midwife Practice in a Professional Bureaucracy' (2004), working paper, University of Michigan Business School.

27. See G. Hamel, Y. L. Doz, and C. K. Prahalad, 'Collaborate with your Competitors—and Win', *Harvard Business Review*, 67/1 (1989), 133–9. An additional important point made by these authors is that the long-term 'winner' in such relationships tends to be the firm that can learn most from its partner.

28. B. Toft and S. Reynolds, *Learning from Disasters* (London: Butterworth, 1994); D. Miller, *The Icarus Paradox: How Exceptional Companies Bring about their own Downfall* (New York: HarperCollins, 1990); D. Elliott, D. Smith, and M. McGuinness, 'Exploring the Failure to Learn: Overcoming the Barriers to Learning', *Crisis Review of Business*, 21/3 (2000), 17–24; J. Fortune and G. Peters, *Learning from Failure* (Chichester: John Wiley, 1995).

9

Making Intelligent Decisions

THROUGHOUT this book we have argued that exceptional managers need both self-awareness and the capacity to reflect. They need intuition and insight about their values and experiences, and the capacity to work with the complex information with which they are daily presented. In this chapter, we focus on rational decision-making models and their potential value to the exceptional manager. We show how they may promote clear thinking and intelligent decision-making on the basis of systematically acquired and ordered information—what we call cognitive competence. We explore this topic by considering the way in which individuals and groups make sense of their world, the mental processes used to process information and acquire knowledge. What does it take to be more 'cognitively competent', and how can this competence be fostered?

In an increasingly complex, ambiguous, and shifting environment, the art and science of decision-making is crucial as managers at every level need both to make sense of, and to communicate, a bewildering flow of information. Few would doubt that the premium placed on managers' ability to process information and extract and use knowledge is greater than ever before—whether in terms of managing strategic transformation (Chapter 3), the management of employee relations (Chapter 4), coping with discontinuous innovation (Chapter 5), identifying and adopting promising practices more generally (Chapter 7), or in processes of organizational learning (Chapter 8). In practice, this means being responsive to the environment and capable of picking up those (weak) signals that may indicate the need for change. Managers must first detect these signals, and then filter, store, recall, and interpret them in a fashion that enables the organization to respond appropriately.[1]

Two seemingly unconnected events, the explosion of the space shuttle *Challenger* in January 1986 and Shell's survival of the world oil crisis in the early 1970s, dramatically illustrate how the quality of decision-making can lead to very different organizational outcomes. The explosion of *Challenger* has been widely attributed to the poor decision-making capabilities of NASA. Conversely, Shell weathered the 1973 oil crisis and associated recession much better than most rivals as a result of far-sighted decision procedures that enabled its managers to respond promptly and with foresight as events unfolded.[2]

In both cases, we see managers faced with enormously complex information and called on to make far-reaching decisions. As we show later, NASA illustrates a number of critical human limitations associated with decision-making. Perhaps most fundamentally, there are limits to the amount of information individual managers (and others) can process. Because of these limitations, they rarely reach optimal solutions. Moreover, research has shown that groups, too, often make less than optimal decisions. Fortunately, however, as this chapter lays out, there are a number of remedies that managers can deploy to counteract these shortcomings, including decision aids to help individuals overcome personal biases and other constraints, and strategies to help groups arrive at more rigorously derived conclusions.

Organizational Decision-making in Practice

As every manager knows, organizational decisions are rarely taken by individuals in isolation. On the contrary, they are inherently social and political in nature. This means that fundamental differences in understanding and belief must somehow be reconciled, either through explicit negotiation or through a tacit process. By better understanding the nature of the key assumptions that individuals bring to the wider organizational arena, we can begin to aid the decision-making process, fostering negotiation among differing stakeholders and stakeholder groups.

Our starting point is the natural limit to managers' abilities to process information. In familiar situations, faced with large quantities of complex information from disparate sources, individuals almost inevitably fall back on rules of thumb (known as 'heuristics') and develop simplified internal representations (known as 'mental models') of the problem they are trying to address. One such rule of thumb, known as the 'availability heuristic', implies that events and outcomes will be judged more frequent or probable to the extent that past examples can be easily recalled. So a retail manager would be more likely to judge that a major competitor will fail in the next year if similar failures have recently been covered in the press. According to the 'representativeness heuristic', an employee who looks and acts like a 'high-flyer' (e.g. smartly dressed and quick to offer forthright opinions in meetings) will be judged and treated as such irrespective of his or her true abilities. These tendencies have an enabling effect on decision-making in the sense that they allow quicker conclusions. The other side of the coin is that they can also damage it by introducing biases that can become blind spots, leading in turn to poor judgements and choices.

The finite information-processing capacity of the human brain has forced us to revise the classical or 'rational choice' view of decision-making, which historically has underpinned much economic and management theory.[3] It is now generally accepted that individual managers think about decision problems and evaluate possible responses using two complementary processes:

- a largely automatic, pre-conscious process which involves developing and using rules of thumb/heuristics; and
- a deeper, more effortful process of detailed analysis.

In Table 9.1 we illustrate how using heuristics can lead to a variety of biased judgements. These include a tendency to overestimate the predictability of past events ('hindsight bias'), a failure accurately to recall how past events unfolded ('logical reconstruction'), overestimation of the chances of desirable outcomes ('wishful thinking'), the tendency to overestimate the ability to influence outcomes ('illusion of control'), and distortions of judgement arising from the availability heuristic, as mentioned earlier. In turn, these biases can lead decision-makers to construct inadequate mental models of the problems they are dealing with, the net effect of which is that their decisions are poor ones.[4]

However, while rules of thumb thus have evident disadvantages, managers who rely solely on detailed analysis are not necessarily better off. Here the danger is of being overcome by sheer quantity of information, or 'paralysis-by-analysis'. To make up for these twin disadvantages, the exceptional manager needs to be able to switch back and forth between rules of thumb, or 'habits-of-the-mind', and 'active thinking', a process referred to as 'switching cognitive gears'.[5]

Yet the ability to switch gears in this way is difficult. Individuals differ markedly in the way they acquire and organize information and knowledge—in effect, they have varying 'cognitive styles'. Two aspects of cognitive style, roughly corresponding to the rule-of-thumb and analytic

Table 9.1. *How selected heuristics and biases affect strategic decision-making*

Heuristic/bias	Effects
1. Availability	Judgements of the probability of easily recalled events are distorted
2. Selective perception	Expectations may bias observations of variables relevant to strategy
3. Illusory correlation	Encourages the belief that unrelated variables are correlated
4. Conservatism	Failure to revise sufficiently forecasts based on new information
5. Law of *small* numbers	Overestimation of the degree to which small samples are representative of populations
6. Regression bias	Failure to allow for regression to the mean
7. Wishful thinking	Probability of desired outcomes judged to be inappropriately high
8. Illusion of control	Overestimation of personal control over outcomes
9. Logical reconstruction	'Logical' reconstruction of events which cannot be accurately recalled
10. Hindsight bias	Overestimation of predictability of past events

Source: C. R. Schwenk, 'The Cognitive Perspective on Strategic Decision-Making', *Management Studies*, 25 (1988), 41–55. Reproduced by kind permission of the publisher. ©Blackwell Publishers Ltd.

approaches discussed above, have come in for considerable attention from researchers: intuition ('immediate judgement based on feeling and the adoption of a global perspective') and analysis ('judgement based on mental reasoning and a focus on detail'). Researchers disagree whether managers can combine analytic and intuitive approaches at the same time, or whether the two are mutually exclusive. If indeed individuals are capable of switching, then it should be possible to train those with a marked preference for one approach to recognize when it makes sense to switch to the other. To the extent that people are unable to combine styles, however, teams will need to be carefully chosen with a view to forming a mix in which individuals complement each another and thereby compensate for their respective weaknesses.[6] This is an issue to which we shall return.

While we can understand the basis of these natural weaknesses, organizations struggle to take account of them in decision-making. What we now know from a considerable volume of research is that that the various biases tend to predominate at different stages of the decision-making process. Consider, for example, a manager faced with the question of whether or not significantly to expand the business. Early in the decision-making process, when they are identifying the nature of the problem, people typically look for information that confirms their initial beliefs. As noted earlier, the effectiveness of the initial judgement depends on the representativeness of the analogies people draw with other similar situations, leading them to prefer some alternatives from the outset and treat others in more negative terms. It is then easy to justify favoured alternatives on the grounds that they do not involve complex trade-offs. From the outset our manager is likely to favour either a growth or consolidation strategy, which means that he or she will tend to focus attention on information that supports the basic preference for, say, growth. As they generate alternatives, individuals use their initial beliefs to anchor or restrain their judgements. Thus, faced with, for example, a newspaper article suggesting that a major competitor would make an ideal target for acquisition on account of its current financial performance, our manager is unlikely to revise his or her estimates concerning future revenue streams in the light of additional historical data (acquired through subsequent library research), depicting a more pessimistic outlook over time. In the final evaluation stage, decision-makers use analogies to justify their point of view, potentially leading them to overestimate the relevance of past experiences, give only partial descriptions of strategic alternatives, and devalue or dismiss vitally important information. Relying on intuition can also lead managers to put too much confidence in their decisions, fostering a misdirected search for certainty and a consequent 'illusion of control'. Convinced as to the 'correctness' of the decision, our manager is thus most unlikely to depart from his or her initial preference.[7]

As we shall see, these problems are often compounded by a process known as 'group polarization', in which in an attempt to diffuse feelings of personal responsibility groups come to favour overly cautious or overly risky alternatives. Too much cohesion within the group can also result in the phenomenon known as 'group-think'—a strong convergence of beliefs that are dramatically out of step with objective reality.[8]

Unfortunately, the cumulative result of these processes is the all-too-familiar 'good money after bad' syndrome, or 'non-rational escalation of commitment to a failing course of action', in which instead of dumping misconceived initiatives, managers go to ever greater lengths to try to make them work. The Millennium Dome project is one good example; another is Prudential's refusal to cut the losses of its ill-fated estate agency chain until they had reached £300 million. In both cases, if senior managers had had the courage to terminate the projects as soon as the problems came to light, they would have released the resources to invest in alternative, potentially more successful ventures. Unfortunately, it is often only with the benefit of hindsight that managers become aware of the true nature of the underlying problems, trapped by the limitations of their individual and collective psychological make-up, the inbuilt unwillingness or inability to jettison existing strategies being reinforced by group processes working to boost joint commitment.[9]

These key issues generate a number of dilemmas for managers as decision-makers, which research is only just beginning to address. What, for example, is the right mix of individuals for effective team-level decision-making? To what extent and in what ways do decision-making teams with similar characteristics and attributes perform better or worse than more diverse ones? How can managers develop mental models that are both sufficiently stable to enable them to act under conditions of risk and uncertainly (that is, using heuristics and mental models), and yet flexible enough to allow for timely updating in the light of changing circumstances? Finally, how do managers avoid becoming paralysed by information overload without succumbing to myopia or being tricked by blind spots? It is to these questions we now turn.

What Can we Do to Improve Individual Judgement and Decision-making?

We have highlighted some of the constraints that influence individuals and groups as decision-making units. How can managers use this knowledge to improve the quality of their decision-making? First, we illustrate techniques that can be used by individual managers to sensitize themselves to their own particular biases. We then go on to consider ways in which groups can overcome some of the more general problems associated with individual-level decision-making.

The Framing Bias

Consider the choices offered in panel A of Table 9.2 and note which option you prefer. Now do the same thing for panel B. If, like most people, you chose A and D respectively, you have selected two diametrically opposed options and fallen foul of the phenomenon known as 'framing bias'. The reason for this 'preference reversal' is that, disconcertingly, the decision-making of most individuals is not neutral but directly affected by the way in which alternatives are presented or 'framed'. Faced with positively framed alternatives (where gains are emphasized relative to losses, as in panel A), people almost always choose the safer option (plan A). However, when exactly the same information is negatively framed (i.e. losses are emphasized relative to gains, as in panel B), they go for the riskier alternative (plan D). In fact, the riskiness of plans A and C is identical, and likewise plans B and D are formally identical. What happens is that a change in the way the problem is framed alters the reference point of the viewer. In panel A, the effect of the positive frame is to emphasize the potential gains and make decision-makers averse to taking risks that would damage them. Conversely, the negatively framed version of the problem focuses attention on losses, which encourages a riskier strategy.[10]

How can managers minimize the risk of falling foul of such biases? We consider the relative merits of two alternative approaches: the 'frame analysis worksheet' and 'causal cognitive mapping'.

The Frame Analysis Worksheet

Several tools and techniques can help the reflective manager fruitfully reconsider the ways in which they and their colleagues make decisions. The 'frame analysis worksheet' developed by Russo and Schoemaker is a

Table 9.2. *Illustration of the framing bias*

Panel A

A large car manufacturer has recently been hit with a number of economic difficulties, and it appears as if three plants need to be closed and 6,000 employees laid off. The vice-president of production has been exploring alternative ways to avoid this crisis. She has developed two plans:

Plan A: This plan will save one of the three plants and 2,000 jobs

Plan B: This plan has a one-third probability of saving all three plants and all 6,000 jobs, but has a two-thirds probability of saving no plants and no jobs

Which plan would you select?

Panel B

Plan C: This plan will result in the loss of two of the three plants and 4,000 jobs.

Plan D: This plan has a two-thirds probability of resulting in the loss of all three plants and all 6,000 jobs, but has a one-third probability of losing no plants and no jobs.

Which plan would you select?

Source: M. H. Bazerman, 'The Relevance of Kahneman and Tversky's Concept of Framing to Organizational Behavior', *Journal of Management*, 10 (1984), 333–43. Reproduced by kind permission of the publisher. ©Blackwell Publishers Ltd.

The issue of issues the frame addresses (in a few words):

- where to relocate a fast print and photocopying business

What boundaries do I (we) (they) put on the question? In other words, what aspects of the situation do I (we) (they) leave out of consideration?

- the relocation is to be within 8 miles of the town center
- buying not considered
- won't consider another town/country

What yardsticks do I (we) (they) use to measure success?

- profitability and good working conditions

What reference points do I (we) (they) use to measure success?

- the profitability of my business in its current location

What metaphors — if any — do I (we) (they) use in thinking about this issue?

- you've got to be where the customers are

What does the frame emphasize?

- attracting new small customers
- continuing as before
- keeping costs low

What does it minimize?

- change of business/market segment

Do other people in the fast print and photocopy industry (fill in your own field) think about this question differently from the way I (we) (they) do?

- some would try and get a space in a big department store

- some would focus on building relationships with largish organizations such that the exact location of the business itself was immaterial to high turnover

Can I (we) (they) summarize my (our) (their) frame in a slogan?

- I am being forced to relocate and want to carry on my business in the same town

Figure 9.1.   Example of a frame-analysis worksheet

Source: P. Goodwin and G. Wright, *Decision Analysis for Management Judgment* (Chichester: John Wiley, 1998), 350. Reproduced by kind permission of the publisher. © John Wiley & Sons Ltd.

form of formalized 'devil's advocacy', designed to encourage managers to consider their framing of issues by challenging them to give explicit answers to the following questions:

- Which aspects of the situation might you have left out of your deliberations?
- What particular features of the problem does your frame emphasize?
- How might other people think about the problem and what issues might they highlight?

Figure 9.1 shows an example of the frame analysis worksheet in action. The example, taken from *Decision Analysis for Management Judgment* by Paul Goodwin and George Wright, concerns a small printing and photocopying business that needs to relocate its office because the existing site is to be redeveloped. The owner has decided to rent alternative accommodation and is actively considering seven possibilities. Clearly, the owner's primary reference point is 'the good profitability of my business in its current location'. As Goodwin and Wright point out, the perceived attractiveness of the various options will be likely to vary depending on whether the profitability of the present office is well above or below the overall company average. If the profitability of the office in its current location is high, the owner might look at the alternative locations in a negative light (fearing they will undermine current performance), and eschew risks as a result. If on the other hand profitability is low, the proprietor may see the alternatives as boosting current performance and be prepared to countenance riskier options. What this technique does is to foster *multiple* frame awareness, sensitizing managers to different ways of looking at decisions.[11]

Causal Cognitive Mapping

Earlier we noted that one of the ways people cope with information overload is by formulating simplified representations of reality, or 'mental models'. 'Cognitive mapping' is a means of revealing the structure and content of these models. Over the years, a wide range of procedures has been devised for this purpose, and they are being applied to an increasingly broad spectrum of strategic management problems. Here we shall confine our attention to one particular form of cognitive mapping technique, causal mapping, as an aid to strategic decision-making, focusing again on framing bias.

The purpose of causal-mapping techniques is to capture the ways in which individuals and groups understand patterns of influence, causality, and system dynamics. These patterns can be represented most conveniently in diagrammatic form, hence the term 'causal mapping', but more complex maps are often best depicted in mathematical form, using matrix algebra. By way of illustration, consider the cause map shown in Figure 9.2. This diagram represents the beliefs of one of the participants in a recent study investigating the potential of causal mapping for overcoming framing bias in strategic investment decisions. In this study, faced with decision scenarios similar in form to the plant-closure problem outlined earlier, a control group was subject to statistically significant framing effects that did not occur in a comparable group which undertook a causal-mapping exercise before making their decisions. These findings, based on a sample of advanced-level undergraduate business and management students, were replicated in a follow-up study working with middle and senior managers on a 'live' issue in a real business setting.

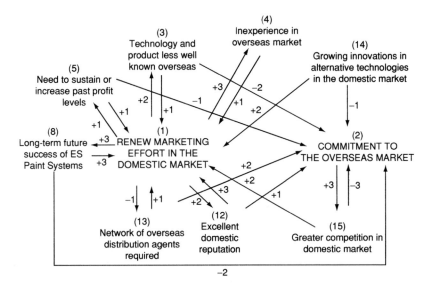

Figure 9.2.   Example of a causal cognitive map elicited from a participant in study 1 of the framing experiments conducted by Hodgkinson and colleagues, 1999

Source: G. P. Hodgkinson and A. J. Maule, 'The Individual in the Strategy Process: Insights from Behavioural Decision Research and Cognitive Mapping', in A. S. Huff and M. Jenkins (eds.), *Mapping Strategic Knowledge* (London: Sage, 2002), 211; reproduced by kind permission of the publisher. © Sage Publications Ltd.

In both studies, participants played the role of board directors making strategic investment choices. They had access to detailed background information on the history of the company and the decision dilemma. As expected, in both studies participants exposed to negatively framed versions of a problem showed a marked preference for riskier alternatives than their positively framed counterparts. Conversely, participants exposed to positively framed versions became more risk averse. Interestingly, however, the participants who drew up a causal map before making their decisions showed no evidence of framing effects. This suggests that causal mapping can usefully help strategists to confront their mental models and strip out biases arising from framing.[12]

In sum, both the frame-analysis worksheet and the causal-mapping process oblige the decision-maker to think and reflect on decision problems at a deeper level than he or she would otherwise do. In so doing, the decision-maker is obliged to confront problems from multiple frames or perspectives, thereby attenuating, if not eliminating, framing bias.

How Can we Improve Group Decision-making?

Using the frame-analysis worksheet and the causal-mapping process, reflective managers have the opportunity to think more profoundly about the way in which they make decisions. But for most complex decisions in organizations, it is groups rather than individuals who are the prime movers. The old adage 'two heads are better than one' suggests that groups are likely be more reflective and better decision-makers, the implication being that in a group idiosyncrasies and biases of individuals are ironed out. Unfortunately, this is often not the case. Consider the NASA case referred to at the beginning of this chapter.

A detailed analysis of the verbal interchanges that occurred at NASA during the ill-fated *Challenger* mission illustrates the powerful effects that dysfunctional group dynamics can exert on decision-making. There is strong evidence to suggest that 'group-think' lay at the heart of the problem. As mentioned earlier, group-think is the tendency of decision-making groups to become overly cohesive to the extent that collective decision-making loses touch with 'reality'. At NASA, although key staff were aware of technical problems with the notorious 'O'-ring seals in the fuel tanks, the launch went ahead. It seems that as the countdown started, senior staff (Level II management) felt increasing pressure to achieve the launch on time. In turn, this brought pressure to bear on the engineers who wanted to delay the flight. While acknowledging the engineers' concerns, the Level III team failed to pass on vital new information to Level II managers to ensure the launch went off as planned. Had this information come to light, the launch might well have been abandoned. In essence, what happened in the *Challenger* case was that constructive 'dissent' was effectively suppressed, with the tragic consequences that were all too visible.[13]

Fortunately, as with individuals, there are a number of tools and techniques that can be used to enhance the quality of group decision-making. While there are no panaceas, we briefly highlight four structured ways of improving decisions made by groups: (*a*) strategies for attaining the optimum team mix, (*b*) Delphi methods, (*c*) group decision support systems, and (*d*) scenario planning.

Team Mix

One obvious way of improving the decision-making capabilities of groups is to make sure that they contain an appropriate mix of cognitive styles, knowledge, experience, and personality characteristics conducive to high-quality debate and functional (as opposed to dysfunctional) interpersonal relationships.

There is some evidence that decision-making teams with a diversity of backgrounds (age, job tenure, education, functional position, and so on) are better placed to make innovative decisions than relatively homogeneous teams, by virtue of the greater variety of cognitive resources they have at their disposal. Assuming it is possible to identify an optimum combination of individuals, this is potentially a very effective strategy for improving decision-making capacity. There are two aspects that need to be considered in this respect: the knowledge and decision-making capabilities of individual team members, and the interpersonal awareness/understanding of basic group dynamics within the team. While it is clear that the best mix of knowledge and thinking styles will vary depending on the nature of the problem and time-scales involved, in our experience having one or two group members who are interpersonally sensitive to the process of the group and the way that it functions can make an enormous difference to decision-making quality.

To achieve a good team mix for decision-making, then, companies need to select individuals for their specialist task knowledge/skills and/or interpersonal savvy, or they need to train and develop them in those qualities, or a combination of both.[14]

Delphi Methods

The second set of approaches, Delphi methods, involves expert panellists predicting future events and their effects by means of an anonymous questionnaire. The results of the inquiry stage are fed back to the same experts in the form of probabilistic data, accompanied by any relevant supplementary information, such as trade press or government reports, allowing them to reconsider their views in the light of the collective information. The aim is to reach group consensus in a way that encourages reflection and learning, while minimizing the possibilities of defensiveness and distortion that can arise from face-to-face interaction, through polarization, group-think, and other potentially dysfunctional group processes.

A major strength of Delphi is the anonymous nature of the information-gathering process. Having individuals make initial judgements in isolation gets round a number of potentially problematic group dynamics, not least the tendency for overly forceful individuals to dominate proceedings. However, although Delphi methods continue to be used for forecasting and aggregating expert opinion more than fifty years after their invention, the research evidence of their effectiveness is equivocal.[15]

In sum, Delphi methods may be appropriate where managers believe that some group members are motivated to manipulate others, or where the wider group dynamics encourage polarization, group-think, or other dysfunctional effects.

Group Decision Support Systems

The third approach comprises a combination of methods, collectively termed Group Decision Support Systems (GDSS), that are used by a facilitator to support negotiation *towards* a decision. In a typical GDSS, between ten and fifteen computer terminals are networked and controlled via a master workstation. Using the master workstation, the facilitator has sole access to the inputs of participants and determines which aspects of the information are displayed to the wider group. The facilitator is thus able to screen out or 'sanitize' the inputs of individual participants, in such a way that information is shared at a deeper level than would typically occur using Delphi methods, while ensuring that potentially dysfunctional group dynamics of the sort discussed above are kept to a minimum. A common feature of many GDSS is the use of visual display techniques for summarizing the various inputs of group members. Increasingly, for example, causal-mapping techniques, such as those described earlier as a basis for improving individual decision-making, form an integral component of GDSS.[16]

Scenario Planning

A fourth approach to improving the quality of group decision-making is scenario planning. A key danger for individuals and groups alike is that they can become too dependent on the mental models that represent their understanding of their organization and its environment. Once formed, these simplified representations of reality become *the* reality for individuals and groups, shaping their day-to-day actions. There is growing evidence that these mental models remain relatively static even in turbulent environments, where their filtering action all too often prevents managers noticing changes in business conditions until they are obvious. Unfortunately, by that time it may be too late to take remedial action—as in the cases of 'strategic drift' discussed in Chapter 2.

Highly participative in nature, scenario-planning methods oblige decision-makers explicitly to consider changes in the world and what they mean for their businesses. Rather than attempting to predict the future, scenario-based methods use speculation and judgement to gain fresh insights and 'bound' future uncertainties.[17] Consider the case of Royal Dutch/Shell, which we highlighted in the introduction to this chapter. According to Pierre Wack, it was through the pioneering work of a number of leading exponents of scenario techniques at Shell that the company was able to weather the financial crisis caused by soaring crude oil prices in 1973. Considered use of scenario-based techniques throughout the previous decade to ponder medium- to long-term developments in economic, social, technological, and political fields enabled the organization to detect the start of the crisis earlier than rivals and quickly roll out contingency plans.[18]

By way of a second illustration, take the case of Knight-Ridder's Philadelphia Newspapers, which in the early 1990s upgraded its printing presses at a cost of $300 million. Soon after making the investment, the company began to realize the potentially devastating impact the Internet could one day have on its business, and managers turned to scenario planning to explore the potential effects. Facilitators began by developing a master list of seventy-four fundamental drivers (social, political, technological, and economic forces) that would probably determine the longer-term shape of the newspaper industry. These key drivers were rated by senior managers in

terms of their relative importance in terms of shaping the future and classified into 'trends' (i.e. forces reckoned to be predictable in direction and
impact within the given time-frame) and 'key uncertainties' (i.e. forces
deemed to be unpredictable). From this material, senior managers developed
a series of scenarios, or stylized portraits depicting a range of plausible futures. They used a 2 × 2 'scenario framework' (traditional versus new business
model on one axis, minor versus major changes in the use of information by
consumers on the other) to generate four major 'scenario blueprints': 'Business as usual ... with a twist'; 'Unbundling of information and advertising';
'Consumers in control'; and 'Cybermedia'. The scenarios were written from
the perspective of a historian in the year 2007. Through these scenarios,
Philadelphia Newspapers picked up valuable early signals of future developments, and when in 1999 Xerox announced a breakthrough in electronic
delivery enabling newspapers to be printed cheaply in remote locations, the
company was able quickly to take the necessary corrective action.[19]

Key Messages and Conclusions

Clear thinking and intelligent decision-making on the basis of systematically acquired and ordered information—cognitive competence—is a prerequisite of exceptional managerial performance in all domains. But, as we
have seen, this is not as straightforward as it sounds. Human rationality is
'bounded', and even the most reflective manager is prone to biases as a
result of incomplete understanding. Heuristics, or rules of thumb, enable
individuals to assimilate rapidly complex information, much of which is
incomplete. But the same heuristics have the corresponding disadvantage
of oversimplification and dangers of poor judgement and choice. We have
also illustrated the potentially powerful dysfunctional effects of framing.
At the group level, the individual problems we have identified can be
greatly compounded through processes such as group-think, which was
at the heart of the *Challenger* disaster.

Fortunately, as we have shown, there are a number of strategies, tools,
and techniques that can greatly improve the quality of individual and
group decision processes. However, it is important to note that the techniques discussed above are highly dependent on context—especially the
degree to which the culture of the organization, together with its wider
external political, legal, economic and social environment, are conducive
to their use. Returning full circle, the importance of context—and the lack
of panaceas—are well illustrated by recent events at NASA. Unfortunately,
the tragic events with which we began this chapter are not the end of the

story. On 1 February 2003 there was a second catastrophic failure when the space shuttle *Columbia* exploded on re-entry into the earth's atmosphere, once again killing the entire crew. As we saw in Chapter 8, organizations do not always manage to overcome their past mistakes. The Columbia Accident Investigation Board (CAIB) concluded after a thorough investigation that, as with the previous *Challenger* disaster, NASA's history and culture had contributed as much to the second tragedy as technical failure.[20] As a result, NASA embarked on an urgent action plan to change the safety climate and culture across the whole agency.[21]

This chapter has demonstrated that managers need help in acquiring and using information to think through alternative options and come to effective individual and group decisions. As observed in Chapter 3, to excel in strategy-making, managers must be able to translate their understanding of the organization's unique resources and competitive position into focused and purposive action, thereby avoiding the danger of falling victim to the unquestioned assumptions and industry norms that all too often misdirect the behaviour of individuals and wider organizations. Rational models may not always be possible or practicable, but where attainable, they offer clear guidance to the reflective manager. Striving for rationality is a vital prerequisite for ensuring the continuous improvement of organizational decision processes and, ultimately, the long-term survival of the company.

Notes

1. Hodgkinson and Sparrow maintain that such competence is crucial to strategic responsiveness and the organization's capacity to learn and renew itself: see G. P. Hodgkinson and P. R. Sparrow, *The Competent Organization: A Psychological Analysis of the Strategic Management Process* (Buckingham: Open University Press, 2002).

2. The way in which Shell developed its decision-making and foresight capabilities has been documented in a series of informative articles and books over many years by a number of former senior staff intimately involved in the process. See e.g. P. Wack, 'Scenarios: Uncharted Waters Ahead', *Harvard Business Review*, 63/5 (1985), 73–90; P. Wack, 'Scenarios: Shooting the Rapids', *Harvard Business Review*, 63/6 (1985), 131–42; K. Van der Heiden, *Scenarios: The Art of Strategic Conversation* (Chichester: Wiley, 1996); P. Schwartz, *The Art of the Long View* (Chichester: Wiley, 1998).

3. In the words of Herbert Simon, managers are characterized by 'bounded rationality', which means that decision-making can only ever partially resemble a rational process, within the limits imposed by the mind. For a fuller explan-

ation of this important concept, see H. A. Simon, *On the Models of Man: Social and Rational* (New York: Wiley, 1957).

4. It does not follow that the use of heuristics invariably results in such biased information processing. Indeed, recent research has identified a particularly powerful form of heuristics, known as 'fast and frugal heuristics', which in a number of cases outperform conventional computer algorithms in judgement and decision-making tasks. For a detailed discussion see G. Gigerenzer, P. M. Todd, and the ABC Group (eds.), *Simple Heuristics that Make us Smart* (New York: Oxford University Press, 1999).

5. A number of researchers and theorists have discussed such dual approaches to information processing. See e.g. M. R. Louis and R. I. Sutton, 'Switching Cognitive Gears: From Habits of Mind to Active Thinking', *Human Relations*, 44 (1991), 55–76; G. P. Hodgkinson and Sparrow, *The Competent Organization: A Psychological Analysis of the Strategic Management Process* (Buckingham: Open University Press 2002).

6. These definitions of analysis and intuition are taken from C. W. Allinson and J. Hayes, 'The Cognitive Style Index: A Measure of Intuition-Analysis for Organizational Research', *Journal of Management Studies*, 33 (1996), 119–35, p. 122. The question of whether analysis and intuition are bi-polar opposites along a single continuum of styles or alternative strategies that can be deployed at will has been debated by a number of authors. See e.g. S. Epstein, R. Pacinini, V. Denes-Raj, and H. Heir, 'Individual Differences in Intuitive-Experiential and Analytical-Rational Thinking Styles', *Journal of Personality and Social Psychology*, 71 (1996), 390–405; G. P. Hodgkinson and E. Sadler-Smith, 'Complex or Unitary? A Critique and Empirical Reassessment of the Allinson-Hayes Cognitive Style Index', *Journal of Occupational and Organizational Psychology*, 76 (2003), 243–68; J. Hayes, C. W. Allinson, R. S. Hudson, and K. Keasey, 'Further Reflections on the Nature of Intuition-Analysis and the Construct Validity of the Cognitive Style Index', *Journal of Occupational and Organizational Psychology*, 76 (2003), 269–78; G. P. Hodgkinson and E. Sadler-Smith, 'Reflections on Reflections ... On the Nature of Intuition, Analysis and the Construct Validity of the Cognitive Style Index', *Journal of Occupational and Organizational Psychology*, 76 (2003), 279–81. For a broader discussion of cognitive style and related concepts, see G. P. Hodgkinson and P. R. Sparrow, *The Competent Organization: A Psychological Analysis of the Strategic Management Process* (Buckingham: Open University Press, 2002); S. Streufert and G. Y. Nogami, 'Cognitive Style and Cognitive Complexity: Implications for I/O Psychology', in C. L. Cooper and I. T. Robertson (eds.), *International Review of Industrial and Organizational Psychology* (Chichester: Wiley, 1989).

7. For further discussion of the nature and role of heuristics and biases over the entire decision-making cycle in the context of organizational decision-making, see C. Schwenk, 'Cognitive Simplification Processes in Strategic Decision Making', *Strategic Management Journal*, 5 (1984), 111–28; T. K. Das and B. S. Teng, 'Cognitive Biases and Strategic Decision Processes', *Journal of Management Studies*, 36 (1999), 757–78. For a more detailed discussion of the illusion of control and

related concepts, see E. J. Langer, 'The Illusion of Control', *Journal of Personality and Social Psychology*, 32 (1975), 311–38; B. Fischhoff, 'Hindsight and Foresight: The Effect of Outcome Knowledge on Judgment under Uncertainty', *Journal of Experimental Psychology: Human Perception and Performance*, 1 (1975), 288–99.

8. Group polarization effects and group-think are discussed extensively in P. R. Kleindorfer, H. C. Kunreuther, and P. J. H. Schoemaker, *Decision Sciences: An Integrative Perspective* (Cambridge: Cambridge University Press, 1993). Irving Janis coined the term 'group-think', a concept which has now become commonplace in everyday management parlance (see e.g. I. L. Janis, *Victims of Groupthink: A Psychological Study of Foreign Policy Decisions and Fiascos* (Boston: Houghton Mifflin, 1972)). A more recent review of group-think research is provided by W. W. Park, 'A Review of Research on Groupthink', *Journal of Behavioral Decision Making*, 3 (1990), 229–45.

9. 'The escalation of commitment' phenomenon was developed and has been discussed extensively by B. M. Staw, 'The Escalation of Commitment to a Course of Action', *Academy of Management Review*, 6 (1981), 577–87. For a review of wider research findings on escalation, see B. M. Staw, 'The Escalation of Commitment: An Update and Appraisal', in Z. Shapira (ed.), *Organizational Decision Making* (Cambridge: Cambridge University Press, 1997).

10. Our understanding of 'framing bias' is due largely to the pioneering work of Kahneman and Tversky. See e.g. D. Kahneman and A. Tversky, 'Choices, Values and Frames', *American Psychologist*, 39 (1984), 341–50; A. Tversky and D. Kahneman, 'The Framing of Decisions and the Psychology of Choice', *Science and Public Policy*, 211 (1981), 453–8. For a fuller explanation in the context of managerial and organizational decision-making, see M. H. Bazerman, 'The Relevance of Kahneman and Tversky's Concept of Framing to Organizational Behavior', *Journal of Management*, 10 (1984), 333–43; P. Goodwin and G. Wright, *Decision Analysis for Management Judgment* (Chichester: John Wiley, 1998).

11. For further details of the development and application of the frame-analysis worksheet, see J. E. Russo and P. J. H. Schoemaker, *Decision Traps* (New York: Doubleday, 1989). Despite the technique's popular appeal, it is important to note that the frame-analysis worksheet, like a number of decision-aiding techniques, has not been systematically evaluated through rigorous research. In the words of Goodwin and Wright: 'Overall, skilful use of Russo and Schoemaker's frame analysis worksheet *may* prompt "multiple frame awareness" which can be used to challenge whether the decision maker's current or usual frame is, in fact, the most appropriate. However, evaluations of the worksheet's effectiveness have not yet been conducted. It is perhaps too early to say whether it can truly promote creative decision making and overcome mechanization and inertia in decision making' (Goodwin and Wright, *Decision Analysis for Management Judgement*, 351).

12. For further details of these studies and subsequent debate see G. P. Hodgkinson, N. J. Bown, A. J. Maule, K. W. Glaister, and A. D. Pearman, 'Breaking the Frame: An Analysis of Strategic Cognition and Decision Making under Uncertainty', *Strategic Management Journal*, 20 (1999), 977–85; G. P. Hodgkinson and A. J.

Maule, 'The Individual in the Strategy Process: Insights from Behavioural Decision Research and Cognitive Mapping', in A. S. Huff and M. Jenkins (eds.), *Mapping Strategic Knowledge* (London: Sage, 2002), 196–219; G. Wright and P. Goodwin, 'Eliminating a Framing Bias by Using Simple Instructions to "Think Harder" and Respondents with Managerial Experience: Comment on "Breaking the Frame" ', *Strategic Management Journal*, 23 (2002), 1059–67; G. P. Hodgkinson, A. J. Maule, N. J. Bown, A. D. Pearman, and K. W. Glaister, 'Further Reflections on the Elimination of Framing Bias in Strategic Decision Making', *Strategic Management Journal*, 23 (2002), 1069–76;

13. For further details, see J. K. Esser and J. S. Lindoerfer, 'Groupthink and the Space Shuttle Challenger Accident: Towards a Quantitative Case Analysis', *Journal of Behavioral Decision Making*, 2 (1989), 167–77.

14. Unfortunately, research in this area is by no means clear-cut. On one hand, more homogeneous groups will have a better understanding of each other and are therefore likely to reach quicker decisions. While this is likely to be beneficial over the short term, on the other hand, there is evidence to suggest that where performance criteria are more long-term in nature, teams which are heterogeneous are likely to perform better. Ultimately, it is likely that what constitutes the optimum mix of the team will vary in accordance with the nature of the problem to be addressed and the team's history. Clearly, in situations where complex issues are being considered, a greater diversity of task knowledge and skills can only enrich understanding. In situations involving relatively simple problems, on the other hand, such diversity is likely to hamper decision-making effectiveness, bringing unnecessary detail to bear on the analysis of the problem. Teams which have been together for extended time periods are likely to benefit from the introduction of new members with contrasting backgrounds, whereas younger teams are likely to gel more quickly if composed of individuals from similar backgrounds. Background similarity, however, poses significant dangers of its own. For instance, one of the dangers confronting teams made up of individuals with highly similar education and training and/or functional backgrounds is that they are likely to develop myopic thinking, leading in turn to a lack of awareness of significant factors that ought to be taken into account in making important decisions. A detailed consideration of the many studies investigating the link between background characteristics and the effectiveness of top management teams is clearly beyond the scope of this chapter. For detailed reviews see S. Finkelstein and D. C. Hambrick, *Strategic Leadership: Top Executives and their Effects on Organizations* (St Paul, MN: West Publishing, 1996); G. P. Hodgkinson and P. Sparrow, *The Competent Organization*.

15. Delphi methods were first introduced in the 1950s at the Rand Corporation. According to Kleindorfer and colleagues, controlled experiments have shown that, applied appropriately, these techniques can lead to significant improvements in judgement and decision-making (see Kleindorfer, Kunreuther, and Schoemaker, *Decision Sciences*, n. 8). However, Goodwin and Wright argue that experimental tests have shown mixed results in respect of the improvement of judgemental accuracy. They maintain that while Delphi techniques improve

performance over simple averaging processes, they rarely outperform the best member of the group (P. Goodwin and G. Wright *Decision Analysis for Management Judgement* (Chichester: John Wiley, 1998)).

16. A number of useful illustrations of cause mapping combined with wider GDSS approaches have been documented and evaluated. See e.g. C. Eden, 'On Evaluating the Performance of "Wide-band" GDSS's', *European Journal of Operational Research*, 81 (1995), 302–11; I. Clarke, W. Mackaness, B. Ball, and M. Horita, 'The Devil's in the Detail: Visualising Analogical Thought in Retail Location Decision-Making', *Environment & Planning B: Planning & Design*, 30 (2003), 15–36.

17. For an overview of scenario-planning techniques more generally, see K. Van der Heijden, *Scenarios: The Art of Strategic Conversation* (Chichester: Wiley, 1996); K. Van der Heijden, R. Bradfield, G. Burt, G. Cairns, and G. Wright, *The Sixth Sense: Accelerating Organizational Learning with Scenarios* (Chichester: Wiley, 2002). A recent survey of UK managers revealed scenario planning to be one of the top three most popular approaches in use in strategy workshops or away days (see G. P. Hodgkinson, G. Johnson, R. Whittington, and M. Schwarz, *The Role and Importance of Strategy Workshops: Findings of a UK Survey* (London: Advanced Institute of Management Research and Chartered Management Institute, 2005)). However, as with many of the other techniques that purport to improve group and individual decision-making discussed in this chapter, scenario-based techniques have received only limited rigorous research attention in terms of their evaluation. See e.g. P. J. H. Schoemaker, 'Multiple Scenario Development: Its Conceptual and Behavioral Foundation', *Strategic Management Journal*, 14 (1993), 193–213; G. P. Hodgkinson and G. Wright, 'Confronting Strategic Inertia in a Top Management Team: Learning from Failure', *Organization Studies*, 23 (2002), 949–77; G. P. Hodgkinson, *Toward a (Pragmatic) Science of Strategic Intervention: The Case of Scenario Planning*, AIM Working Paper Series, WP No. 012-September-2004, ESRC/EPSRC (UK) Advanced Institute of Management Research (AIM), London Business School (available online at: http://www.aimresearch.org/012wp.html).

18. For further details of this case see Wack, 'Scenarios: Uncharted Waters Ahead', and 'Scenarios: Shooting the Rapids' (n. 2).

19. For further details of this case see P. J. H. Schoemaker and V. M. Mavaddat, 'Scenario Planning for disruptive technologies', in G. S. Day, P. J. H. Schoemaker, and R. E. Gunther (eds.), *Wharton on Managing Emerging Technologies* (New York: Wiley, 2000).

20. See *Assessment and Plan for Organizational Change at NASA* (2004; available online at: http://www.nasa.gov/pdf/57382main_culture_web.pdf).

21. The *Columbia* disaster has been extensively analysed from a range of perspectives in W. H. Starbuck and M. Farjorn (eds.), *Organization at the Limit: Lessons from the* Columbia *Disaster* (Malden, MA: Blackwell 2005).

10

Cooperating across Boundaries

COMPANIES are becoming increasingly joined-up places. There may have been a time when high-performing individuals, or even high-performing teams, could make a real and lasting difference on their own. Now, much of the value creation in companies takes place as a consequence of the relationships between people, often people in different functions, businesses, geographies, and countries. The impact is felt in many different ways. The value from mergers and acquisitions is rarely realized unless groups and individuals in both companies are able to work closely with each other. The increasingly sophisticated needs of consumers cannot be met unless employees from sales and marketing, research, and production are able to pool their joint ideas and resources to come up with innovative products and services. The needs of global supply chains and global buyers are fulfilled only if a company can join up its product or service offering by integrating employees from across the globe.

As Chapter 5 shows, innovations, particularly those that are discontinuous, involve multi-functional teams working together to bring new insights into products and service. Yet managing across boundaries is by no means unique to those trying to handle radical innovation. Chapter 7 demonstrates that productivity improvements and the sharing of promising practice take place across the boundaries of business units and the company. Increasingly, innovation, the sharing of leading practices, and productivity improvements are the result of what people do and communicate across boundaries, whether between teams, functions, businesses, or indeed between the company and its customers and partners.[1]

At the same time, the extent and typography of these boundaries are becoming ever more complex. Team memberships morph and reconfigure as talent rapidly moves around the company; functions are renamed, realigned, and reconstituted; and business units change their name and their shape with alarming regularity. Value is now created as much outside a company as within, as suppliers, partners, and outsourcers all become part of an ever more complex value chain.[2] Managers always had to manage across boundaries, but now the borderlines are porous rather than impervious, and fluid and dynamic rather than static.

How does the exceptional manager cope with what GE's previous CEO Jack Welch termed 'boundarylessness'? As part of an ongoing study, we framed this question to the executives in a number of high-performing firms where managing across boundaries was a central part of their success, and where those boundaries were becoming increasingly complex. What were the issues they faced, and how they had gone about solving them?[3] Here we focus on four companies:

- BP, the oil super-major. Among comparable firms, BP has the lowest unit costs and the highest return on capital employed, and in 2003 delivered after-tax profits of over $1 billion a month on annual revenues of $130 billion. The challenge for BP CEO Lord John Browne and his executive team is to manage across the boundaries of 120 independent, autonomous business units scattered across the globe.

- Nokia, the mobile phone and network equipment company, which in 2004 had a 28 per cent share of the mobile-phone business and a market value that had increased sevenfold in five years. At Nokia, CEO Jorma Ollila and his senior executives have the task of managing across the boundaries of an organization currently based on global IT and service platforms and a modular organizational structure which is constantly being re-formed and reconfigured.

- OgilvyOne, the world's largest direct-marketing agency, part of WPP. To deliver global service to its multinational customers, the executive team led by CEO Reimer Theddens must develop skills and configure processes across a physically fragmented, talent-rich organization.

- The Royal Bank of Scotland (RBS), the fifth largest retail bank in the world by market capitalization. In managing the steady ascent of RBS in both size and efficiency, the boundaries CEO Fred Goodwin and his team have mastered are the cultural and organizational ones that separated the original RBS and new acquisitions such as NatWest.

The Journey of Corporate Renewal

As reflective practitioners, the executives we interviewed described the kinds of dilemma that they continually run up against. One of the most important was managing the tension between the autonomy of separate business units, partners, or functions, and the need to combine resources across boundaries.[4] As executive teams, they were well aware that, given too much autonomy, functions, business units, or partners drift away from each other, limiting the value that can be created through knowledge sharing. At the same time, they realized that too much integration and control was also counterproductive, the dead hand of bureaucracy stifling entrepreneurship and the sharing of ideas and insights alike.

Yet these executives were aware that managing these two tensions, shown as the two axes of performance quality in Figure 10.1, was by no means straightforward. Consider the journey their companies had made over the previous decade. For most of them, it was a journey of corporate renewal. In this journey, the initial goal was to build performance in the operating businesses or functions. In the mid-1990s, for example, Browne and the executive team of BP found themselves in the bottom left-hand corner of the performance quadrant. BP had neither high-performing business units, nor integration and synergy between them. In previous decades, like many companies, BP had grown rapidly, adding businesses to meet specific market needs. By the 1980s it contained a rag-bag of businesses, of which some were performing well, but many others were not. Moreover, because they had grown as separate units, the businesses had little holding them together. Integration across the group was weak.

During the 1990s BP's strategy was to clean up and rationalize its portfolio, moving business units from the lower-left to the lower-right-hand side of the model. Where units failed to improve, the company either closed them or sold them on. The focus on performance enabled each business to identify and unleash its entrepreneurial talent as it was liberated from centralized bureaucracy and control. By the 1990s the focus of executive attention had changed. As Browne put it:

> The organization that we evolved from 1995 onwards was founded on several simple concepts. [Premise] number one was our observation that people worked better in small units, because the closer you can identify people with objectives and targets, the better things happen. So we started off with what we came to call the 'atomistic structure', so that the big, longer-term targets of the company could be divided and deployed into smaller units that could take full ownership of these targets.

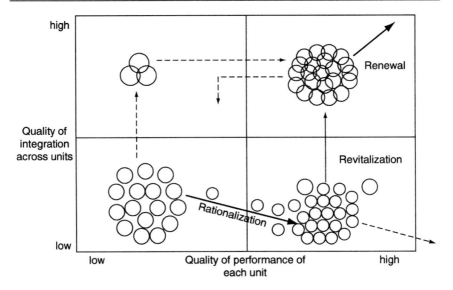

Figure 10.1. The journey of corporate renewal

As a group, BP was moving from bottom-left to bottom-right quadrant of the model in its journey of revitalization. It had gone from the point of bankruptcy to world class by focusing firmly on smashing the monolith and creating a strong performance culture in the business units. But the very process of creating autonomy and freedom had generated tensions of its own. Browne's adviser Nick Butler noted:

> BP was a collection of fiefdoms. These fiefdoms were extremely separate: they lived in separate buildings, had separate management systems and different philosophies. The fiefdoms did not mix, and the people barely came together at the top.

Executives at other companies were reflecting on similar issues. Butler's words were echoed by OgilvyOne CEO Reimer Theddens:

> Historically, Ogilvy had been a fragmented organization of talented people. Before 1997, having entrepreneurial units was better—it was absolutely right in those days. It allowed us to bring different people with different skills to grow the company. But over time, what had begun as a means to enable the different divisions in the company to grow and develop, turned into factions that would not work together to benefit the whole, but engaged in backbiting and individualism.

The Drivers of Integration

By the first years of the new century, the challenge for the executive teams at BP and OgilvyOne was no longer boosting the performance of the autonomous operating units, pushing accountability down to individual managers, and promoting entrepreneurship. The new challenge was to integrate the diverse units—to begin to manage across boundaries.[5] As Browne put it:

> [BP's] second premise was contradictory to the first, and this was our observation that any organization of scale could create proprietary knowledge through learning...So the question was now could you get independent atomistic units to work together to share information, to learn, and to retain learning.

Among Browne and his colleagues, the conviction was growing that creating a learning organization was about people working across boundaries. The lack of integration between business units and functions was becoming an increasingly obvious handicap in a joined-up world. At OgilvyOne, the message was forcibly brought home to Theddens in 1996 by a Henley Forecasting Centre report on the company's clients. It included remarks such as, 'the creative guy was brilliant, but did not seem to integrate with the rest'. Customers wanted a 'single face' wherever they bought the company's services, yet they increasingly saw OgilvyOne as fragmented and poorly set up to deliver global capability. The challenge was encapsulated by a major project from American Express: to roll out the American Express Blue credit card worldwide across multiple media in six months. How could the company make such a project work across its dispersed geographies and structures? For Theddens and his team, this was a problem that entailed hard creative thinking.

For OgilvyOne, the principal driver of integration was the service demands of global customers. In other companies, the momentum came from within. Take Nokia, where the executive team had come to the conclusion that central to the company's innovative capacity—on which it depended to keep ahead of the pack—would be its ability to support cooperative working within and across development teams.

Backtracking a little, after overcoming the crises of 1988 and 1995, Nokia had forged ahead of Motorola, until then the undisputed leader in mobile phones. By 2000 it had achieved spectacular growth and in 2001 was able to weather the telecoms storm through its well-honed ability to bring a stream of new products to the market. A key element in the company's strategy was to master the nascent 'mobile multimedia' market. In October 2003, for example, it launched N-Gage, 'a gaming device that happens to have a mobile phone in it'. Operational capabilities in areas such as logistics, manufacturing, vendor management, and marketing clearly played a part in Nokia's superior performance. However, managers believed that the core was the company's ability to use the vehicle of new-product development to evolve seamlessly alongside changing technologies and markets. In a world of digital convergence, this pitched Nokia against a wide variety of companies including giants such as Microsoft and Motorola on the one hand and eager new contenders for the application space such as Sony, Canon, and Nintendo on the other. The team concluded that to compete against such rivals required the meeting of minds and ideas from across the whole company, and indeed from its many partners. In other words, integration was key to the speed and accuracy of product development.

Managing cooperatively across company boundaries was also key for RBS. In 1995 RBS acquired NatWest in the largest takeover in British banking history. The management challenge was of corresponding size. The biggest IT integration of its kind ever in the financial sector, it entailed migrating NatWest's 466 IT systems to RBS's much smaller one, at the same time as handling 18 million customer accounts worth £158 billion and their huge attendant transaction volumes without missing a beat. So critical a transition could only take place on the basis of strong and implicit trust between the executives of both companies.

To sum up, in their various ways all our companies faced the need to integrate across organizational boundaries as the next stage of renewal. For BP, it was a question of capitalizing on the group's experience and learning. For OgilvyOne, the drivers of integration were primarily external, as large customers demanded a 'single face' across the globe. For RBS, growing primarily through merger and acquisition, integration of new competencies and talents was at a premium. At Nokia, meanwhile, the imperative for new products and services could only be satisfied by deep sharing of knowledge and insights from across the divisions and businesses of the company, and by teams of people being prepared and able to share their own unique ideas and inspirations. For all of these companies, then, if they were to move on working across boundaries, then cooperation had to become the norm. It was not an option.

The Changing Nature of Integration

At one level, there is nothing new here. The need to manage across boundaries to counterbalance internal divisions is an old chestnut. But today's circumstances create some new possibilities and render some historical ones less important.

The most important new integrator is the Internet.[6] At BP, for example, much of the information shared across the business units is web-based. And use of the web is not limited to young hires. Deputy chairman Rodney Chase, a thirty-year BP veteran, checked the message board daily and was an active user of the intranet. At OgilvyOne the intranet likewise provided the vehicle for rapid integration of the worldwide offices and business streams. The technology may have been new, but the sentiments date back to founder David Ogilvy. 'I prefer the discipline of knowledge to the anarchy of ignorance. We pursue knowledge the way a pig pursues truffles,' wrote David Ogilvy. In this case, 'truffles' was the living product of years of documentation designed to capture the knowledge of the company. All employees have access to the database via the intranet, and sixty knowledge officers across the offices oversee its use and development. At Nokia, the global integrated IT platform enabled business groups to share information moment by moment. And similarly at RBS, the global platforms created a common set of processes and practices. Information-sharing has always been at the heart of managing across boundaries, but now technology allows organizations to respond to the need for integration in ways that would have been unthinkable even five years ago.

Meanwhile, some formerly important integration tools have become less significant: staff relocation and structured career paths, for example. In the past, in companies as diverse as Unilever, Matsushita, and Hewlett-Packard, managers who had worked in different functions, businesses, or geographic locations turned their collective personal networks into the glue that held the company together.[7] Although such networks are a powerful tool for socializing people and building organizational cohesion, they are now less common—in part because lifetime careers and on-demand mobility of employees can no longer be assumed.[8]

Then, the drastic pruning of middle managers that many companies undertook in the 1990s deprived them of an important but unrecognized source of organizational integration. The mid-level managers who once played boundary-spanning and coordination roles are gone.[9]

But perhaps the most important change has been in management philosophy and individual attitudes to authority. In the past, the management of boundaries was primarily managed through vertical processes and roles. The way to encourage different businesses, functions, or geographical units to share resources and coordinate their activities was to bring them under a common boss and a common planning and control system.[10] Managers now see such structures as overly cumbersome and bureaucratic. At the same time, the attitudes of employees towards authority have shifted perceptibly over the last decade.[11] In many hierarchical companies, the wishes of senior managers were read as a symbol of authority and power. Managers did as they were told. Now employees, particularly younger employees, are more questioning of authority and less susceptible to the use of power and coercion in the managerial dynamics. As 'volunteer investors', they are less likely to bow to authority.[12] Their aspirations are to become more self-determining, more autonomous, and more questioning. In building organizational purpose and cohesion, leaders are increasingly finding that the developmental needs of employees are as crucial to success as the operationalization of strategy.

Although managers have always recognized the relevance of mechanisms for horizontal integration, in practice they have seen them as secondary reinforcements to the primary vertical processes. In a significant change, companies are now moving away from the traditional mechanisms of hierarchy and formal systems to manage across borders, relying instead on horizontal processes that overlay integration on sub-unit autonomy and empowerment. The secondary has now become primary.[13]

In each of the companies we studied, the executive team had a clear agenda for integration between units, often based on a set of management tools and processes designed to pull the organization back together again. Explaining the importance of these processes in RBS's integration of NatWest, CEO Goodwin noted:

> We are taking the integration concept and model and making ourselves more efficient . . . We have to prioritize across the group how we are going to cooperatively develop systems and processes that are world-class and efficient and that will have an impact on the bottom line . . . Each business has its initiatives that are either income-generating or cost-reducing.

We believe that these integration systems, practices, and processes are key to managing across boundaries; without them, companies remain fragmented and atomistic. But while *hard bonds* of integration through tools and techniques are crucial, they are underpinned by what we might call *soft bonds*. We heard the concept from OgilvyOne's Theddens, who observed that 'in a more complex market, you need "soft bonds" between people—people who like to work together'.

The Challenge for the Exceptional Manager

For the exceptional manager, we believe that managing across all kinds of boundaries requires the active building of both hard and soft bonds.[14] In the journey of corporate renewal shown in Figure 10.1, many companies now find themselves in the bottom-right quadrant. When we asked executives from these firms how they bridged the boundaries, we found both hard and soft bonds of integration. Perhaps surprisingly, they believed that the softer bonds had most impact on their capacity to manage across boundaries. In managing these soft bonds, they believed three elements to be crucial:

- First, they championed the practices and processes that supported networks of cooperative relationships between different groups of people both within and outside the company. They had an understanding of what was needed to maintain the knowledge within the firm, and also what was needed to create innovation. While their role in supporting these norms of cooperation was complex, they believed their personal behaviour with their peers and their attitudes to co-operation made a significant difference.
- Next, they believed that the reflective conversations that took place across the boundaries were crucial. They described how in their own behaviours they acted as role models for making possible creative dialogues and conversations.
- Finally, they understood that their personal attitudes to others, their 'theory of the firm', profoundly influenced the way they crafted the practices and processes of the firm. They understood that a culture of cooperation required a mindset of cooperation.

Supporting a Network of Cooperative Relationships

We found that in these companies the complex structure of hierarchical and formalized roles was supplemented by a vast network of friendships and social ties that criss-crossed the organization.[15] Executives believed that these cooperative relationships were crucial to the way in which boundaries were bridged and knowledge shared.

They described a time when these cooperative relationships between people from different functions or businesses would have grown over decades through job rotation, shared development, and training experiences. While some of these processes still had a role to play, executives in our companies had augmented them with a new set of practices and processes that accelerated social integration and supported the building of these complex networks of relationships.

They also understood that the benefits of networks of cooperative relationships come from balancing strong friendships (or what have been termed strong network ties) with weaker ties based on looser acquaintance. Strong ties typically occur between people who spend time with each other, sharing their views and developing reciprocal understanding. In such relationships, knowledge which is difficult to describe or to teach another person (i.e. tacit knowledge), is developed and exchanged. The network ties that occur between people in different parts of the company, or with those outside the company, are typically weak ties, since they are likely to meet less often and know each other less well. However, these multiple, weak network ties that criss-cross a company can bring real benefits. It is often these relationships across boundaries that shape fresh insights and perspectives, and that lead to the creation of new ideas and ultimately innovative products and services. Much individual and organizational learning occurs through the vehicle of these weak company-spanning ties.[16]

It was no surprise to find that these companies had many practices and processes for supporting cooperation in common. So, for example, the development of cooperative relationships through the use of executive training programmes or team building was relatively common. However, beyond these general 'leading-practice' processes, there were also what we termed 'signature processes' to denote the unique way in which the senior executives supported cooperative working.[17]

At Nokia, for example, the complex networks of both strong and weak ties within groups and between groups of people were crucial to the regular updating of the Nokia portfolio. We saw how the Nokia team was adept at supporting strong network ties both within and across team boundaries. Within the modular product teams, for example, the software developers had built strong ties over years of close collaboration. They socialized frequently, knew each other well, and were able to develop and share a high degree of complex tacit knowledge. The senior executives at Nokia were at great pains to keep the teams intact even through the company's frequent reorganizations. Mikko Kosonen, who heads strategy, described it thus:

> One of the distinctive characteristics of Nokia is the organizational architecture. It is *avant garde*. It fits with the turbulence and an opportunity-rich environ-

ment. Reconfigurable, modular, reusable capabilities . . . reusability depends on standardization, working with existing repositories.

Creating both strong and weak relationship ties across Nokia's internal boundaries was also deemed crucial. The organizational architecture that Kosonen referred to, as well as a whole portfolio of practices and processes, made this possible. Through these structures, practices, and processes, employees had an opportunity to bring their ideas and insights to other groups within the company. For Nokia this ensured that knowledge flowed across the company, a concept which managers believed was essential in the company's complex, ever-changing environment.

Faced with the need to build both strong relationship ties capable of retaining deep tacit knowledge and weak relationship ties to bring insight, the executive team had developed a unique structural architecture that they constantly reconfigured to align the competencies of the company with the changes in the environment. These structural reconfigurations were typically carried out at speed. For example, in 2003 Nokia Mobile was restructured from two business units to nine, with two horizontal processes, in a matter of months. This near-instant reorganization was possible because it involved moving modular teams of people with shared competencies bodily from one part of the business to another. Teams could be as small as six people, or as large as hundreds, and the reconfigurations typically took place around nodal points at which the technologies become entangled. As Mikko went on to say, 'We use reorganizations as a means to shuffle the pack. People learn new jobs, they are stretched. The modularity ensures that the relationships stay—it is the job change that breaks the old way of working.'

At BP a 'signature process' was the concept of 'peer assist' and 'peer challenge'. As described earlier, in the journey of corporate renewal, BP had broken itself up into 150 autonomous business units. The resulting focus on performance had enabled business units to identify and unleash their entrepreneurial talent. On the other hand, on the path to integration the challenge for CEO Browne was 'how could you get independent atomistic units to work together to share information, to learn and to retain learning'. The answer in part came from a highly innovative organizational structure termed 'peer groups'. These consisted of clusters of up to thirteen business units from across the globe, grouped together roughly by market, whose business heads were tasked to develop not only their own capability and performance, but also those of the other business units within the group.

'Peer assist' had been developed to encourage groups of managers from similar businesses to drive learning and share knowledge across the company. Subsequently, 'peer challenge' broadened the approach to embrace the traditional vertical performance-management and resource-allocation processes.[18]

In the past, BP business-unit managers agreed an annual performance contract with top management which it was then up to them to meet however they liked. 'Peer challenge' added the condition that before finalizing the contract with Browne and his colleagues, managers must have their plans approved by their peers, too. 'The peers must be satisfied that you are carrying your fair share of the heavy water buckets,' said deputy chief executive Chase. 'The old issue of sandbagging management is gone. The challenge now comes from peers, not from management.'

Polly Flinn, a senior manager, put it this way: 'peer challenge is about convincing people in similar positions to support your investment proposal knowing that they could invest the same capital elsewhere, and going eyeball to eyeball with them, and then having to reaffirm whether you have made it or not over the coming months or quarters'. In an added twist, BP has extended the peer process even further. The three top-performing business units in a peer group have been made responsible for improving the performance of the bottom three. 'We had "not invented here" raised to an art form', said Chase. With 'peer assist' and 'peer challenge', on the other hand, 'What we have raised to an art form is that if you have a good idea, my first responsibility is to share it with my peers, and if I am performing poorly, I will get the peer group to help me.'

The executives in these four firms understand that cooperative relationships are the soft bonds that hold their fragmented companies together. These relationship ties will form naturally, developing on the basis of proximity ('whom I sit next to') and similarity ('who is like me'). But while natural ties are important, there is a danger that they simply reinforce the old silos and divisions of the company. In our integrated companies, we saw that executives were heedful about considering the practices and processes that build, shape, and protect the network of relationships that can potentially form a bridge between functions, businesses, and geographies. In doing so, they made three crucial contributions.

- They understood the importance of good, positive cooperative relationships across an integrated company. They took great pains to ensure that they were personally seen to create and maintain relationships with people throughout the firm. By doing so, they set the expectation that networks of relationships were key to success.

- They were conscious of the need to build strong cooperative relationships both within teams and across businesses and functions. As a consequence, they worked hard to develop and support practices and processes that created the context for people to meet. In a sense, they 'engineered' proximity.
- They were aware of the many barriers to cooperative working—typically the promotion system, remuneration and bonus processes, and job structure—and worked hard to ensure they were eliminated and replaced by processes and practices that encouraged cooperative networks of relationships.

Supporting with Reflective Conversations

Networks of relationships across invisible organizational boundaries play a crucial role in creating the soft bonds of integration. But while the spread of these networks is the structure of integration, they are simply conduits; avenues through which ideas and knowledge, insights, and theories flow. The speed and extent of new-product development at Nokia, for example, did indeed depend on the extent to which people with different mindsets and knowledge were able to meet each other in structures and processes such as the modular architecture. But meeting was not sufficient at Nokia. The extensive product portfolio was the result of the *content* of these relationships: in other words, what was actually said, how it was heard, and the commitments that were made as a result of these conversations.

Pursuing the goal of 'knowledge management', as we noted in Chapter 7, many companies have installed IT-based systems that are essentially databases for sharing information across the organization. However, our executives acknowledged that these systems were only the first step in establishing a truly shared repository of company knowledge. They described how the heart of working cooperatively across the company was not simply the result of an IT system or knowledge-management technology. Rather it was the result of reflective, purposeful conversations. It is through these reflective, purposeful conversations that companies develop new ideas, share knowledge and experiences, and enhance individual and collective learning.[19]

In all four companies, managers participated in rich, reflective conversations that were characterized by both analytical rationality and emotional authenticity. At OgilvyOne managers believed that the deep conversations between Theddens and the executive team about the company's future were crucial to success. At BP people like Polly Flinn shared many thoughtful conversations with peers on how to meet their daily challenges. At RBS Goodwin used his daily morning meetings with his executive team to create a flow of reflective conversation which is credited with creating much of the energy that went into the integration of the NatWest acquisition.

It is our observation that conversations in many companies are dehydrated and ritualized, having neither analytical rigour nor emotional authenticity. Essentially 'set pieces' in which participants go through the motions, they take place within a framework of tightly defined agendas that constrain the opportunities for exploration or discovery. Some of these conversations are a proxy for downward hierarchical communication, often of information of which the junior is already aware.

Reflective executives believe that purposeful conversations are crucial to cooperative working across the boundaries of a company. Those in our companies used a portfolio of conversational styles (see Figure 10.2). On some occasions they focused on *disciplined debate*. With its roots in Socratic thought, these disciplined conversations are essentially hypothesis-testing. Conversants ask questions like: 'What are the assumptions behind this proposal?'; 'What data or evidence do we need to prove these

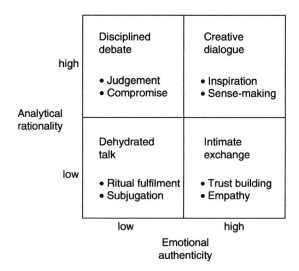

Figure 10.2. A typology of conversations

assumptions to be false?'; 'What do we believe to be true that is actually untrue?'

This was the kind of disciplined conversation we heard at BP. Chase commented: 'We are a deeply questioning team. We constantly inspect what we do in order to find out if in fact it is the exercise of laziness or prejudice.' The focus on intellectual rigour is a reflection of Browne's deeply held convictions. 'Unless you can lay out rational arguments as the foundation of what you do, nothing much happens', is his constant refrain. We found the same focus on disciplined debate at RBS. This is how Goodwin described the morning meetings, the locus for many critical conversations:

> My direct reports and I meet at 9.30 every day for about one hour...the presumption is that anything that has happened the day before or something is happening in your diary for the coming day, you will share it with your colleagues...Generally you are not allowed to take papers to the morning meeting, so you have to know what you are talking about.

Disciplined debate is crucial to the 'soft bonds' that hold companies together. But to be effective, it needs to have both a 'Socrates' to pose the questions, and information to underpin it. At BP Browne embodies the belief in rigour and rationality: 'Rigour implies that you understand the assumptions you have made—assumptions about the state of the world, of what you can do, and how your competitors will interact with it.' The second requirement for disciplined debate is relevant conversation. 'There is no point in just changing a process,' explained David Watson, a group vice president at BP. 'It has to start with changing the fabric—the information. If it is the same information, we will get the same conversations. So we have to provide different information for different conversations.'

Executives in these high-performing companies believe that rationality and analytical rigour are crucial. But they also understand that the soft bonds that bridge boundaries with empathy, mutual understanding, and trust need something else. *Intimate exchanges* are the foundation for building such deep, trusting relationships. This is particularly crucial when the relationship is being built across the company boundaries. At OgilvyOne, for example, we heard two people carrying on a series of deepening exchanges over five weeks before deciding to merge their companies. Over this period Nigel Howlett, chairman of the London office, met Tim Carrigan to discuss the acquisition of Tim's company, NoHo Digital. Howlett and Carrigan met for at least a half-day a week to talk — about their families and children, their personal hopes for the future, their fears and apprehensions, the way they liked to work, and their philosophy of leadership. Amazingly absent from these conversation was any mention of commercial issues. Those were dealt with separately, through the more rational and disciplined conversations between the finance professionals of both companies. What Howlett and Carrigan had was deep, intimate conversation about themselves and their relationship. Howlett reflected: 'We invested a lot of time before we even signed the letter of intent.' Only after the management teams were on board did the two of them proceed to the full-scale acquisition.

As senior executives of the two companies, their conversational role-modelling had a profound effect on *creative dialogue*. Increasingly, employees of the two groups began to meet informally. NoHo employees were rapidly integrated into OgilvyOne's Friday morning breakfast meeting in the London office, where up to ninety people met to talk about topics of mutual interest. As OgilvyOne creative director Rory Sutherland commented: 'The most important role of the manager at OgilvyOne is to create friendships.' As a consequence, once the acquisition of NoHo had been given the go-ahead, the integration of skills and competencies was rapid and successful, and by October 1999 *Adweek* described the company as 'one of the premier models of how a traditional ad agency can operate successfully in the non-traditional world of cyberspace'.

One of the essential features of vertical, bureaucratic role-based relationships is depersonalization. When horizontal boundary-bridging relationships become the norm, the first requirement is to repersonalize the workplace: to recognize that employees are real people, that they have feelings and emotions that affect their work, and to legitimize the role of these feelings and emotions in the day-to-day functioning of the company. Beyond legitimizing emotions, it is also necessary to create space and time for conversation to occur. To give expression to this need, the OgilvyOne off-site meetings are typically held in the chateau that belonged to David Ogilvy in France. More than the beauty of the place, the location personalizes Ogilvy's larger-than-life figure—his creative passion, his legendary curiosity, his capacity for friendship and love, his personal generosity—and it generates a very different level of authenticity in conversations than is possible in the company's boardroom. Over time, these conversations have matured into intense, often very personal creative dialogues between Theddens and the members of the executive board about the purpose of the company, the nature of creativity, and the meaning of brands.

In creating a context for good conversation, these exceptional managers described what they believed to be crucial:

- They consistently made time to have conversations with those around them. In some cases they played the 'Socrates' role of questioning and analysing. This was the style adopted by Goodwin at RBS. Others took a more emotional, involving tone, like Howlett at OgilvyOne. Their conversational style reflected their own personal style. Yet while their styles were different, each was fundamentally committed to the importance of reflective conversation and creative dialogue.
- They gave time and attention to these conversations. The notion of the 'busy manager' endlessly involved in activity is anathema to real conversation (a topic we return to in Chapter 11). They were prepared, like OgilvyOne's Howlett, to set aside time for regular talk that carried on from one occasion to the next.
- In these conversations, we found that exceptional managers were prepared and able to be authentic, to 'be themselves'. Their authenticity was crucial to the depth and richness of the conversation, particularly to intimate exchanges. But it also served a role in creating the foundation of trust and respect that lubricated the networks of relationships so crucial to managing cooperatively across boundaries.

Values and Assumptions

In our four high-performing companies, the structure of the relationship networks criss-crossing the organization created a vehicle for the soft bonds to form. Rich, deep, thoughtful debates and conversations provided the forum for ideas to be exchanged and assumptions to be tested. But beneath each of these there is one more challenge that the exceptional manager faces in working across boundaries. Network structures are primarily a challenge of process and practices. Conversational protocols are a challenge of time and space. The third challenge is of an altogether different nature and scale. It is a challenge of the mind, of the fundamental assumptions that executives have about the motives and intentions of others.

The network structures may be in place, the conversations happening, but are people actually cooperating with each other across the boundaries of the company? And if so why are they cooperating? We discovered that in the four companies many of the senior executive team members held clear views on the subject. Fundamentally, they believed that people were capable, willing, and able to cooperate.

Such an assumption is important, for it flies in the face of dominant attitudes in many of today's companies—and of much management theory. For most economic institutions, the underlying assumption (often unarticulated) is that people work with each other out of self-interest. In this view, individuals (and therefore employees) seek to maximize their own personal gain, rationally choosing the best means to serve their goals. In extreme form, the assumption is that individuals are not only motivated to satisfy their own desires, they are also essentially indifferent to how their actions affect others. The role of society, the company, or indeed an executive then becomes one of controlling selfish self-interest through the rules of morality or the procedures of justice and fairness.

Our starting assumptions about the intention of others creates a self-fulfilling cycle. In Figure 10.3 the development of this self-fulfilling cycle is illustrated. For example, an executive whose assumption about human behaviour is that people are basically selfish will attempt to check their selfishness through practices and processes designed for surveillance and control. These practices and processes themselves begin to shape the norms of behaviour, and ultimately what becomes legitimized behaviour, and what is delegitimized. In this way selfishness breeds selfishness (just as the converse is true: trust breeds trust). The language and metaphors

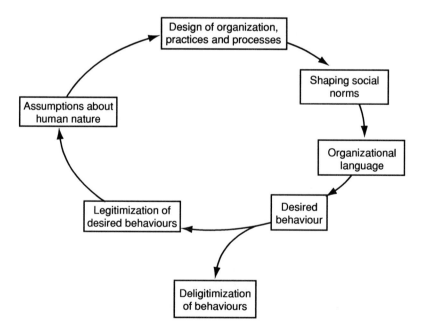

Figure 10.3. The self-fulfilling prophecy

managers use unconsciously serves to reinforce the tendency. For example, many performance-management practices and processes pit
people against each other and discourage cooperation (for more on the
pitfalls of performance management, see Chapter 6). The language of the
battlefield and competition is not the language of cooperation.

The Self-fulfilling Prophecy

In these companies we saw many ways in which cooperative rather than
selfish behaviour was encouraged. Talking with a group of executives at
London Business School, BP's Chase explained it this way:

> In our personal lives—as fathers, mothers, brothers, or sisters—we know how
> much we would like to help someone close to us succeed. Why didn't we believe
> that the same can happen in our business lives? That is the breakthrough, and
> you get there when people take enormous pride in helping their colleagues to
> succeed.

For Chase, the reality was that people could behave cooperatively with
each other. The issue for him was not so much what companies can do to
support cooperation, but rather what they often inadvertently do to kill it.

The challenge for exceptional managers is then how to stop killing
cooperation: how to build the company into an arena for evolutionary,
spontaneous cooperation. To do so they have to have to come head to
head with the cooperation killers—the structural, process, and cultural
impediments. The horizontal processes at Nokia and BP, for example, are
intended to lay a solid foundation for cooperation. When coupled with
rich and reflective conversations, the basis has been laid for a cooperative
mindset based on assumptions of trustworthiness and authenticity.

While this is crucial, we also saw executives playing a fundamental role
in supporting cooperative relationships through their language and behaviour, based on their assumptions about human nature. For example,
they were prepared to bring into conversation the notion of personal
values. They did this both with regard to the company, and in the description of their own beliefs and behaviours.

We heard a striking example at BP. In 1997 Amnesty International ac-
cused BP of funding private armies in Colombia, alleging that these security forces had been responsible for widespread extrajudicial executions,
torture, and disappearances of civilians. At that time the question, 'What
is your personal Colombia?' echoed in the minds of all BP executives.

Memories of the incident affected every decision made subsequently by an executive and shaped a new outlook regarding BP's role as a business. As a business-unit leader explained:

> When we talked to the outside world the oil industry was seen as big and powerful, dirty and secretive and grey—and we did not want that. We didn't want to be an unknown player in a big sector not known for goodness or as a force of goodness.

This was the starting point for a set of values and beliefs which were called 'a force for good'. Four actions underpinned the sentiment: a real focus on safety; environmental care; freedom from discrimination; and investment in the community from which people come. Tangible actions included Browne's speech on climate change at Stanford University and BP's withdrawal from the Global Climate Coalition, a Washington-based lobbying and public relations organization that opposed government intervention on climate change. Being a force for good was about having 'goals that are worth pursuing for everyone; that have to do with making society better as a result of participation than if we had not been there,' as Chase remarked.

The executive team at Nokia also had a strong collective view about their values and assumptions. Over its 140-year history, a set of societal values had deeply embedded themselves within Nokia. As Olli-Pekka Kallasvuo, executive vice president for mobile phones, observed: 'To some extent culture is not created. It happens... In addition the top seven or twelve people follow the Nokia values in practice. They make reference to the values, they talk about them. There is a lot of informal communication.'

'Respect' was seen as particularly central to the leadership values of Nokia. It was apparent in the ways in which partnerships with suppliers were created and sustained. It was also apparent in the day-to-day behaviour of managers. Management encouraged every kind of discussion, but not disrespect or behaviour behind people's back. As J. T. Bergqvist, head of IP mobility, explained: 'If someone says, "I think that X is not performing," we would encourage him or her to talk directly to the person. We encourage respectful peer relationships.' The capability to behave in a respectful manner was a crucial selection criterion for people entering the company. As a consequence, managers spent what seemed a disproportionate amount of time exploring the personal values of candidates during the interview process. As the organization globalized, however, the emphasis on values emerged as a real benefit. Olli-Pekka summed it up:

Despite the 'me-me-me' era, I believe people want to be part of something meaningful, something they can be proud of, where they can contribute... That's why values are so important. Nokia is an emotional journey. People join us because it's a bit special.

In building the cooperative mindset, these exceptional managers were prepared to question their own assumptions and to live by a set of personal values:

- They had a 'point of view' about their personal assumptions of human nature. For those best able to manage across boundaries, these assumptions were based on the belief in the basic goodness of man and the role that cooperative relationships play in the natural order. They understood that people were capable of behaving in a cooperative manner without the transactional element at its core.
- They lived on a daily basis a set of values and virtues that had respect for others at the core. This was apparent in what they said, but more importantly, in how they behaved. They understood that a purpose such as 'increasing profits by 12 per cent' was not compelling for employees. They realized that most people come to work in a positive spirit; concepts such as 'a force for good' provide a frame of values and assumptions in which cooperation and the positive spirit more generally can flourish.

Many executives are faced with the legacy of the 'silo mentality': business units competing with each other, executives failing to trust others, individual employees seeking to maximize their own self-interest. Yet in this complex, ever-changing world, where innovation is key, they are called on to move to the top-right corner of the renewal matrix. In this quadrant, innovation, the sharing of promising practices, and the push for productivity will more and more be the result of the collective rather than individual endeavour. Increasingly, value will be created in the relationships between people.

As we have seen in this study of high-performing companies, many have come from a heritage of fiefdoms and competition between units. And yet the executive team of each firm has had the will and commitment to take positive action to move from a company of baronies to a more cooperative way of working. In this journey, they have understood that the 'hard bonds' of reporting relationships can play a role. But more important are the 'soft bonds' of the many practices and processes that bring people together—'peer assist' at BP that encourages and supports cooperative relationships between people in disparate parts of the company, or the modular architecture of Nokia that keeps important teams intact over long periods of time. Executives in these firms have seen the company less in terms of the 'hard bonds' of power and responsibility, and more in terms of the 'soft bonds' of friendships and relationships. They have also understood that in shaping the practices and processes that support cooperation, bringing promising practices from outside the company can be important. But more important still is their capacity to craft and shape practices and processes based on their own values and assumptions, to support and champion 'signature processes'.

But beyond the crafting of practices and processes, these executives fundamentally believed that cooperative relationships could only flourish in their companies if they themselves behaved cooperatively.

Notes

1. For an overview of how business structures are changing, see e.g. S. L. Brown and K. M. Eisenhardt, *Competing on the Edge: Strategy as Structured Chaos* (Boston: Harvard Business School Press, 1998).

2. This point is made forcibly by C. K. Prahalad and V. Ramaswanny, *The Future of Competition: Co-creating Unique Value with Customers* (Boston: Harvard Business School Press, 2004).

3. These have been written up as a series of case studies by Lynda Gratton and Sumantra Ghoshal: 'Our research method was a two-stage process. First, we sought to acquaint ourselves with the company by collecting an array of secondary sources to create a preliminary picture of the company and the industry. The data were important in establishing both the overall structure of our study and for developing an understanding about the specific areas of business where managing across boundaries appeared to be key. We then interviewed the CEO and most of the members of each company's executive committee. We also interviewed executives in different functions at different levels, including operating-level managers actually involved in day-to-day activities. The interviews lasted a minimum of one hour and a maximum of two-and-a-half hours. Our approach was essentially collaborative and participative. We encouraged the interviewees to take an active part in the research process and to share their insights and understandings with us as reflective practitioners. In effect, the interviews became an open conversation through which the manager's experience and knowledge of the organizational process and practices were combined with our ongoing interpretation and evolving theories. Our working assumption was that executives are willing to respond truthfully, that they are intelligent and smart, and that they are reflective about their own practice and can make judgments about it.'

4. For a rich description and analysis of this tension in the specific context of large, diversified global companies, see C. K. Prahalad and Y. Doz, *The Multinational Mission: Balancing Local Demands and Global Vision* (New York: Free Press, 1987).

5. This sequential process of performance improvement—first building the strength of the units and then building integration mechanisms across them—was described in S. Ghoshal and C. A. Bartlett, 'Rebuilding Behavioral Context: A Blueprint for Corporate Renewal', *Sloan Management Review*, 37/2 (1996), 32–43.

6. The impact of the web on integration opportunities can be easily inferred from the analysis of R. L. Daft and R. H. Lengel, 'Organizational Information Requirements, Media Richness, and Structural Design', *Management Science*, 32 (1986), 554–71. For a more focused discussion on the role of IT in facilitating communication, see A. D. Shulman, 'Putting Group Information Technology in its Place: Communication and Good Work Group Performance', in S. R. Clegg, C. Hardy, and W. R. Nord (eds.), *Handbook of Organization Studies* (London: Sage, 1996), 357–74.

7. For an overview of how these managerial career structures created integration opportunities, see H. Gunz, *Careers and Corporate Cultures* (Oxford: Blackwell, 1989).

8. This point was forcibly made by Rob Goffee and Gareth Jones in their *Harvard Business Review* article, 'Why Should Anyone be Led by You?', Vol. 78, Issue 5, 62–70.

9. The important but often ignored role of middle managers in organizational integration has been described in R. M. Kanter, *The Change Masters* (New York: Simon and Schuster, 1983).

10. Such vertical processes of organizational integration lay at the heart of the divisionalized organizational model: for perhaps one of the richest and best-known expositions, see A. D. Chandler, *Strategy and Structure: Chapters in the History of American Industrial Enterprise* (Cambridge, MA: MIT Press, 1962).

11. These demographic trends have been described in L. Gratton, *The Democratic Enterprise* (London: FT/Prentice Hall, 2004).

12. We explore the concept of the 'volunteer investor' in L. Gratton and S. Ghoshal 'Managing Personal Human Capital: New Ethos for the "Volunteer" Employee", *European Management Journal*, 21/1 (2003), 1–10.

13. See J. Galbraith, *Designing Complex Organizations* (Reading, MA: Addison-Wesley, 1973). In the context of large, global companies—of the kind that are used to illustrate the arguments in this chapter—the use of such horizontal mechanisms has been described in C. A. Bartlett and S. Ghoshal, *Managing across Borders: The Transnational Solution* (Boston: Harvard Business School Press, 1988).

14. Our focus in this chapter is on the challenges of internal integration across existing and established units within large, complex organizations. Clearly, there are other important integration contexts—that of integrating strategic alliances, joint ventures, upstream and downstream partners on the value

chain, and so on. While these contexts are not the subject of this chapter, interested readers can find comprehensive treatments of such topics elsewhere—in Y. Doz and G. Hamel, *Alliance Advantage* (Boston: Harvard Business School Press, 1998), on integration across strategic alliances and partnerships, for example. Even within the organization, integration of new ventures poses a unique set of challenges, which we do not deal with here. Readers interested in this specific topic can find an outstanding analysis in C. Christensen, *The Innovator's Dilemma* (Boston: Harvard Business School Press, 1997).

15. For a useful overview of network structure, see M. Kilduff and W. Tsai, *Social Networks and Organizations* (London: Sage, 2003).

16. For a broader description of how these cooperative processes can work, see J. Nahapiet, L. Gratton, and H. Rocha, 'Knowledge and Relationships: When Cooperation is the Norm', *European Management Journal.* Vol 2 (2005), pp. 3–14

17. The concept of 'signature processes' is described in more detail in L. Gratton and S. Ghoshal, 'Beyond Best Practice', *Sloan Management Review*, 46/3 (2005), 49–57.

18. A more detailed description of BP's 'peer assist' and 'peer challenge' can be found in S. Ghoshal and L. Gratton, 'Integrating the Enterprise'; *Sloan Management Review*

19. We have described the extent and typology of these conversations in L. Gratton and S. Ghoshal (2002) 'Improving the Quality of Conversations', *Organizational Dynamics*, Winter 2002, 31/3, 209–23.

Overcoming Busyness

THE lack of energetic and focused action-taking by managers is a pervasive problem in companies. Research shows that only about 10 per cent of managers take persistent and purposive action to achieve their goals. It is not that the other 90 per cent do not know what to do: most have clearly defined projects and goals and possess all the knowledge and resources they need for taking action. The problem is that, even though they know what to do, they simply do not carry it out.

Over the last five years, we have researched action-taking by managers in several related projects. Beyond a longitudinal study of 130 managers in a global airline that was the focus of an article in *Harvard Business Review*,[1] we have carried out an empirical survey covering 250 managers in a large oil company in the US and have written detailed case studies on action-taking in the context of specific large projects in twelve major companies.[2] More recently, we shadowed twenty managers from ten different organizations as they went about their daily work. In each of these studies, we came across instances of both purposeful action-taking and what we have come to call 'active non-action', that is, busyness that has no productive outcome. Our analysis has revealed three major traps that lock managers into non-action.[3]

The first is the trap of *overwhelming demands*. Many managers get caught in webs of expectations that completely overwhelm them. The demands of their day-to-day work leave no time for reflection or prioritization and, as a result, they lose sight of what really matters. They spin their wheels and achieve little of significance.[4]

The second is the trap of *unbearable constraints*. Many managers feel squeezed in narrow corsets of rules and regulations and come to believe that they have too little space for autonomous action. Focusing on the factors that limit their ability to act, they pay little attention to what they actually can do. They become reactive and lose the capacity to create and pursue worthwhile goals under their own steam.

The third trap of non-action is *unexplored choices*. Being focused on the demands and constraints of their jobs, a majority of managers develop tunnel vision. With their attention entirely focused on immediate needs and requirements, they fail to perceive and exploit their freedom to make choices and to seize opportunities to take the initiative.

From this research, we have identified specific ways in which managers can avoid or overcome all three traps of non-action (see Table 11.1). We shall describe these ways in the remainder of this chapter, but we must make one point clear at this stage: while in most cases managers can overcome the traps within the framework of their existing employment—either by modifying the work context or by changing their own perceptions of their work—there are some situations in which the only way to break out of the bind is to change jobs.

We describe the experiences of Thomas Sattelberger, former operations director of Lufthansa, the German airline, in more detail later. One of Germany's highest-profile HR managers, Sattelberger had high hopes of creating the country's first corporate university. He pursued the dream initially at Daimler-Chrysler, but in the end concluded that the gap between his vision and the priorities of top management was too wide. So he moved to Lufthansa, where the atmosphere was more receptive and he could finally achieve his goal.

Without denying the relevance and significance of the situations that render people powerless to take purposeful action, in this chapter

Table 11.1. *Overcoming the traps of non-action*

The trap of overwhelming demands	The trap of unbearable constraints	The trap of unexplored choices
• Develop an explicit personal agenda	• Mapping relevant constraints	• Being aware of choices
• Slow management: reducing, prioritizing, and organizing demands	• Accepting trade-offs	• Involving key players to expand choices
• Structuring contact time	• Selectively breaking rules	• Building personal knowledge and competencies
• Shaping demands: managing expectations	• Tolerating conflicts and ambiguity	• Enjoying the freedom to act

we focus on what they can actually do within their existing jobs. In the last analysis, truly impossible situations are relatively rare. In most cases, thoughtful and determined managers can manage the demands, constraints, and choices of their existing jobs to carve out space for purposive action.

Overcoming the Trap of Overwhelming Demands

In most instances, managers who find themselves caught in the trap of overwhelming demands do so not because of their work situation per se, but because of the way they deal with expectations.[5]

Typically, they take demands for granted without asking whether they make sense, whether they can be influenced, and what can be done to reshape them. Consumed by demands and constantly under pressure, these managers do not make the time to ask themselves the most fundamental question: 'Am I busy on the right things?'

The simple fact is that it is easier to be busy than not. A highly fragmented day is often also a very lazy day. It is easier to respond to each new request, to chase the latest query, and to complain about overwhelming demands than to set an order of priorities and stick to it.

Most managers can overcome habitual fire-fighting.[6] To do so, however, they must first overcome what is probably the most difficult hurdle: the desire to be indispensable. Most often, managers who complain that they have too little time actually thrive on the sense of importance they derive from their busyness. They enjoy being at the centre of frantic activity. The last thing they want to have is more time—time to reflect on what they are doing.

An Oxford graduate with an MBA from London Business School, Jessica Spungin found herself caught in this trap when she was promoted to associate principal (AP) at consultancy McKinsey's London office in 2000.[7] As an AP, consultants are expected to take on more responsibilities of the partnership group, juggle multiple projects, serve as 'inspirational team leaders', and play an active role in office life. Already handling two major client projects, after her promotion Spungin was also asked to co-lead McKinsey's recruitment programme at UK universities and business schools, participate in an internal research initiative, serve as a senior coach for six business analysts, run an office party for 750 people, get involved in internal training, and help out on a new project for a health-care company. This is how she described a nightmare week:

I flew to the US on a Sunday night to be there for an 8.30 meeting the next morning on the research project, did a full day in New York on Monday, including some work on my banking client, got on a plane the same night to the Middle East, getting there on Tuesday afternoon, did a meeting and a dinner with my other client that night, worked in Tel Aviv through Thursday, and took the midnight flight back to the US, arriving at 5 a.m. Friday morning for a full day of meetings. I was supposed to go back to the hotel on Friday night to pick up my bags and head home to London, but I arrived at the hotel, crashed on the bed and didn't wake up until the next morning.

Soon Spungin hit the wall. In her first round of upward feedback from the three project teams she had worked with as an AP, she was rated second from bottom among her peers. One comment read: 'Jessica is really effective when she sits down with us, but she hardly ever does it.'

Spungin began to see that part of the problem was her own lack of confidence with her new position and her own success. She reflected: 'I never said "no" to people asking me to help out on stuff in case they thought I couldn't cope; I never said "no" to a client who wanted me to be there for a meeting, regardless of the flying involved. I drew the boundaries based in what I thought was expected of me, not on the basis of what I was good at, what was important, or what I could physically do.'

Spungin is one of the managers we studied who was able to overcome the trap of overwhelming demands. How she did so illustrates the ways in which managers can actively shape and influence the demands they confront in their jobs.

Developing an Explicit Personal Agenda

The first requirement for loosening the constraint of overwhelming demands is to develop a clear personal agenda.[8] As opposed to those who are vague about their objectives, effective action-takers build a precise idea of what they want to achieve in their jobs. They transform general aims such as growth, profit, providing the best service to customers, or personal career success into clear long-term goals—a vivid mental picture of the desired end-state, including a concrete understanding of how to get there.

The starting point for Spungin's recovery was the recognition of what she really wanted to achieve: she wanted to be a partner at McKinsey. It was a difficult agenda to commit to; as she remarked, 'Saying "I want to be a partner" is a bit like saying to someone "I love you"—it always makes you vulnerable. The chances are that you won't make it, and you want to avoid the heartbreak.'

Once she developed clarity about what she really wanted, the consultant could begin to visualize her life as a partner. One of the most important outcomes of this visualization was that she started to think in longer time blocks: instead of thinking only about the next three to six months, as she had done before, she started thinking in terms of one to five years. 'When you think you will be out in a year, you don't plan for the next horizon,' she noted. 'When you start thinking in terms of five years, you can prioritize.'

Having changed her mode of thinking, Spungin started to take proactive steps to assert control over her own development and task portfolio. As an expert in corporate banking thanks to an earlier stint at Citibank, she had slipped into the routine of accepting one banking project after the other, even though she realized she was not enthusiastic about the sector. In the context of longer-term job and career development, it became very clear to her that banking was not where she wanted to be. Instead, she decided to focus on the organizational practice, which dovetailed well with continuing work with her industrial client, a project that she really enjoyed. This focus on the functional and client side of her work then allowed her to bring a similar focus to other areas.

While reacting to demands distracts managers and makes it hard for them to see the big picture, a personal agenda has precisely the opposite effect. It allows them to integrate the diverse and loosely related goals they have for their short-, medium-, and long-term responsibilities into one broader master plan. As a result, personal agendas allow managers to relate immediate priorities to their own longer-term aspirations. A personal agenda is much more motivating and exciting then merely responding to everyday demands. It is, therefore, the first and most essential requirement for freeing oneself from the trap of overwhelming demands.

Slow Management: Reducing, Prioritizing, and Organizing Demands

With her new focus, Spungin went on to reorganize the work of her personal assistant. In the past, given her frantic schedule, her assistant would often take decisions for her—telling team members seeking a meeting that she was busy, for instance. Now she got her assistant to provide daily updates on meetings and discussions, so that she herself could make the call about what to participate in. In her mind, clients and the teams associated with them came first. Behind them she prioritized recruiting, the research initiative, and the coaching role. As it turned out, the non-client work mostly peaking at different times of the year, she could see how she could manage it alongside client work as long as she set aside half a day a week for 'other things'.

Many of the demands that managers accept as given are actually discretionary in nature. They see more demands than there really are because they fail to recognize that some of the things they do are actually choices rather than requirements. Those who take purposeful action, by contrast, check thoroughly what is actually a demand and what they can chose to do or not do. Thereby they not only reduce demands on their time, they also systematically streamline their routine work. They create space for tasks that are important for their own agenda instead of doing what they like, are familiar with, or find easiest to do; and they resist the temptation to jump impulsively from one thing to another.[9] As Spungin learned, 'in order to achieve speed in the work that matters, one must practise slow management.'

Structuring Contact Time

Managerial work is interactive and interdependent by nature. Managers rarely work on their own. The problem is that interacting with people is not only time-consuming but exhausting; it is the chief source of the multiple interruptions about which managers often complain.[10] A typical trap of non-action is getting caught up in intensive interactions with many different people.

Most managers spend much more time with their direct reports than is really necessary or even desirable. Younger managers, in particular, often fall victim to the fallacy of wanting to be seen as a 'good boss' and caring about subordinates by being unrestrictedly available.[11] This, in part, was the source of Spungin's problems—in trying to look accessible, she had in fact become highly inaccessible to those who really needed her time, and at those points of time when they needed it most.

Slowly she brought more structure to her contact time. Depending on the state of play in each project, either the team with her industrial client or the team with her healthcare client would come to the forefront. She became very explicit with each team about what she was going to do, spending more time on one team and less on the other, and then switching. By choosing priorities, phasing projects, and refocusing, she was able to devote more time to mentoring and coaching her teams. As a result, her 2002 feedback review—exactly one year after she was rated second from bottom in her peer group—rated her second from top.

Shaping Demands: Managing Expectations

Many managers constantly worry about whether they are meeting the expectations of others. Trying to please everyone, they tend to be absorbed in speculation about what others expect, the best strategy for meeting those expectations, and the consequences of not meeting them. They constantly monitor comments, feedback, and even the looks of others to interpret whether they are indeed living up to what they think others want. Ultimately, they fail, not only because they find little time to pursue their own agenda, but also because in trying to please everyone they typically end up pleasing no one.

What Spungin learned at McKinsey was that wanting to make something happen inevitably meant that she could not meet everybody's expectations. Initially, she discussed her options with several senior colleagues, but most of their suggestions only reflected what they needed most from her. Then she took a different tack: 'It made a big difference when I stopped and thought about what I wanted, rather than focusing on pleasing my mentors—of which there were many. They were important to me, but if I was going to succeed, I had to do it by being me, not many bits of lots of them.'

Having stopped trying to please everyone, she could then also work actively to both shape and respond to the demands she chose to meet. With clarity of her own objectives, she could become more proactive—presenting her own goals and ideas in advance, so that they would influence what others expected of her. Also, having chosen to focus on a few of the demands, she could go beyond trying to meet them and do everything she could to exceed them.

In June 2003 Jessica Spungin was made a partner in McKinsey.

Overcoming the Trap of Unbearable Constraints

One manager in a large telecommunications company we studied epitomized the trap of unbearable constraints: 'Already doing my day-to-day job often drives me and my people to our limits. No one is willing to give us more resources—people, money, and equipment. For a long time I have been wanting to introduce a quality-control system. That would really help us reduce errors and complaints and save us more time. And I would if I could get the resources. But given the situation, I do not see how I could do that—I do not see how I could do anything else or more than what I am currently doing.'

Contrast this with the experience of Sattelberger. Recall that Sattelberger had left Daimler-Chrysler for Lufthansa because he was unable to achieve his goal of creating a corporate university at the former; he fully anticipated doing so at the latter. His vision was to build corporate Germany's most progressive human-resource management capability, which he visualized as a temple with three pillars—one for each stream of organization and people-development measures that he wanted to build, while the roof was the university that would tie the pillars together and give the HR and organization-development work robustness and visibility. He anticipated that Lufthansa would already have the foundation of effective operational HR processes on which he could immediately start building this temple. What he discovered instead, however, was a complete mess. The operational HR processes were in disastrous disarray.

Without effective processes, it was futile to think of creating a corporate university. But Sattelberger did not give up. It took him two years of exhausting work to 'clean up the pigsty', but during that period he built the network and credibility he needed to erect his temple, once the foundation was in place. And so he did. The first corporate university in Germany—the Lufthansa School of Business—came into existence in 1999.

The way Sattelberger went about relaxing the initial constraints illustrates some of the key strategies managers can adopt to overcome the trap of unbearable constraints.

Mapping the Constraints

The first strategy is to develop a clear map of the constraints as a preliminary to thinking through systematically how they can be overcome. Instead of lamenting limitations in general, purposeful managers identify with some precision the specific constraints that hinder their ability to achieve their goals. With the aid of such mapping, they often discover that some of the constraints they presumed to be critical do not actually matter very much. They can then concentrate their energy on overcoming those constraints that are indeed killers for their cause.

Sattelberger identified two constraints as critical for his ambition to build the HR-OD 'temple'. The first was a general lack of understanding among the airline's technically orientated senior managers of the strategic role that HR could play in achieving the company's vision and purpose. To overcome this constraint, he chose what he described as an 'emergent strategy'. He never spoke about his vision as a whole; that would have frightened off most of his stakeholders. Instead, he created commitment for specific initiatives, projects, and programmes that were the building blocks of his temple. By delivering tangible results, slowly and incrementally he created trust and belief in his case that HR development (and eventually the university) could play a vital role in supporting corporate strategy and stimulating organizational development and change. Over time, he noted, 'they started seeing the whole picture'.

Shortage of resources was the other critical constraint. Lufthansa was in the middle of a strategic cost-saving programme that required every area to reduce total costs by 4 per cent a year for the next five years.[12] From Sattelberger's point of view, 'This meant that investing in anything other than the absolute essentials was not on the agenda at all.'

Sattelberger urgently needed half a million dollars to proceed with a company-wide initiative that he saw as central to his vision. To generate some income, Sattelberger came to an agreement to rent out Lufthansa's existing training facilities. But that was not enough, and the controller was adamant that official policy was sacrosanct. Seeing that his vision was in danger of foundering, Sattelberger took the matter to Lufthansa CEO Jürgen Weber. Sattelberger said: 'I explained to Weber that the initiative was vital for the company's future and to the development of business-driven HR in the company, and that the dogma on cost reduction would kill both. We had several conversations. Finally, Weber said, "For God's sake, do it, but do it right and stick to your budget".'

Sattelberger had to work hard, but his was not a unique case. Just as they shape demands, purposeful managers also systematically loosen constraints and broaden their freedom to act. Their strategies depend on the nature of the constraints in question. Some try to generate resources by winning one top-level sponsor. Others build a broader network of relationships to access needed material and non-material resources such as money, information, advice, and competencies. What they all have in common is a critical awareness of the pinch-points for their project and the ability to work systematically and strategically to overcome or work round them.

Accepting Trade-offs

Not all constraints can be overcome, however, no matter how hard or persistent the effort. When they run up against immovable barriers, most managers respond in one of two equally ineffective ways.[13] Some just give up, feeling hurt and frustrated in the process. Others bang their heads against the wall. They try again and again, essentially repeating the same arguments over and over, ultimately frustrating everyone else.[14]

Purposeful managers, too, do not always get what they want and need for their projects. However, they deal with constraints much more flexibly. While never losing sight of their overall ends, they tend to be far more willing to accept trade-offs. For every intention, there are 'must-haves' and 'nice-to haves'. Purposeful managers develop a great deal of clarity on the distinction between the two and accept compromises on the 'nice-to-haves' much more readily than their strong-headed colleagues. At the same time, they fight much harder on the 'must-have' elements.

Sattelberger coped with many setbacks, accepting significant delays and even cancellations of different parts of his initiative. He put aside his vision for the first two years to 'clean out the pigsty'; he worked to increase earnings to relax resource constraints; and he started with much less than he expected—but he never allowed his vision to wither.

Selective Rule-breaking

Most managers just obey rules, procedures, and directions. They accept formal regulations as given and define their activities around them. Purposeful managers take a more active stance towards both the formal rules of the organization and its informal norms. Not only do they question standing rules that they believe to be outdated or inappropriate, but they also break the rules or find a way around them when it is absolutely necessary for achieving their goals.

There is a subtle but profound difference, however, between wholesale and selective rule-breaking. Mavericks who flout all rules can rarely achieve the centrality within the network of relationships among key organizational members that they need for pursuing significant initiatives. The challenge is to conform to some rules in order to earn the legitimacy and credibility to break others. In Sattelberger's words, 'You have to be loyal to the company and not get into guerrilla warfare. But at the same time you must remember that nobody thanks you for following the rules. But they do thank you for doing a fantastic job.'

In most organizations, it is often the informal, unwritten norms and regulations that are greater barriers to purposeful action than the formal rulebook.[15] Being explicit and limited to specific areas, formal rules are paradoxically often less restrictive than informal ones developed through cultural norms, habits, and shared expectations that tend to blanket all aspects of behaviour. Further, not being explicit, they also often become undiscussable. As a result, they tend to be much more pervasive and pernicious in shaping and constraining individual action.

The cultures of most companies inhibit purposeful action-taking on the part of their managers. The culture of frenzy—of celebrating busyness—that characterizes some young high-technology companies is as much a hindrance to the reflective and persistent pursuit of goals as the bureaucratic cultures of some old and established corporations.[16] Similarly, while a culture of strict top-down command and control certainly limits the scope of individual initiative, so does an extreme consensus-orientated team culture.

More than by breaking formal rules, purposeful managers succeed by challenging the web of informal restrictions arising out of unspoken cultural norms. Typically, they break the code of silent adherence by making these rules explicit and exposing them to debate. Entrenched dogmas survive only as long as they remain unquestioned. Purposeful managers unshackle themselves by making these restrictions visible and, therefore, untenable.

Tolerating Conflicts and Ambiguity

Most managers try to avoid conflict and in case of disagreement attempt to avert confrontation by changing their opinion or diplomatically not speaking their mind. As a result, they spend a lot of time figuring out strategies for navigating around potential conflicts and confrontations. The cost of this superficial harmony is that they lack positive freedom to act and are constrained by their own insecurity. Purposeful managers, by contrast, do not shy away from conflict. The best of them follow the dictum 'disagree, but do not become disagreeable'; but all prefer the authenticity of open debate to the conspiracy of silent disharmony.

Sattelberger had several serious arguments with Lufthansa's controllers and senior management. He believed that their focus on cost reduction was necessary, but risked becoming counterproductive if taken to extremes. Although concerned to build good, stable relationships with colleagues, he had no compunction about engaging in direct confrontation when his vision seemed in danger of stalling. On occasion, he deliberately provoked conflicts in order to win attention for his agenda at top-management level. As he put it: 'You have to fight for new standards. You can't do that if you are never willing to engage in direct and difficult conversations.'

Willingness to engage in conflict to shield and nurture an important goal requires a well-developed capacity for living with ambiguity. In organizations of any size and complexity, conflicts—particularly on important issues—rarely find instant resolutions. Typically, there is a process of escalation and a period of uncertainty, and purposeful managers need stamina to sustain their commitment through these difficult times. As Sattelberger observed, 'There is a limit to how far and how fast you can push. Eagerness beyond this limit is counterproductive. People get pissed off. You have to grit your teeth and carry on. You cannot allow this tension to drain your energy. You have to learn to live with this uncertainty if you want to start something new.'

Overcoming the Trap of Unexplored Choices

Managerial jobs are indeed subject to both demands and constraints. At the same time, they are also essentially discretionary in nature.[17] All managers have some degree of choice with regard to both the goals they can pursue and the means for pursuing them. Often managers do not recognize this freedom because they have fallen victim to the trap of unexplored choices. First, they do not recognize their choices. Secondly, even when they can perceive alternatives, they do not exploit their ability to explore them. Purposeful action-takers, on the other hand, avoid this trap by being aware of their choices, by expanding their opportunities and freedom to act on those choices, by developing personal competencies that both create choice and enhance their ability to make things happen, and by learning to enjoy the freedom and responsibility that choice brings with it.

To illustrate how managers can overcome the trap of unexplored choices, consider the example of Dan Andersson, a mid-level manager in ConocoPhillips. In 1992 Andersson was part of a Conoco team that was exploring the possibility of entering the Finnish market, a move that would require breaking a monopoly that had reigned since 1947. Budgeted at $1 million, it was considered a capital-light project. The first task was to set up storage facilities that would allow Conoco to import its own petrol. After several months of intense search, the team eventually found an existing tank terminal that Shell had abandoned decades ago. While rusty outside, the tanks, built in the 1920s, appeared to be clean and usable inside.

After months of intensive work with the city authorities, the team won approval for leasing the facility. Success seemed close, and the team was jubilant. Then came what seemed to be a fatal phone call from Conoco's laboratory: there was too much carbon in the steel for the tanks to qualify for storing petrol.

The first reaction of every member of the team to this hammer blow was to give up. There was no other facility in Finland that Conoco could buy, and without its own storage facility it could not break into the market. There appeared to be no alternative but to abandon the whole idea.

Andersson, on the other hand, came up with a seemingly absurd idea: building a new storage terminal from the ground up. He told us: 'One simply does not build new tank terminals any more. Nobody would even consider such a proposal. However, I did not see any other way to break the monopoly. This was the only way we could import our own petrol. So I started exploring this option.'

Eventually, Andersson managed to convince Conoco's management to build the new tanks, even though it meant making an investment of six times the original budget. When the first Conoco ship arrived at the harbour, city representatives, hundreds of spectators, Finnish TV, and Conoco top management were there to celebrate. 'This big event when the first load of imported petrol arrived was the emotional success,' Andersson recalled. 'The economic success followed.'

Being Aware of Choices

Why did Andersson think of building new storage as an option while most of his team did not? In fact, the option to build was only one of several alternative plans Andersson had up his sleeve. As he put it: 'Even when the whole team, including me, was totally excited about the idea of upgrading the old Shell tanks and everything appeared to be going smoothly, I had thought about three alternatives. Plan B was to build a new facility. Plan C was to create a joint venture with a competitor, and plan D was to find an investor for the tanks. Yes, we had a single official option—but in my mind we had the other three possibilities, too.'

Intellectually, there was nothing unique or particularly special about any of these alternatives. Yet, in the given context, others did not even see them. They were outside the team's mandate. Everyone else's vision was limited to the boundaries of the official mandate; Andersson's was not.

This kind of blindness is not unusual; it often prevents managers from taking purposeful action.[18] As we have seen in other chapters, managers develop a level of loyalty to and identification with their companies, strategies, and assigned tasks that leads them to take the givens as unalterable. As a result, they perceive few choices—and indeed little need for choices in the first place.

Crucially, Andersson's commitment was to the underlying purpose of the project—breaking the state-owned monopoly. So instead of starting from the budget as given, he started from breaking the monopoly as given. He constantly scanned the environment for possible obstacles and for strategies that would help him to overcome them. His different framing allowed him to see more choices.

Involving Key Players to Expand Choices

Purposeful managers are not only more aware of their choices; they also consciously create choice by generating opportunities and expanding their space for taking autonomous action.

One of the ways of expanding freedom to act is by generating ideas through conversations and interactions with others.[19] Managers without a strategic agenda of their own carry out their tasks and limit their conversations to their day-to-day work problems. With their goals in the forefront of their minds, purposeful managers constantly explore the perspectives of others and generate new choices by involving others.

This is what Andersson did to overcome a potentially fatal flaw in his proposal: the only land available to site the new terminal was severely contaminated. By involving local officials, the landowner, and a variety of other people in his agenda, he was able to find an ingenious way for Conoco to take over the land without assuming historical liability. It was only with the participation of external stakeholders that such a creative solution could have been arrived at. No one in Conoco could have generated it unaided.

Within the organization, managers can expand their opportunities for autonomous action-taking by co-opting their superiors into their agenda. Many managers avoid open and honest discussions with their bosses about their own freedom because they do not want to be seen as too pushy. Often they feel insecure about their performance and lack the self-confidence to ask such questions.

By contrast, purposeful managers engage their bosses in candid discussions about the scope of their jobs and roles. In most instances, such discussions expand their opportunities and space for action. Typically, bosses tend to see a job as bigger, and as providing more opportunities for innovation, than do the job-holding managers themselves. Often the boss is able to take a more detached view of the job than the junior manager, and thereby open up more freedom, choices, and opportunity for purposeful action.

In this case, Andersson created a series of interactions with his bosses that helped him both to develop his alternative plan and to secure their commitment to it. With the support of the local authorities, he persuaded the company's senior team to visit Finland for face-to-face discussion of the problems and opportunities. 'Once my boss got involved with the touch and the feel, once he saw the land, met the people, and got a sense of what the battle was like, he started sharing our feelings,' Andersson recalled. He added: 'We did not discuss the budget. Instead we explored possibilities and created commitment to the solution. The budget discussion came much later.'

Building Personal Knowledge and Competencies

For purposeful managers, another means of expanding the domain of choice is learning—building specific knowledge and competencies.[20] The most effective of these managers invest in developing two different kinds of competencies: a set of general skills and deep, expert knowledge in one specific area. This combination helps them generate and exploit choices in three different ways.

Greater knowledge and competence help them to identify choices more effectively.[21] A deep understanding of the company and its businesses, for example, is often a prerequisite for perceiving opportunities for self-generated and autonomous action. Especially important is the understanding of the invisibles—decision-making processes, informal rules and norms, interpersonal relationships, and historically developed social dynamics—that influence how ideas are received and acted on.[22] With a rich and deep understanding of these invisibles, a manager can intuitively sense the right way to present a proposal and the extent to which it can be pushed at a particular point in time.

An intimate understanding of the company is also necessary for understanding different perspectives and positions, including those of key stakeholders in any particular initiative. Managers narrowly focused only on their own jobs often do not understand the concerns and biases of others and are therefore unable either to empathize with them or to present their ideas in a form that would chime with the perspectives of key influencers.

Managers known for their knowledge and competence enlarge their freedom of action by virtue of their credibility within the organization. Compared with colleagues who lack a field of expertise, managers who are experts in particular topics or functions develop more opportunities simply because they are more sought after for advice and for joint work. At the same time, their ideas and opinions carry more weight.

How did Andersson manage to persuade top management to invest six times more than originally planned in the Finnish venture? One reason was the solid base of credibility he had established thanks to in-depth research and expertise about the Finnish market. 'I was the only one with a deep understanding of the political and economic structures of the region. I knew everything about all the earlier efforts of our competitors to enter the market, and about why they failed. It was that deep knowledge that allowed me to develop a convincing business case. I could show that the investment would be paid off within five years.'

As Andersson's experience demonstrates, an additional benefit of competencies lies in competent managers' enhanced confidence in actually exploiting their own ability to choose. Many managers hesitate to exercise choice, even when they are aware it exists. Without the confidence born of competence, they can be overwhelmed with anxiety by the responsibility and risk that inevitably go with autonomous action. Often they fail to take the initiative because they are insecure in their decisions, do not trust their own judgement, and feel that they need direction or backing for their choices. In contrast, managers who believe that they have the necessary knowledge and competence feel more confident of being able to deal with unforeseen incidents or difficult tasks and find it easier to take decisions.

A Bias for Action

Ultimately, perhaps the attribute that most decisively differentiates executives who actively manage their work contexts from those who fall victim to the three traps is their general attitude towards choice and the responsibility that it implies. Purposeful managers have a bias for action simply because they enjoy choice and the freedom to act.

This difference between those who enjoy freedom of choice and those who are haunted by it becomes particularly salient during phases of major change. In companies undergoing change, managers have to work in relatively turbulent and unstructured environments. It was under these conditions that we could see the differences in attitude most sharply.

Facing exactly the same circumstances, those who enjoyed freedom pushed out the scope of their jobs, expanded their area of choice, and pursued highly ambitious goals. Those who did not enjoy the freedom reacted to the perceived lack of structure by becoming disoriented, then paralysed.

Managers who are ill at ease with the freedom to act need constraints and clearly defined demands. Unstructured, chaotic environments make them feel intensely uncomfortable. One manager in a company undergoing radical restructuring told us: 'Somehow the entire process was diffuse, and there was no transparency....So I had very limited possibility to make any plans. Long-term goals were clearly inappropriate, and even in the short term I felt unable to influence anything.' The lack of predictability and structure, together with insecurity about requirements and roles, made him feel much more constrained than in the pre-transformation phase of bureaucratic controls. The ambiguity of choice made him feel anxious, stressed, and threatened. Like several similar colleagues, he reacted to the lack of structure by feeling paralysed and powerless.

A bias for action is not the special gift of a few; most managers can develop it as a capacity.[23] Spungin's story demonstrates what a difference a personal agenda can make. Andersson did not always enjoy freedom of choice. His experience and newly developed competencies changed his view and gave him the energy and willpower to explore his choices. This is precisely the sentiment he shared with us in his analysis of why and how he pursued his idea so relentlessly. 'After I started to develop an active stance, I learned to like it,' he explained. 'Now I actually search for situations that go beyond my scope and enjoy catching the opportunity of the moment. Having a vision and making decisions is fantastic and exciting. Somehow this gives me a kick.'

It is a bias for action that distinguishes managers who make important things happen—exceptional managers—from those who succumb to the traps of non-action. Purposeful action has less to do with the working context and more to do with a way of seeing and dealing with those contexts. This is the profound insight of Joseph Schumpeter, the Austrian economist who gave us the theory of creative destruction. What differentiates the entrepreneur from others?

> Most people go about their normal, daily business and have sufficient to do thereby...A minority, with a sharper intelligence and a suppler imagination, see numerous new combinations....It is a still smaller minority that acts...The new combinations will always be there; the truly indispensable and decisive will always be the deed and the energy of the entrepreneur.[24]

Notes

1. See H. Bruch and S. Ghoshal, 'Beware the Busy Manager', *Harvard Business Review*, 80/2 (2002), 62–9; and H. Bruch and S. Ghoshal, *A Bias for Action: How Effective Managers Harness their Willpower, Achieve Results, and Stop Wasting Time* (Boston: Harvard Business School Press, 2004).

2. See http://www.ecch.com/ for the published case-study material.

3. The framework of demands, constraints, and choices as a way to think about managerial jobs was suggested by R. Stewart in her book *Managers and their Jobs* (London: Macmillan, 1967). See also R. Stewart, *Choices for the Manager* (London: Prentice Hall, 1982).

4. 'Management was, is, and always will be the same thing: the art of getting things done,' write Bob Eccles and Nitin Nohria, both professors at Harvard Business School, in their celebrated book *Beyond the Hype*: see R. G. Eccles and N. Nohria, *Beyond the Hype* (Boston: Harvard Business School Press, 1992).

5. Studies on the nature of managerial work are helpful for pointing out the risk of non-action in managerial jobs, yet most of them provide evidence that, even in cases of similar jobs, managers differ noticeably in their extent of action-taking. See J. P. Kotter, *The General Managers* (New York: Free Press, 1982).

6. See C. P. Hales, 'What Do Managers Do? A Critical Review of the Evidence', *Journal of Management Studies*, 23 (1986), 88–115; L. B. Kurke and H. E. Aldrich, 'Mintzberg Was Right! A Replication and Extension of the "Nature of Managerial Work" ', *Management Science*, 29 (1983), 975–84.

7. See also S. Ghoshal and H. Bruch, 'Reclaim your Job', *Harvard Business Review*, 82/3 (2004), 41–5.

8. See Kotter, *The General Managers* (n. 5). The importance of continuously clarifying and deepening one's personal agenda has also been highlighted by P. Senge, *The Fifth Discipline: The Art & Practice of the Learning Organization* (New York: Doubleday, 1990).

9. Typical managerial problems in goal pursuit are getting started, being too easily distracted, giving up in the face of obstacles when increased effort and persistence are needed, or resuming action after disruptions. See P. M. Gollwitzer, 'The Volitional Benefits of Planning', in P. M. Gollwitzer and J. A. Bargh (eds.), *The Psychology of Action* (New York: Guildford Press, 1996), 287–312. Getting started with or resuming an interrupted goal pursuit is rather simple when the necessary actions are well practiced or routine. See J. A. Oullette and W. Wood, 'Habit and Intention in Everyday Life: The Multiple Processes by which Past Behavior Predicts Future Behavior', *Psychological Bulletin*, 124 (1998), 54–74. Often, however, managerial behaviours are not routine. Consequently, persistence, discipline, and overcoming a disinclination to exhibit a certain behaviour become critical to managerial action. See V. Brandstätter, A. Lengfelder, and P. M. Gollwitzer, 'Implementation Intentions and Efficient Action Initiation', *Journal of Personality and Social Psychology*, 81 (2001), 946–60.

10. See F. Luthans and J. K. Larsen, 'How Managers Really Communicate', *Human Relations*, 39 (1986), 161–78; and R. Whitley, 'On the Nature of Managerial Tasks

and Skills: Their Distinguishing Characteristics and Organization', *Journal of Management Studies*, 26 (1989), 209–24.

11. See Stewart, *Choices for the Manager* (n. 3).

12. See 'Lufthansa 2000: Maintaining the Change Momentum', case study prepared by H. Bruch and S. Ghoshal (London: London Business School, 2000); see also H. Bruch and T. Sattelberger, 'Lufthansa's Transformation Marathon: A Process of Liberating & Focusing Change Energy', *Human Resources Management*, 40 (2001), 249–59.

13. See Stewart, *Choices for the Manager*.

14. Several scholars have pointed out that in cases of crisis, failure, or urgency, managers tend to display irrational behaviours, such as the use of behavioural templates, reactiveness, displacement activitites, or more extensive trial and error. See e.g. I. L. Janis and L. Mann, *Decision Making: A Psychological Analysis of Conflict, Choice and Commitment* (New York: Free Press, 1977). Managers try to cope with a problem by using the behavioural plans they already have rather than taking time for analysing, developing, and choosing a satisfactory way out of a precarious situation. For a review on forms of non-action, see H. Bruch, *Leaders' Action: Model Development and Testing* (Munich: Hampp, 2003).

15. See J. A. Chatman, J. T. Polzer, S. G. Barsade, and M. A. Neale, 'Being Different Yet Feeling Similar: The Influence of Demographic Composition and Organizational Culture on Work Processes and Outcomes', *Administrative Science Quarterly*, 43 (1998), 749–80.

16. For a discussion of culture, see E. Schein, *Organizational Culture and Leadership*, 2nd edn. (San Francisco: Jossey-Bass, 1992).

17. Managerial tasks are discretionary and—what is important for action—involve choices, rather than being routinely executed or determined by external factors. Management can, therefore, be distinguished from administration by its ability to select and change. See R. Whitley, 'On the Nature of Managerial Tasks and Skills: Their Distinguishing Characteristics and Organization', *Journal of Management Studies*, 26 (1989), 209–24.

18. See D. M. Rousseau and S. A. Tijoriwala, 'Assessing Psychological Contracts: Issues, Alternatives and Measures', *Journal of Organizational Behavior*, 19 (1998), 679–95.

19. See Stewart, *Choices for the Manager*.

20. Investigating the tactics used by people at work to influence their superiors, coworkers, and subordinates, Kipnis and colleagues found reason to be the most effective one. See D. Kipnis and S. M. Schmidt, 'Upward-Influence Styles: Relationship with Performance Evaluation', *Administrative Science Quarterly*, 33 (1988), 528–42; and D. Kipnis, S. M. Schmidt, and I. Wilkinson, 'Intraorganizational Influence Tactics: Explorations in Getting One's Way', *Journal of Applied Psychology*, 65 (1980), 440–52.

21. See M. Frese et al., 'Personal Initiative at Work: Differences between East and West Germany', *Academy of Management Journal*, 39 (1996), 37–63.

22. This particular competence has been called *organizational awareness* and refers to an individual's ability to understand an organization's informal and formal

structures, unspoken organizational constraints, underlying problems, opportunities, or political forces. See L. M. Spencer and S. M. Spencer, *Competence at Work* (London: Hay McBer Research Press, 1994).

23. See Bruch and Ghoshal, *A Bias for Action* (n. 1).

24. See J. A. Schumpeter, *Theorie der wirtschaftlichen Entwicklung (Theory of Economic Development)* (Leipzig: Duncker & Humblot, 1912), 110.

Taking the First Steps

EXECUTIVES across the developed world are faced with a dilemma. Do they stay on the familiar low road, concentrating on cutting costs and competing on price, or do they strike out on the road less taken, the high road, competing on innovation, value added, and speed? In this book, we have argued that in reality they have no choice. For firms in the developed world, only the high road leads to sustainable long-term prosperity. The steady globalization of manufacturing and services means that there will always be someone, in some corner of the world, capable of delivering at lower cost. In mature economies the high fixed cost base makes it impossible to compete on the basis of cost alone. Moreover, if the citizens of developed countries want to maintain their lifestyles and economic growth rates, they must be employed in companies that are innovative and commercially successful, and thus able to generate profits and pay good wages.

Recognizing the value, indeed the necessity, of going beyond 'business as usual' is a major hurdle in its own right. Most people are more comfortable with what they already know and understand, and managers are no exception. But our starting premise is that managers cannot stay in their comfort zone if that is not providing innovative, high-value-added products and services. To do so, we need a fresh approach to moving upmarket, to creating higher-value products and services, to being more innovative, and to coming up with unique strategies and ways of competing. As we have seen, for some companies, innovation has always been the key to their competitive strategy. But for many, this has not been the case. As we have noted, UK companies have a poor record in both investment in, and exploitation of, R&D and executives are now summoned radically and fundamentally to change their approach.

We believe that at the heart of the new approach—the levers that switch the trajectory of the company from low road to the high road—are the beliefs and actions of the exceptional manager. We make this call for the exceptional manager with care. We have noted that the economic land-scape of the UK has been transformed beyond recognition over the last two decades as Britain has turned itself into one of the most market-orientated and business-friendly economies in the world. Yet, in terms of average firm productivity, the UK still lags the performance of other mature economies such as the US, France, and Germany. We in the AIM Fellowship are clear that the organizational efforts and skills of managers play a significant role in performance; an element in any performance gap will therefore come down to the expertise and abilities of management. By this we mean not only senior executives in major corporations. At all levels of organizations of all sizes, people are engaged in roles and activities which impact on efficiency and innovativeness. In this book, we have considered what it will take for firms to enjoy sustainable success in terms not only of strategic orientation but also of organizational routines and processes, and indeed, the roles and behaviours of individual managers.

Organizational success or failure can derive from many different sources beyond the actions of senior executives. In the early part of this book, we considered the classic answers to achieving strategic success—use strategic planning, choose an attractive industry, use generic strategies, think of resources and competencies, make fast strategic changes, diversify—and came to the conclusion that while these may be of some use, they do not of themselves guarantee success. However, although the challenges managers face are profound, and without doubt there are no simple formulae for success, we should not be pessimistic about the role of management. The first challenge is to accept that change is normal, and transform-ational change sometimes necessary.

So what are the positive actions managers can take? As scholars well versed in the evidence, we distrust catch-all, instant solutions. We make no apology for this, even if some of our conclusions will disappoint those intent on quick fixes. We believe that profound changes are needed if companies are successfully to move to the next level of competitiveness. Among the key challenges are:

A Call to the Exceptional Manager...

Our first, and perhaps overriding, conclusion is that what is demanded is exceptional management. Why exceptional? Simply put, it is our belief that 'business as usual' will inevitably create a downward spiral in the relative performance and comparative position of companies in the developed world. We have described the fundamental and often unrecognized traps of inertia that constrain the manager operating with the 'business as usual' mindset. To break out of the cage of their own assumptions, managers must become more self-critical, more prepared to question what they and others take for granted, more ready to challenge 'the way things are done around here'. In this sense, being an exceptional manager is about focusing as much attention on the exception as on the rule. A major challenge, then; but it does not mean that exceptional managers need to remain a rarity.

... to Address the Challenge of Discontinuous Change

The rate of change that organizations experience is likely to accelerate as their context becomes increasingly dynamic: technology continues to advance, markets fragment, and global competition grows. Such uncertainty puts a premium on the ability of managers to learn to deal proactively with discontinuous change. However, it is not possible to 'manage' these changes in the classic sense of controlling and coordinating. In responding to their context, managers cannot assume the indefinite life of a current business model, however successful it has been in the past. Ultimately any business model, however innovative, will run out of steam. Under these circumstances, managers are called on to transform the business model, and thus to manage innovation beyond small increments of change—beyond the steady state. It is this combination of managing the routine while understanding and investing in transformational strategic change that we believe is crucial. In other words, it is discontinuous innovation that poses the greatest challenge.

As we have seen, discontinuous innovation is much easier for new entrants to an industry starting from scratch than for incumbents with their accumulated baggage of ingrained models and routines. So managers are challenged to find ways of reproducing the entrepreneurial agility of the mould-breakers. We see this as encompassing a cognitive challenge (of awareness), a political challenge (of support), and a technical challenge (of resource development). We believe these challenges can be met, and have described some of the means of doing so. However, as upheavals increase in frequency and amplitude, so does the premium on the ability of managers to learn to deal proactively with change. As we have noted, traditional responses of command and control will not do here. Rather, the task of the exceptional manager is developing and managing the context within the organization from which new ideas can emerge and be carried forward. It is a vitally important one.

...to Emphasize Participation

One of our most important conclusions is that the high road of innovation and value creation demands an employee workforce that is both skilled and actively engaged with and participating in the business of the company. By this we mean engaged in a pluralistic decision-making process, engaged in contributing to both continuous and discontinuous improvement, and engaged in building relational networks within and outside the firm. Exceptional managers are therefore called on to promote direct employee involvement and indirect participation and actively to champion working systems intended to develop and support reciprocal commitment between employers and employees. This requires that employee contributions are underpinned by skills development and training, that employees have opportunities to participate in decision-making and incentives to contribute through their perceptions of employment security, promotion opportunities, and remuneration that is fair. There is a tension to be negotiated between the turbulence and uncertainty of the world outside the organization and the appropriate level of employee security, engagement, and reward within. To strike the right balance, the exceptional manager needs to think systematically about the design of work and the development of skills. Again, however, this is not a matter of following a simple checklist. Rather, it is a matter of operating proactively within a flexible, dynamic framework to create a context that is unique and appropriate to their particular circumstances.

...to Shape the Organizational Context

One of the essential ways in which exceptional managers respond to the challenges of discontinuous innovation is in their shaping of the context within which people work. They do this through their stewardship of the practices, processes, and structures of the organization, both those that deal with the management of people and the operating systems of the organization. As we have noted, British employment relations have been traditionally characterized as 'adversarial'. Moreover, there has been a tendency for British managers to treat employees at arm's length and a general neglect of human-resource issues. We call on the exceptional manager to make more and better use of high-performance work systems. It is our strong belief that by putting some basics in place companies could make real inroads in the productivity gap that consistently separates UK firms from those of the US, France, and Germany. By the basics we mean not only the working practices themselves: recruitment, performance feedback, pay, training, etc. Also important is the way they are carried out. Only by being consistent, just, and fair will they work to create the employee commitment that is key to firms' ability to take the high road to innovation and value creation.

But employee commitment and business performance are determined by a wider range of features than just those concerned with employment relations. The way in which performance is measured is also critical. We have singled out performance measurement because it is a resource-hungry activity that impacts both directly and indirectly on the capacity of individuals and teams to innovate. In the changing circumstances in which managers now increasingly find themselves, it needs to change its function. Exploring the role performance management can play in the ambiguous and fuzzy process of exploration for new ideas and knowledge, we conclude that exceptional managers must learn to see performance measurement less as a control system, more as a vehicle for learning. Treating performance management as learning requires them to be more discerning as to what is measured and what is not, to balance the focus on financial measures of value with non-financial measures, to broaden the measurement methodology to embrace value creation as well as profit, and to learn how to manage innovative performance. We see this as a particular challenge since at the heart of innovation is the need to experiment, to do things differently, and to take advantage of emergent opportunities. The management and measurement of innovative environments is a complex business. However, by seeing performance as a planning rather than a review process, we believe it is possible for the exceptional manager to use performance management as a help rather than a hindrance on the high road to innovation and value creation.

While we have singled out performance management as a key practice affecting innovation, we acknowledge that in reality practices such as these come in 'bundles' of routines, systems, and procedures. A critical issue for organizations is the orientation to, and ability successfully to achieve, change. The dynamic capabilities bundles of practices create are key to the innovative capacity of the company. Dynamic capabilities are shaped by the executive team, but also by employees who carry strategic and operational practices forward. As we have seen, adopting new practices is less straightforward than it might seem; facilitating information flows will be key, as will the capacity of employees to learn from their success and failures.

Organizational innovation means new processes as well as products and services. Historically, UK managers have had a poor record of introducing new ideas on how to organize and manage their businesses. We have emphasized the importance of the role of exceptional managers in ensuring that promising practices are brought into the organization. For example, we would expect the exceptional manager actively to seek out how other companies are addressing the challenges of performance management. However, we have also noted the potential pitfall of following fads and cautioned managers to ensure that promising practices are first understood and evaluated and then shaped to meet the specific context of the organization. Managers must also avoid the trap of being content with 'picking the low-hanging fruit', that is, simply introducing the easy-to-do aspects of a practice, and be sure to adopt the central elements that impact performance. Success in this regard will mean an ongoing learning process for individuals and the organization as a whole.

. . . to Champion a Learning Environment

The high road to innovation and value creation is built on an organization and managers that are capable of meeting the cognitive challenge of radical innovation. This requires them to tune into weak signals inside the firm, to tolerate uncertainty and new ideas, to foster divergent thinking, and to create an organization in which the parts are integrated and capable of learning from each other. The capacity of members of a company to learn quickly and effectively will be crucial to their ability to deal with the many challenges that taking the high road involves.

To build learning capacity, we would encourage the exceptional manager to think systemically about a range of learning initiatives and actively to participate in and champion the learning processes of the company. In particular, we draw attention to the priceless knowledge that is present inside every firm, some of it tacit informal and among ordinary members of the organization, but nevertheless potentially a wellspring of innovation. Without a participative management approach to employees, this tacit knowledge and innovation potential will be lost.

In considering managers' own activities within a learning environment, we pay particular attention to the way the exceptional manager makes decisions. In a complex, ambiguous, and shifting world the manager's capacity to make sense of the context, process information, and acquire knowledge is crucial. Here, it is the combination of the striving for rationality together with the ability to see the significance and potential of the informal aspects of organizations that can be the source of significant new ideas. There are natural limits to any managers' ability to process complex information and also to be aware of and mediate their own biases. We do not argue that managers should rely on detailed forms of analysis that can overwhelm them in data. Instead, we have drawn attention to a number of techniques that can sensitize them to their built-in biases and improve the quality of group decision-making. However, as we have repeatedly emphasized throughout this book, the effectiveness of these techniques and tools is highly dependent on context, especially on the degree to which the internal political environment and culture of the organization is conducive to their use. This is why we actively encourage managers to engage in open debate between themselves and with employees about what should be done and how it should be achieved. Openness and a willingness to debate, listen, and reflect are among the key qualities of the exceptional manager.

In any organization, much of the knowledge that forms the raw material of innovation lies *between* people, in the intricate networks of friendships and social ties that criss-cross the company. The exceptional manager has a key role to play here in developing an organizational structure and fostering networks that enable diverse people to come together to exchange ideas. The exceptional manager does not dismiss or ignore these more informal aspects of organization but seeks to understand, nurture, and gain benefit from them.

. . . to Act as a Role Model to Others

In much of this book, we have called on the exceptional manager to be the architect of what goes on around her; specifically to be actively involved in designing and implementing innovative practices and processes. However, beyond the role of organizational architect, we have described a crucial part for managers to play in nurturing and promoting through their behaviour the way that others engage in innovative endeavour. We have highlighted a number of behaviours as being particularly crucial to fostering an innovative climate. One is the way in which managers engage in reflective conversation with others. Our emphasis here is in balancing the rational, analytical data described earlier, with emotional authenticity and empathy. It is within these creative dialogues that new ideas and knowledge are created. Another key behaviour is the skill with which the exceptional manager navigates action-taking. Most managers are faced with overwhelming demands and, at times, unbearable constraints. The way that they navigate through these potential traps sends out clear and unambiguous messages to others about how they should behave. Our message to managers is to mediate the overwhelming demands by developing an explicit personal agenda, slowing down by reducing and organizing demands, so as to find the space to challenge themselves and to manage the expectations of those around them so that they do the same.

Our call in this book is for managers to strive to be exceptional. By this we mean exceptional in their capacity to build and support a unique context capable of innovation, but also exceptional in their personal knowledge and competencies, and in the values and attitudes they bring to their work. It is about stepping out of the comfort zone of 'business as usual' and displaying the qualities of commitment and trust that they will expect of others. Fundamentally important here is the general attitude towards choice and the responsibility that it implies. As we have seen, this bias for action is not a special gift of a few; most managers can develop it. It is, however, the bias for action that distinguishes managers who make important things happen—exceptional managers—from those that succumb to the traps of non-action and imprisonment in existing routines. It is the exceptional manager who has developed a way of seeing and addressing the context of innovation that helps the company journey on the high road. In the exceptional manager, we have seen that beneath the action orientation lie fundamental assumptions about the capacity, willingness, and ability of others to grow and to cooperate. It is these assumptions that fuel the emphasis on participative management and form the basis for creative dialogue. In taking the high road to innovation, the exceptional manager is called on to build on these assumptions and values and to nourish the relationships that will be key to the future success of organizations operating in the high-value-added, high-innovation sectors that offer the UK the prospect of long-term sustainable growth.

Index

3M 96, 97, 107, 117–18
ABB 94
accounting, and changing nature
    of 110–11
acquisitions, and buying technical
    capability 101–2
action-taking:
    and active non-action 223
    and bias for action 238–9,
        250
    and exceptional management 230
    and overcoming overwhelming
        demands 225–6
        developing personal agenda 226–7
        managing expectations 229
        prioritizing 227–8
        structuring contact time 228
    and overcoming unbearable
        constraints 229–30
        accepting trade-offs 231–2
        mapping constraints 230–1
        selective rule-breaking 232–3
    and overcoming unexplored
        choices 234–5
        awareness of choices 235–6
        building personal knowledge/
            competencies 237–8
        involving key players 236–7
    and rarity of 223
    and toleration of ambiguity 233–4
    and toleration of conflict 233
    and traps of non-action 223–4
        overcoming 224
added value:
    and competitiveness 3, 4, 35
    and international comparison 31
adversarialism, and employment
    relations 64–5, 246–7

AIM Fellowship 244
Air France 48
airline industry 46
    and easyJet business model 54–6
Alfred Herbert 64
Amazon.com 121
ambidexterity, organizational 107, 120,
    130 n2
Amnesty International 217
analysis:
    and decision-making 282
    and reflective conversations 212–13
Andersson, Don:
    and awareness of choices 235–6
    and bias for action 239
    and building knowledge/
        competencies 238
    and involving key players 236–7
    and overcoming unexplored
        choices 234–5
Argyris, Chris 158
Arthur Andersen 166
assumptions:
    and cooperative relationships 215–17
    and organizational culture 12–13
    and reflective conversations 212–13
audit society 127, 134 n41
authority, and changing attitudes
    towards 206

B&Q, and employee consultation 74
Bain 166
Bank of England 24
Bank of Santander 56
Beach, Dennis E. 162
behaviour, and assumptions
    about 215–17
Bergqvist, J. T. 218

bias, and decision-making 11, 16, 180,
    182–3, 193
Bic 90
Bland, Christopher 97
Booz-Allen & Hamilton 164
boundaries, managing across 199–200
    and assumptions about
        behaviour 215–17
    and autonomy/control tensions 201
    and changing boundaries 199–200
    and corporate renewal 201–2
    and importance of 206, 210, 215
    and integration:
        changing nature of 205
        drivers of 203–4
        hard/soft bonds 205
    and internal divisions 202
    and networks of cooperative
        relationships 207–8, 210, 211,
        219–20
    and promotion of cooperation 217,
        219–20
    and reflective conversations 211–12,
        215, 250
bounded rationality 11, 193–95 n3
BP 168
    and managing across boundaries 200
        cooperative relationships 209–10
        corporate renewal 201–2
        integration 203, 205
        internal divisions 202
        peer assist 209–10
        peer challenge 209
        reflective conversations 211, 217
        values 217–18
    and organizational learning 163, 208
    and success of 6
BP Exploration, and employee
    consultation 74
brainstorming, and radical
    innovation 93
Branson, Richard 5, 97, 118
brewing industry, and diversification
    of 51

British Airways 43, 48, 99
British Telecom 22, 97
Browne, Lord John 162, 200, 201, 203,
    209, 213
business innovation 89
business models:
    and changing 52, 54, 56, 57
    and components of 54
    and easyGroup 54–6
    and limited life of 56
Business Process Re-engineering
    (BPR) 139
Business Serve, and dynamic
    capabilities 170, 172
Butler, Nick 202

Canon 204
capital intensity, and productivity 29
Carrigan, Tim 213–14
Castorama 74
causal-mapping, and decision-
    making 187
Center for Business Knowledge 165
Challenger space shuttle 178, 179,
    189–90
change:
    and acceleration of 245
    and action-taking 250
    and recognizing need for 138
    and strategy development 8–10, 50–2
    see also innovation; radical
        innovation; transformational
        change
chaos, and innovation 14
Chaparral Steel, and organizational
    learning 160–2
Chartered Institute of Personnel and
    Development 76
Chase, Rodney 162, 205, 210, 213, 217
choices, overcoming unexplored 234
    and awareness of choices 235–6
    and building knowledge/
        competencies 237–8
    and involving key players 236

Ciba Specialty Chemicals, and dynamic
    capabilities 169–170
Clinton, Bill 44
cognitive competence, and decision-
    making 178, 193
cognitive mapping, and decision-
    making 187, 189
Coles, David 128
collaboration 140–1
collective bargaining 82
Columbia Accident Investigation Board
    (CAIB) 194
Columbia space shuttle 194
communities of practice 150
    and knowledge dissemination 167–8
Company Law Review 109
comparative advantage 21–2, 28–9
competencies, and business
    strategy 49
Competition Commission 24
competition policy 24
competitiveness:
    and challenge of 34–5, 37
    and comparative advantage 21–2,
        28–9
    and competitiveness agenda 19
    and definition of 28
    and foundations of 3–5, 15
    and individual/collective
        development 156
    and innovation 3, 4, 35, 80, 107, 243
    and low-cost approach to 3–4, 29, 36,
        47, 243
    and management 4, 19
    and market reforms as
        handicap 18–19
    and productivity 28
        international comparison 29–30,
            244, 247
        labour market participation 30–1
        variations in 31–2, 44 n24
    and public policy 36
    and sectoral differences 31

complexity theory 100 n5
Confederation of British Industry
    (CBI) 73, 76, 77
conflict, and action-taking 234
conformity:
    and communities of practice 166
    and strategy development 13–14
constraints, overcoming
    unbearable 229–30
    and accepting trade-offs 231–2
    and mapping constraints 230–1
    and selective rule-breaking 232–3
consultation, and employment
    relations 72–4
contact time, and action-taking 233
control:
    and management 14
    and performance
        measurement 109–10, 123–4
cooperation:
    and assumptions about
        behaviour 216–18
    and employment relations 63
    and exceptional management 249
    and performance measurement 119
    and promotion of 217–18
    and reflective conversations 211–15,
        250
    and relationship networks 207–8,
        211
    see also boundaries, managing across
coordinated economy 21–2
corporate performance:
    and business failure 5, 7
    and business success 6–7
    and impermanence of success 8
corporate renewal, and managing
    across boundaries 201–2
corporatism 20
cost, and competitiveness 3–4, 29, 36,
    47, 244
Costa 88
Creative Entrepreneurs Club 140

creativity:
  and performance measurement 115
  and radical innovation 93

DaimlerChrysler 168
data overload:
  and decision-making 180
  and performance
    measurement 114–15, 128
D'Aveni, Richard 50
decision-making 179–83
  and analysis 180
  and biased judgements 180
  and cognitive competence 178, 193
  and cognitive styles 180–2
  and escalation of commitment 183
  and exceptional management 244
  and group improvement in 189–90,
    193
    Delphi methods 190–91, 197
    Group Decision Support
      Systems 190–91
    scenario planning 192
    team mix 190
  and group polarization 183
  and group-think 183, 189, 191, 193
  and human limitations 179
  and individual improvement in 184,
    194
    causal cognitive mapping 187–9
    frame analysis worksheet 184–7,
      190 n11
    framing bias 184, 196
  and information overload 183
  and information-processing
    limitations 180
  and intuition 182
  and organizational outcomes 179
  and radical innovation 99
  and rational choice view of 180
  and rules of thumb
    (heuristics) 179–80, 183, 195 n4
  and social and political nature of 173

and strategy development:
  bias 10
  incrementalism 11
  institutional norms 13
  organizational culture 12, 14
  process of 11
  resource dependence 14
  role of experience 11–12
Dell 165
Delphi methods 197
  and decision-making 192
demands, overcoming
    overwhelming 225–6
  and developing personal
    agenda 226–7
  and managing expectations 229
  and prioritizing 227
  and structuring contact time 228
Deming, W. Edwards 139
Deming Plan–Do–Check–Act cycle 111
Department of Trade and Industry, and
    Innovation Review (2004) 87–8
DHL UK 128
Diageo 94, 96, 99, 101
differentiation, and business
    strategy 47–8
diversification:
  and business strategy 50–1
  and transformational change 53
double-loop learning 158
Dow Chemical 166
Drucker, Peter 109–10
dual structures, and radical
    innovation 99
dynamic capabilities 169–73, 247–9
  and Business Serve 171–2
  and Ciba Specialty Chemicals 170
  and flexibility 172
  and Oticon 169–70
Dyson, James 119

easyCinema 55
easyGroup, and business model 54–6

easyJet 27, 43, 42, 121
  and business model 54–6
Egg (online bank) 87
Eisenhardt, Kathy 123, 124
Electronic Arts 102
electronic point of sale systems
      (EPOS) 114
Employment Act (1980) 23
employment relations:
  and basic principles of 69–72
  and cooperation 63
  and economic performance 80
  and employee expectations 62,
      70, 72
  and employee participation 246
    conditions for 80–1
    consultation 72–4
    partnership arrangements 75
  and flexibility of 79
  and High Performance Work
      model 63, 80, 247
    as benchmark 79
    constraints on 67–8
    difficulties in evaluating 78–9
    employee involvement 73
    extent of implementation of 78
    practices of 76–7
    support for 76
  and importance of 62
  and individual managers 82
  and institutional context 64
    adversarialism 65
    managerial style 66
    multi-level collaboration 82
    trade unions 65–6
    training and development 67
    work intensification 80
  and institutions of 63
  and lack of focus on 67–8
  and lessons for companies 81
  and middle management 81, 82
  and payment systems 71
  and policy evaluation 72

and policy implementation 72
  and productivity 81
  and strikes 21, 64
  and trust 64, 66, 80–1
  and wider strategic goals 77
Employment Tribunals 69
Engineering Employers' Federation 76
Enterprise Act (2000) 22
enterprise resource planning (ERP) 148
Ericsson 102
Ernst & Young 110, 163
European Commission 76
European Union:
  and competition policy 22
  and National Information and
      Consultation Directive 73
  and Single Market Programme 24,
      38 n13
expectations, and action-taking 223
experience:
  and decision-making 11
  and organizational culture 12–13
external scanning capability, and
      radical innovation 94–5

factor accumulation, and economic
      growth 21
financial performance, and priority of
      strategy over 44
financial services, and deregulation 22
flexible working 63
Flinn, Polly 210, 212
foreign direct investment (FDI), and
      manufacturing 4
Forrester, Jay 159
framing, and decision-making 187
  frame analysis worksheet 184–7,
      196 n11
  framing bias 184
France:
  and indicative planning 20
  and productivity 28
Fraser Institute 24

generic strategies 47–8, 59 n9, 10
Germany, and productivity 30
GlaxoSmithKline 89, 110
Global Climate Coalition 218
Goodwin, Fred 200, 206, 212, 213
Goodwin, Paul 187
Gross Domestic Product, and
    international comparison 29–30
Group Decision Support Systems 191
group polarization, and decision-
    making 183
group-think, and decision-making 183,
    189–90, 193

Haji-Iaonnou, Stelios 54–5
Hamel, Gary 98, 171
heuristics 195 n4
  and decision-making 179–80, 193
Hewlett-Packard 166, 205
hierarchy 206
High Performance Work (HPW)
    model 63, 80, 146, 247
  as benchmark 79
  and constraints on:
    demands on managers 68
    institutional pressures 68
    lack of focus on employment
      relations 67–8
  and difficulties in evaluating 75–9
  and employee involvement 73
  and extent of implementation
    of 74–8
  and practices of 76–7
  and support for 76
Horton, Bob 6
Howlett, Nigel 213–14
human-resource management
    (HRM) 142
hyper-competition, and business
    strategy 50

IBM 52
Icarus paradox 9

idea generation, and radical
    innovation 94
income inequality 23
incremental change:
  and steady-state innovation 90
  and strategy development 8, 10
incubators, and radical
    innovation 99–100
indicative planning 20
indispensability, and overcoming desire
    for 225–6
industrial relations, see employment
    relations
industry effect, and strategy 46, 59 n6
industry groups 150
inequality 23
information technology:
  and integration 205
  and knowledge management 164–6,
    211
  and performance
    measurement 111–12
infrastructure, and public
    investment 24–5
Innocent fruit juices 91
innovation:
  and competitiveness 3, 4, 37, 87, 107,
    243
  and corporate transformation 87
  and dynamic capabilities 179
  and economic growth 26
  and Innovation Review (DTI,
    2004) 88
  and management control 14
  and market innovation 121
  and nature of 107
  and organizational constraints 89
  and performance
    measurement 117–18
    constraining creativity 120
    control emphasis of 121–2
    efficiency focus of 120
    focus on critical measures 123

hindering adaptability 121
hindering cooperation 119
implications for strategic
    management 124
internal focus of 120
measuring inspiration 119
nature of innovations 119
nature of processes 118
reframing 121
target-setting 119
time-scale 110
what to measure 113, 123
and process innovation 88
    and product development 88
    as random process 88
    and science base 24
    and Total Factor Productivity 29
    and typology of 89
    see also radical innovation; steady
        state innovation
inspiration, and performance
    measurement 119
institutional norms, and strategy
    development 13–14
institutions:
    and competitiveness 36–7
    and coordinated economies 20–1, 22
    and employment relations 64–7
    and market economies 20
    and reforms of:
        competition policy 24
        infrastructure 24–5
        international comparison 26–7
        labour market 22–4
        privatization 22, 38 n6
        significance of 27
integration, and managing across
    boundaries 203–7
Intel:
    and constructive confrontation 98
    and corporate venturing unit 99
International Knowledge Management
    Network (IKMN) 164

Internet, and integration 205
intuition, and decision-making 182
investors, and performance
    measurement 109, 110
Ishikawa 139
ISO 9000, and total quality
    management 146

Jensen, Michael 113
Jobs, Steve 5
joint ventures, and acquiring technical
    capability 102
Juran, Joseph 139
just-in-time (JIT) 142, 143, 148

Kallasvuo, Olli-Pekka 218
Kaplan, Robert 113
Knight-Ridder 192
knowledge:
    and dissemination of 166–7
    and knowledge management 164–66,
        168, 211
    and local nature of 167–8
    and managers 173–4
    and political nature of 156, 157, 166,
        173
    see also learning
knowledge economy 109–10
knowledge management 211
    and communities of practice 167–8
Knowledge Management Forum 164
Kosonen, Mikko 208–9
Kraft General Foods 88
Kwik-Fit Financial Services 147

labour market:
    and institutional reforms 26
    and participation rates 30–1
labour relations, see employment
    relations
lean production 111, 143, 145,
    149
    and Toyota Production System 139–40

learning:
  as bridging concept 157, 162, 174
  and context of 156
  and double-loop learning 158
  and dynamic capabilities 169–73
    Business Serve 171–2
    Ciba Specialty Chemicals 170
    flexibility 172
    Oticon 179–80
  and exceptional management
  and innovation 88
  and knowledge:
    dissemination of 166–7
    local nature of 167–8
    political nature of 156, 157, 167, 173
  and knowledge management 164–66,
      168, 211
    communities of practice 167–8
  and managers 173–4
  and organizational learning 157–9
    BP 162–3, 203
    Chaparral Steel 160–2
    Rover 159–60, 173
    successful implementation 163–4
    weak ties 208
  and performance measurement 108,
      122, 125–7
legislation, and performance
    measurement 109
Lego 93–4, 100–1, 102
literacy, and United Kingdom 25
London International 46
London Rubber Group 46
long-range planning 45
Lufthansa 48
Lufthansa School of Business 230

McDonald's 91
McKinsey 166, 225–6
management:
  as career aspiration 5
  and challenges of 244
    transformational change 245–6

and competitiveness 4, 19
and contribution of 4–5, 14–15, 243–4
  corporate failure 5, 7
  corporate success 6–7
and control 14
and exceptional management:
  action-taking 250
  decision-making 249
  dynamic capabilities 247–8
  employee involvement 246
  employment relations 246–7
  fostering cooperation 249
  learning environment 248–9
  managerial practices 247–9
  need for 244–5
  organizational innovation 248
  performance measurement 247
  reflective conversations 250
  shaping organizational
    context 246, 248
  transformational change 245–6
and qualities required 178
and reflective management 151–2
and strategy development 11–13, 15
and Total Factor Productivity 29
and weaknesses of 35
managerial practices 151–2
  and adoption of 138
    deployment 151
    embedding 151
    sustaining 152
  and alliance and network
    management 141
  and confusion about 138–9
  and evaluation of 139
    adaptation 148
    foundation practices 149
    identification of 138
    organizational fit 148
    practices as bundles 142–4
    recognizing promise 145, 147
    sources of knowledge about 149–51
  and exceptional management 247–8

and mindfulness 142, 153
and pitfalls for integration of 137
and recognizing need for change 138
and reflective management 141–2
Manpower Services Commission
    (MSC) 23
manufacturing:
    and employment relations 64–5
    and foreign direct investment (FDI) 4
Marconi 95
    and decline of 8
market economy 21–2
market innovation 121
market reforms, as competitive
    handicap 18–19
Marks and Spencer 43, 52
    and business model 52–3
    and corporate venturing unit 99, 100
    and decline of 8
    and strategic drift 9
Matsushita 205
measurement systems, see performance
    measurement
Microsoft 168, 204
middle management:
    and employment relations 81, 82
    and role of 7
Millennium Dome 183
Miller, Danny, and the Icarus paradox 9
mindfulness, and managerial
    practices 142, 152
minimum wage 22–3
Monsanto 168
Motorola 203, 204
motor-sport industry, and radical
    innovation 95
multinational enterprises, and
    productivity 33

NASA, and decision-making 179,
    189, 193
national champions 20
nationalization 20

NatWest 200, 204
Nestlé 88
networks:
    and alliance and network
        management 141
    and knowledge dissemination 166–7
    and managing across
        boundaries 207–11
    and radical innovation 92, 102–3
    and reflective conversations 211–15
Nichia Chemical 90
Nintendo 93, 204
Nissan 4
NoHo Digital 213–14
Nokia 44, 96, 99, 145
    and managing across boundaries 200
    cooperative relationships 206–7
    integration 203–4, 205
    values 218–19
Nonaka, I. 164–5
North West (England) Automotive
    Alliance 140–1
Norton, David 62

Ogilvy, David 205, 214
OgilvyOne:
    and internal divisions 202
    and managing across boundaries 200
    integration 203, 205, 206
    reflective conversations 212,
        217–20
Ollila, Jorma 200
One-world 140
Organization for Economic
    Cooperation and Development
    (OECD) 26
organizational ambidexterity 107, 120,
    130 n2
organizational culture:
    and radical innovation 96–99
    and strategy development 12–13
    and values 217–19
organizational fields 13

organizational learning 157–9
 and BP 162–3, 203
 and Chaparral Steel 160–2
 and Rover 159–60, 173
 and successful implementation 163–4
 and weak ties 208
 see also learning
Oticon, and dynamic capabilities 169–70
outsourcing 36

Palm 91
paradigm innovation 89
partnering, and acquiring technical
  capability 102
partnership arrangements, and
  employment relations 75
part-time work 63
Pasteur, Louis 88
payment systems, and employment
  relations 71
peer assist, and BP 168, 209–10
peer challenge, and BP 210
performance measurement:
 and challenges of 112
  data overload 114–15, 128
  multiple measures 114
  perverse incentives 115–16
  what to measure 113
 and exceptional management 247
 and external drivers of:
  changing basis of value 110
  changing nature of work 109
  investor pressure 109
  legislative requirements 109
  regulatory environment 109
 and innovation 107–8, 112, 129
  focus on critical measures 123
  implications for strategic
   management 124
  what to measure 123, 125–6
 and innovation, dilemmas in 117–18
  constraining creativity 120
  control emphasis of 121–2

  efficiency focus of 120
  hindering adaptability 120
  hindering cooperation 119
  internal focus of 120
  measuring inspiration 119
  nature of innovations 119
  nature of processes 118
  reframing 121
  target-setting 119
  time-scale 121
 and internal drivers of:
  organizational factors 110–11
  organizational improvement 111
  technological developments 111–12
 as learning system 108, 122, 125–7
 and managerial practices 146
 and managing through 126–8
  performance analysts 127
  performance planning 126–7
  systems thinking 127–8
 and pervasiveness of 108
performance reviews 126
performance-related pay 71
personal agendas, and action-
  taking 226–7
perverse incentives, and performance
  measurement 115–16
Pfizer 88
Philadelphia Newspapers 192
Phoenix consortium 159
Porter, Michael 18
 and management weaknesses 36
portfolio management, and
  transformational change 53
position innovation 89
Post Office 22
poverty 23
Power, M. 127
Prêt à Manger 91
prioritizing, and action-taking 227–8
Private Finance Initiative (PFI) 22, 24
privatization 22, 38 n6
process innovation 88, 89

and radical innovation 90
and steady-state innovation 90
product development, and
    innovation 88
product innovation 89
    and radical innovation 90
    and steady-state innovation 90
productivity:
    and competitiveness 28
    and employment relations 81
    and international comparison 29–30,
        244, 247
    and labour market participation
        rates 26, 27
    and multinational enterprises 33
    and public sector 39 n21
    and Total Factor Productivity 29
    and trade unions 65
    and variations in 31–4, 40 n24
Prudential 91, 183
public investment 24–5, 36
public policy:
    and competitiveness 36
    and corporate strategy 36
public sector, and productivity 39 n21
punctuated equilibrium 8

quality certification 146

radical innovation 90, 103
    and challenge of 93, 245–6
    and the cognitive challenge 93–4
        external scanning capability 94–5
        fostering of divergent thinking 97
        idea-generation process 94
        promoting innovative culture 96–7
        signals from within firm 95–6
    and constraints on 92
    and definition of 90
    and difficulty of 91–2
    and networks 92
    and the political challenge 97–8
        decentralizing seed-funding 98–9

decision-making process 98
dual structure approach 99–100
as strategic necessity 91
and the technical challenge 100
    developing entrepreneurialism 101
    developing new partner
        networks 102
    developing technical
        capabilities 101–2
    skills development 100–1
see also innovation
Raynet 102
reflective management:
    and managerial practices 141–2,
        151–2
    and mindfulness 142
    and reflective conversations 211–12,
        215, 217, 250
regulation:
    and international comparison 27
    and performance measurement 109
research and development:
    and lack of investment in 25, 36,
        38 n16, 87, 243
    and performance measurement 112,
        115
resource dependence, and strategy
    development 14
resource-based view (RBV) 49, 169
restrictive practices 65–6
Ridgway, V. F. 113
Robert Bosch 102
Robert Wiseman's Dairies 144
Roche 98
    and strategic vision process 101
Rose, Ian 160
Rover, and learning within 159–60, 173
Rover Learning Business 159
Royal Bank of Scotland:
    and managing across boundaries 200
        integration 204, 205, 206
        reflective conversations 212, 213
    and strategic probes 56–7

Royal Bank of Scotland (*cont.*):
  and success of 6–7
  and transformational change 53
Royal Sun Alliance 99
rule-breaking, and overcoming
     unbearable constraints 232–3
Russo, J. E. 184
Ryanair 27, 46, 54, 121
  and radical innovation 91

Saatchi & Saatchi, and diversification
     of 51
Sainsbury 52
  and business model of 46, 48
Sanford Berol 114
Sattelberger, Thomas 224
  and mapping constraints 230
  and overcoming unbearable
     constraints 230
  and selective rule-breaking 232
  and toleration of conflict 233
  and toleration of uncertainty 234
  and trade-offs 232
scenario planning, and decision-
     making 192–3
Schoemaker, P. J. H. 184
Schön, Donald 158
Schumpeter, Joseph 239
science base, and innovation 25
Scottish & Newcastle Breweries 144
Sega 93
Senge, Peter 158–160, 162
service profit chain 146
Seton Scholl Healthcare 46
shareholder value 44, 68
Shell 98
  and decision-making 178, 179, 192
  and external scanning capabilities 95
Single Market Programme (EU) 24,
     38 n13
six sigma 111
skills and education 23, 36, 246
  and productivity 30

and radical innovation 100–1
and upward trends in 66–7
Smart car 91
Smith & Nephew, and transformational
     change 53
social capital 145
Society of Motor Manufacturers and
     Traders 150
Sony 94, 204
Sorrell, Martin 51
Southwest Airlines 46, 54, 121
Spungin, Jessica:
  and bias for action 239
  and developing personal
     agenda 227–8
  and managing expectations 229
  and overwhelming demands
     on 225–6
  and prioritizing 227–8
  and structuring contact time 228
SSL International 46
Star Alliance 140
Starbucks 88, 91, 121
steady state innovation 87, 89–91
  and management of 88
  and networks 102
  see also innovation
strategic drift 9
strategic planning 43–4
Strategos 94
strategy
  and business model 54–6
  and conventional prescriptions
     for 45
  differentiation 47–8
  diversification 50–1
  embedded competencies 49
  generic strategies 47–8, 59 n10
  hyper-competition 50
  imitation 48
  industry effect 46, 59 n7
  limitations of 58
  resource-based approach 49, 169

strategic group membership 46–7, 59 n8
strategic planning 45–46
and definition of 43, 57 n1
and development of:
  bias 12
  institutional norms 13–14
  organizational culture 12–14
  resource dependence 14
  role of experience 11–12
  incremental approach 10
  patterns of 8–10
  public policy 36
  similarities in 13
  strategic planning 45–6
and dynamic nature of 44, 52, 169–73
and priority over financial performance 44
and routine 52
and strategic probes 56
and transformational change 52–4, 56–7, 87
strikes 23, 64
Sutherland, Rory 214
systems thinking, and organizational learning 158

Takeuchi, H. 164
technology:
  and performance measurement 111–12
  and Total Factor Productivity 30
Tesco, and transformational change 53
Theddens, Reimer 200, 202, 203, 206, 212
total factor productivity (TFP), and components of 30
total productive maintenance (TPM) 142, 148
total quality management (TQM) 111, 142, 146, 148
Towers, John 159, 160
Toyota 4

and Toyota Production System 139–40
trade unions 18, 19, 22, 23
  and employee consultation 73
  and employment relations 64, 65–6
trade-offs, and overcoming unbearable constraints 231–2
Trades Union Congress (TUC) 73, 76, 77
training 23
Training and Enterprise Councils (TECs) 23
transformational change 9–10
  and business models 52, 53
  and challenge of 245–6
  and radical innovation 87, 90
  and strategy development 8, 56–7
trust, and employment relations 64, 66, 80–1

Unilever 94, 205
Unipart 22
United Kingdom:
  and competitiveness:
    challenge of 37–38
    competitiveness agenda 19
    foundations of 3–4, 13
    low-cost approach to 3–4, 29, 34, 47
    productivity 29–30, 244, 247
    productivity variations 31–3, 40 n24
    sectoral differences 31
  and foreign direct investment (FDI) 4
  and institutional reforms:
    competition policy 24
    competitiveness 36–7
    infrastructure 24, 27
    international comparison 28–9
    labour market 22–4
    privatization 22, 38 n6
    significance of 27
  and managerial complacency 138
  and market reforms as handicap 18–19

United States, and productivity 30
universities, and management
        courses 5

value, and changing basis of 110
values, and organizational
        culture 217–19
venture units, and radical
        innovation 100
Viagra 88
Virgin 89, 96
    and innovative culture of 97
visualization, and action-taking 227
Vodafone 96

Wack, Pierre 192
Wage Councils 23
Walkman 94
Watson, David 213
Weber, Jürgen 231
Welch, Jack 5, 200
welfare-to-work 23

WF Electrical 116,
        119
Wheelwright, Steven 111
Whirlpool 98
Whitbread, and transformational
        change 53
Woodroffe, Simon 118
work:
    and changing nature of 109–10
    and intensification of 67
Workplace Employment Relations
        Survey (WERS) 77
world class manufacturing 111
World Economic Forum 26
        Global Competitiveness Report
            (2000) 36
WPP 51, 96, 200
Wright, George 187

Xerox 166, 167, 193

Yo Sushi 118

	DATE DUE		